Instructor's Resource Manual

for

Sternberg and Williams

Educational Psychology

prepared by

Mary Ann Rafoth
The Center for Educational and Program Evaluation
Indiana University of Pennsylvania

with assistance from
Jill Cieslinski
Danielle DeAngelis
Tim Borick
Tracy Motter
Karen M. Wolff

Allyn and Bacon
Boston London Toronto Sydney Tokyo Singapore

TABLE OF CONTENTS

Preface

Welcome to the instructor's manual for *Educational Psychology* by Robert Sternberg and Wendy Williams. I hope you will find that the manual enhances your use of this innovative and comprehensive text. The instructor's manual is organized by chapter. *Chapter-at-a-Glance* tables at the beginning of each section will help you integrate the resources in this manual with the text as well as the Test Bank, Transparency Packet, and Supplemental Video that are part of the complete instructional package from Allyn & Bacon. Each chapter supplement in the instructor's manual contains a detailed chapter outline, a list of transparencies that are applicable to the chapter, several activities to accompany your instruction including instructor directions and student handouts, a listing of additional video and Internet resources to accompany each chapter, and a series of student handouts for class use. Roman numerals and capital letters, as well as bolded headings, in the detailed chapter outlines correspond directly to heading in the textbook. Additional information from the text is included in the outlines in bulleted headings and statements summarized for your convenience. I developed each activity and many of the handouts over my years as an instructor of educational psychology. I have found them to work well in the classroom, to help students gain a deeper understanding of the content, to enable students to more directly see applications of theory, and to generate higher-level thinking and discussions. I hope you will too. I have found that videos greatly enhance student interest and understanding and I encourage you to review the ones that have been suggested. The Internet has also become a valuable resource. I encourage you to preview the sites listed and guide your students' use to supplement the text. In summary, I hope you find the manual helpful in building the analytical, creative, and practical thinking skills that are essential to effective instruction in your students.

Mary Ann Rafoth

Chapter One
Becoming An Expert Teacher; Becoming an Expert Student

The instructor's manual for this chapter contains:
- A *Chapter-at-a-Glance* chart that reviews all chapter related material
- A detailed chapter outline to highlight main points of the chapter
- A list of transparencies from Transparencies - Educational Psychology IV that correspond to this chapter
- Several activities to deepen student understanding
- An annotated list of additional resources including internet sites
- Handouts to accompany your lessons

CHAPTER-AT-A-GLANCE

Chapter Outline	Objectives	Instructional Aids
1.0 The Thinking Triangle p. 5	1. Describe the three parts to the "thinking" triangle.	- Transparency T1 - Handout 1.1 - Test Bank Questions 1-4
2.0 What is an expert teacher? p. 6	1. Discuss how the knowledge of expert teachers differs from nonexpert teachers. 2. Discuss how expert teachers are efficient. 3. Describe what it means to have creative insight. 4. Describe the advantages of expertise.	- Transparency T2 - Handouts 1.2, 1.3, 1.4 - Activity 1.1 - Test Bank Questions 5-21, 41-51, 53-55, 58-60 - Video Segment 1
3.0 What do we know about expert students? p. 21	1. Describe how expert students use effective learning strategies. 2. Describe the incremental view of intelligence. 3. Discuss how having high aspirations helps expert students. 4. Describe perceived self-efficacy, and how it affects students. 5. Describe the importance of pursuing a task to completion. 6. Discuss how expert students take responsibility for self and actions. 7. Describe the expert student's ability to delay gratification.	- Handouts 1.5, 1.6, 1.7, 1.8, 1.9 - Activities 1.2, 1.3 - Test Bank Questions 22-36, 52, 56, 61
4.0 Educational psychology and the creation of expert teachers and expert students, p. 29	1. Describe the various methods of educational psychology research.	- Transparencies T3, T4, T5, T6 - Handouts 1.10, 1.11 - Activity 1.4 - Test Bank Questions 37-40, 57

DETAILED CHAPTER ONE OUTLINE
I. **The Big Picture**
- Opening vignette of Sandy: A first year teacher
    - Discusses the challenges experienced by a first year teacher
    - Describes the influence of Danielle: An expert teacher

- Definition of an Expert Teacher
    - Uses a broad base of organized knowledge and experience efficiently and creatively to solve many kinds of problems that occur in educational settings.
    - Able to motivate students to learn complex information, deal with test anxiety in students, and handle discipline problems effectively.
    - Capitalize on and learn from the experiences of other teachers.

- Definition of an Expert Student
    - Use strategies to help them learn efficiently and are open to challenges and willing to overcome problems to achieve learning goals.
    - When expert students become teachers, they are able to use what they have learned in their career to identify expert and nonexpert students within their classroom.

- The "Thinking" Triangle
    - Refers to a theory of intelligence developed by Robert Sternberg in which intelligence is viewed as having three major aspects.

    - Thinking Analytically – questions that ask you to analyze, compare and contrast, or evaluate concepts or information.

    - Thinking Creatively – questions encourage you to invent, discover, or design.

    - Thinking Practically – questions help you learn how to apply in everyday life what you already know.

II. **What is an expert teacher?**
- How experts differ from nonexperts
    - Reflective thinking – reflect on your progress at teaching, and attempt to understand what you are doing right and doing wrong and why.
    - Develop a list of strategies used by successful teachers for teaching accurate, comprehensive content knowledge:
        Integrate teaching strategies into your own approach.
        Capitalize on your strengths as you lead a class.
B. Expert teachers have expert knowledge
- Experts have and use more knowledge to solve problems.
- Knowledge is based on experience and not necessarily biologically based memory or thinking skills:
    - Classic chess study – experts' stored knowledge allowed them to memorize the chess pieces' patterns more easily, giving them an advantage over novices.
    - Other related studies – experts' main advantage over novices is in having more knowledge about their domain of expertise.
- Types of expert knowledge
    - Content knowledge – knowledge of the subject matter to be taught.
    - Pedagogical knowledge – specific knowledge of how to teach.
    - Pedagogical-content knowledge –specific knowledge of how to teach what is being taught:
        How to explain particular concepts
        How to demonstrate and explain procedures and methods
        How to correct students' naïve theories and misconceptions about subject matter

B. Organization of expert knowledge
- Experts and novices differ not only in the amount of knowledge they have but also in how they organize that knowledge in memory.
- Lesson plans – experts more thoroughly integrate knowledge of content to be taught with knowledge of teaching methods.
- According to Leinhardt and Greeno, lesson plans have three main components.
  - Global plans – information not related to specific lesson content or subject matter:
    - Routines for checking homework
    - Presenting new material
    - Supervising guided practice
  - Local plans – information related to lesson content and subject matter
    - Routines for presenting particular concepts
    - Routines for assessing student understanding of particular concepts.
  - Decision elements – information that makes the lesson plan responsive to expected and unexpected events:
    - Prepares teacher for unanticipated circumstances
    - Use at times when students are not quick to understanding material
- Characteristics of expert lesson plans
  - Enables the expert teacher to teach effectively and efficiently
  - Maximizes the amount of time that students spend learning
  - Knowledge related to teaching content enables the teacher to connect student feedback to lesson objectives
- Characteristics of novice lesson plans
  - Have less complex and less interconnected lesson plans
  - Due to lack of teaching knowledge, they have difficulty generating examples and explanations.
  - Tend to have difficulty relating student questions to lesson objectives.
- Knowledge about the teaching context
  - Expert teachers need knowledge of the social and political context in which teaching occurs.
  - Working effectively with others is as essential as knowledge of how to teach.
  - Expert teachers need to know how to compete effectively for limited school resources.

C. Expert teachers are efficient
- **Experts automatize well-learned skills.**
  - Automatic mental processes- processes that have become well learned and require little effort.
  - Due to increased experience, experts expend less energy accessing mental resources compared to novices.
  - Experts are able to perform tasks effortlessly that novices can only perform with effort.
  - Expert teachers deal with potential discipline problems before they erupt.
  - The ability to automatize well-learned routines does not exist independently from the possession of organized teaching knowledge.
- **Experts effectively plan, monitor, and evaluate their performance.**
  - Metacognitive processes – the process in which one "thinks about thinking"
  - Experts spend more time trying to understand the problem to be solved.
  - Experts are more likely to monitor their ongoing solution attempts, checking for accuracy.
  - Experts are also more likely to update or elaborate problem representations as new constraints emerge.
  - "Reflective practice in teaching" – a focus on thinking about thinking:
    - Expert teachers have a disposition toward reflection – a continuous learning through experience.
    - Reflective teachers use new problems as opportunities to expand their knowledge and competence.

- **The relationship between automatizing well-learned skills and planning, monitoring, and evaluating.**
  - Experts make skills automatic by their ability to be reflective and to think about thinking during problem solving.
  - True experts reinvest mental resources to better understand problems.
  - True experts view complications as challenges which allow them to work on the leading edge of their knowledge and skill.

D. Redefining Problems
- Experts are able to see problems from different perspectives.
- By redefining problems, experts reach insightful solutions.
- Three key ways experts think about problems
  - Experts distinguish information relevant to solving a problem from information that is not relevant.
  - Experts combine information in ways that are useful for problem solving.
- Experts apply to a teaching problem information acquired in another context.
  - Expert teachers are adept at observing and applying an analogy in order to solve a problem.
  - Expert teachers frequently exploit analogies between things that are familiar to their students and things that are new to their students.
  - Having a lot of knowledge that is well organized is essential to an expert's ability.

E. Advantages of Expertise
- To become an expert teacher knowledge, efficiency, and insight are necessary.
- Expert teaching skills are developed through course work and hands-on practice.

F. Implications for teaching.
- Teachers become expert by learning from experience about the content of the subjects they teach, about general methods for teaching, and about specific methods that work to teach their content areas.
- Teachers become expert by growing in efficiency as they "think about thinking" and learn to make daily tasks and routines automatic.
- Teachers become expert by developing their insight and ability to solve problems by understanding the important aspects of problems, understanding how other solutions in the past can be used to solve problems in the present, and understanding how to reorganize problems to make them easier to solve.

III. What do we know about expert students?
A. Expert students use effective learning strategies to help them learn.
- These learning strategies may be acquired through direct instruction from a classroom teacher or from other students.
- Learning strategies may also be invented by the expert student.

B. Memorization Strategies
  - When learning a new strategy for studying, an expert student must work to maintain the strategy.
  - The expert student is to watch for ways to transfer strategies by using them with new material and in new contexts.

C. Evaluating Strategies
- Expert students monitor the effectiveness of their strategies by testing them to see which ones lead to increases in performance.
- Think-aloud protocols:
     Think aloud and methodically state your steps in solving a problem or doing a task. Allows the student to find places where reasoning is not sound or strategy could be improved.
- Table 1.2 : General Strategies for Improving Learning and Performance

- Knowing why – students need to know the purposes of various school tasks and how learning is relevant to their lives now.
- Knowing self – self-assessment can help students understand their own work habits and intellectual preferences.
- Knowing differences – recognizing distinctions among different kinds of work, students can vary their strategies.
- Knowing process – students can plan effective strategies if they recognize the problems for themselves.
- Reworking – taking time to go over work helps students recognize the importance of self-monitoring.

D. Expert students have an incremental view of intelligence
- Incremental view – the belief that intelligence can be increased
  - Students see corrective feedback as an indication that more work and effort are needed to remediate the weakness.
  - Students respond to failure by working harder in the future.
  - Students seek out challenges because these challenges represent learning experiences.
- Entity view – the belief that intelligence is fixed
  - Students tend to take negative evaluations of their abilities and performance as signs that they are not intelligent enough to succeed.
  - Students tend to avoid situations in which they might get negative feedback, and thus, avoid challenges.
- Ames and Archer (1988) study
  - Mastery-oriented beliefs (incremental beliefs) – students with these beliefs were concerned with mastering material:
        Used more strategies and more effective strategies in their schoolwork.
        Were more open to challenging tasks.
        Had a more positive attitude.
        More likely to believe that effort was the key to improvement in performance.
  - Performance-oriented beliefs (entity beliefs) – students with these beliefs were concerned with performing well.

E. Expert students have high aspirations

F. Expert students have high perceived self-efficacy: They believe they are capable of succeeding in school.
- Students attempt more challenging tasks and achieve more academically.
- Previous success at an activity increases perceived self-efficacy.
- Positive social role models have an impact on perceived self-efficacy.
- Self-efficacy tends to be found in particular domains.
- Students tend to be more vulnerable to failure when they try something new compared with when they try to do something they can already do well.

G. Expert students are more likely to complete a task.
- Expert students use many different methods to help them through stumbling blocks and see tasks through.
- Lyn Corno (1989) study
  - Volition – the tendency to continue to pursue a goal
  - Know how to control attention to tasks and eliminate distractions.
  - Know how to manage study time.
  - Know how to control anxiety.
  - Know how to motivate themselves.
- Expert students can learn strategies to help them succeed, and by applying these strategies, expert students can increase their ability to see tasks through to completion.

H. Expert students take responsibility for self and actions.
- Expert students must be able to take responsibility for successes and failures.
- Expert students must be willing to take control of a task, to criticize themselves, and to take pride in their best work.
- Internals – people who tend to take responsibility for their lives.
- Externals – people who tend to place responsibility outside themselves.

I. Expert students have the ability to delay gratification.
- It is essential to learn to see tasks through without immediate rewards.
- Walter Mischel study
  - Children who are better able to delay gratification are more successful in various aspects of their lives.
  - The ability of children to delay gratification can even predict their scores on the Scholastic Assessment Test when they are much older.

J. Implications for Teaching
- Expert teachers work to help their students become expert learners.
- Expert students use strategies to help them learn, know that intelligence can be increased, have high aspirations and see themselves as capable of achieving these aspirations, see tasks through to completion, take responsibility for themselves and their actions, and understand the value of delaying gratification.

IV. **Educational psychology and the creation of expert teachers and expert students.**
- The goal of educational psychology is to take knowledge from the discipline of psychology that is relevant to education and to apply this knowledge in order to improve the quality and outcome of the educational process.

- Educational psychologists develop guiding principles that answer groups of questions on the same topic.
  Principles describe well-known and established relationships between events.
  Theories are scientific explanations for why events happen the way they do

A. Descriptive research – the scientist observes and describes what is happening in a situation without changing the dynamics of the situation.
- A correlation is a relationship between two measured things.
- A positive correlation means that when one of the things increases, the other also increases.
- A negative correlation means that when one of the things increases, the other decreases.
- Researchers try to determine whether the results are statistically significant: the results are not due to random or chance variation.
- A case study is an in-depth observation of one individual.

B. Experimental research
- The scientist designs a test to answer a question and actually changes what happens to people so the effects can be observed.
- The two groups of participants must be roughly equivalent, or chosen at random.
- The students or people in the experiments are sometimes called subjects.
- The groups of people who undergo a change by researchers are sometimes called experimental groups.
- The groups of people for whom nothing is changed are called control groups.
- Both types of research are valuable and important ways to gain information about how to become an expert teacher and how to help students become expert learners.

C. Implications for teaching

- Educational psychology uses science to uncover information that helps teachers solve problems and teach effectively.
- Educational psychology uncovers trends in how teachers teach and how students learn, and develops explanations for these trends so teachers can understand what happens in the classroom and why.
- Teachers can learn from descriptive research and case studies as well as from experimental research performed by educational psychologists and other scientists.

TRANSPARENCIES
- T1   Components of Good Teaching
- T2   Expert and Novice Teachers Think About A Discipline Problem
- T3   Three Types of Correlation
- T4   Correlation Does Not Show Causation
- T5   Possible Correlations: Attentiveness, Achievement, And IQ
- T6   Results of Successful Single-Case Experiments

CLASS ACTIVITIES

Activity 1.1. Reflection on Effective Teaching
Use this handout in conjunction with the beginning of the chapter to help students reflect on the characteristics of effective teachers, their concerns, and their own learning and study needs.

Students may complete the questions in class or as an outside assignment. You may want to have students share their responses in small groups before holding a class discussion. Each group should summarize the characteristics of effective and ineffective teachers in their own learning experiences.

This activity will also provide you with an idea of student learning needs and expectations that you can refer to when discussing the expert student later in the chapter.

Activity 1.2. The Metacognitive Interview
Use this handout to explore the concept of expert student. Students may complete the interview in class and score each other's papers to explore their metacognitive skills.

As an outside assignment, ask the students to interview a student from fifth grade through twelfth grade, create their profile using the forms included and complete the intervention plans.

As a discussion starter ask students whether anyone deliberately taught them memory or study strategies in their educational careers. How did this contribute to their expertise as students? What are the implications of students' level of metacognitive development for classroom teachers?

Activity 1.3. What Is Motivation?
Use this exercise after views on intelligence are introduced to help students explore their own ideas about how such perceptions shape expectations and motivation.

This task may be presented as a "think, pair, share" exercise. Each student should complete the questions on the handout individually either in class or as an outside assignment. Students pair up and share their responses. Finally, each pair shares their common ideas with the class as a whole in a group discussion facilitated by the instructor.

Activity 1.4 Educational Research: Confirming the Obvious?
Use this quiz to begin your discussion of the contributions of research to educational psychology and improved classroom instruction.

After administering the quiz and reviewing the answers lead a class discussion on the importance of research to teaching and learning.

Class Activity 1.1
Reflection on Effective Teaching

1. Describe the most **effective** teacher you ever had.

2. Describe the most **ineffective** teacher you ever had.

3. What are your main concerns/fears/anxieties about teaching as a profession?

4. Under what conditions do you learn best? (Conditions might include types of materials, requirements, involvement with other people, factors in the physical environment, teaching styles, and study skills)

5. What do you hope to gain from this course?

Class Activity 1.2
METACOGNITIVE INTERVIEW

The interview takes about 20 minutes to administer and consists of three parts: Metacognitive Knowledge, Metacognitive Skills and Strategies, and Monitoring and Self-Awareness.

Student _____

Grade _____   Age _____

General Directions: Please respond honestly to all the questions below. The point of this exercise is to find out what you know about good study habits so your teachers can help you study better. Do not be concerned about whether or not your answers are right or wrong. You will not receive a grade on this assignment.

I. Metacognitive Knowledge

INSTRUCTIONS: Below are some descriptions of situations in which a student is asked about memory activities. Please read each description, and think about how *you* would answer the question. Read the four answers labeled "A", "B", "C", and "D". Choose the response that best fits how *you* would answer the question.

1. One day two friends went to a birthday party and they met eight children they didn't know before. I'll tell you the names of the children they met: Bill, Jake, Jane, Sally, Anthony, Jim, Luis, and Cindy. After the party one friend went home and the other went to practice a play that he was going to be in. At the play practice, he met seven other children he did not know before, and their names were: Sally, Anita, David, Maria, Jim, Dan, and Jake. At dinner that night, both children's parents asked them the names of the children they met at the **birthday party** that day. Which friend do you think remembered the most, the one who went home after the party, or the one who went to play practice where he met some more children? Why?
    A. The one who went straight home would remember more, but I don't know why.
    B. The one who went to the play would remember more, because some of the children at the play had the same names as those at the party, so it would remind him.
    C. They would be able to remember both equally well.
    D. The one who went straight home would remember more, because he wouldn't get mixed up by hearing all the other names of the children at the play.

2. If you wanted to phone your friend and someone told you the phone number, would it make any difference if you called right after you heard the number or if you got a drink of water first? Why?
    A. It would help to get the drink because you would have more time to remember the number.
    B. It wouldn't make any difference whether you called right away or got a drink first.
    C. It would be better if you phoned first, but I don't know why.
    D. You should phone first; otherwise, you might forget the number while you went to get a drink.

3. You are asked to remember a list of 10 numbers in order. You are also asked to predict how many numbers in the sequence you will accurately remember immediately after the presentation of the numbers:
    - A. I can remember all 10--no problem.
    - B. I won't be able to remember all 10, but maybe about 6 or 7.
    - C. I can probably remember the first 2 numbers.
    - D. I'm not good at remembering numbers, and I won't remember any of them.

4. If you were trying to remember 10 numbers, as in the question above, which of the following ways do you think would be the best?
    - A. Say all the numbers as quickly as possible.
    - B. Repeat the numbers over and over.
    - C. Try to put the numbers in groups to make it easier.
    - D. Try to think of another number, like an address or locker number, that is the same as some of the numbers.

5. The other day I played a tape for a girl. I asked her to listen carefully to the tape as many times as she wanted so she could tell me the story later. Before she began to listen to the tape, she asked me one question: "Am I supposed to remember the story word for word, just like on the tape, or can I tell you in my words?" Which would be easier for her to do--learn the story word for word, or in her own words? Why?
    - A. Either way would be just as easy.
    - B. It would be easier for her to learn to say it in her own words, because she could explain the general idea. If she had to do it word for word, she might forget some of the words and that would ruin the whole story.
    - C. It would be easier for her to learn to say it word for word, because she would listen to each of the words on the tape very carefully.
    - D. It would be easier for her to learn to say it in her own words, but I don't know why.

6. Look at these two word lists:
    List A: Mary-walk
    Charley-jump
    Joe-climb
    Anne-sit

    List B: boy-girl
    hard-easy
    cry-laugh
    black-white

    Suppose I showed you the two lists of words above (List A and List B) and asked you to learn them so that when I show you one of the words, you can tell me the other word that goes with it. For example, when I show you "boy", you would tell me "girl". Do you think one of these lists would be easier to learn than the other one? Why?

    - A. No. Both lists would be equally difficult to learn.
    - B. List B would be easier to learn because it is more meaningful.
    - C. List B would be easier to learn, but I'm not sure why.
    - D. List A would be easier to learn because the names might remind you of a few friends you have.

7. Jenna skimmed through a chapter in her science book before reading it. Juan started reading immediately. Which student will better remember what was read? Why?
   A. Jenna will remember more because she knew what the chapter was about before she read it.
   B. Juan will remember more because he didn't waste time and started reading right away.
   C. Jenna and Juan will remember the same amount.
   D. Jenna should remember more, but I don't know why.

8. Andrew likes to mark important things in his book with a yellow marker when he is reading. Susan does this, too. She marks everything, sometimes whole paragraphs. Andrew only marks main ideas and important words. Who will remember more? Why?
   A. Susan will remember more because she marked more information.
   B. They'll both remember the same amount.
   C. Andrew will remember more because he only marked what he wanted to remember.
   D. Andrew will remember more, but I'm not sure why.

II. Metacognitive Skills and Strategies

INSTRUCTIONS: Below are some descriptions of situations in which a student is asked about memory activities. Please read each description and think about how you would study in that particular situation. Read the four answers: "A", "B", "C", and "D". Choose the one that is most like what *you* would do.

9. A student in class is told to read and study a section from one of the class' books. The student is told that he/she will be quizzed on the material. **If it were I:**
   A. I would read the story and take notes by writing important points of the story.
   B. I would read the story and try to put it in my own words.
   C. I would read the story once.
   D. I would read the entire story twice.

10. The teacher is introducing a new lesson. She writes some key words on the board and tells students what they mean. She also talks about the topic and tells the students some information. **If it were I:**
    A. I would copy the key words down.
    B. I would copy the key words down and try to write the definitions the teachers gave next to them.
    C. I wouldn't write anything down--I'll remember it or wait for a review sheet.
    D. I would copy the words and definitions and try to write down the main ideas the teacher was saying as well.

11. A student is shown a set of pictures of common objects arranged in a row on cards like those shown below. The goal of the task is for the student to recite the list of pictures in order, from left to right, when the pictures are no longer in view. The student is given two minutes to study the pictures, and his or her study behavior is observed. How much the student remembers is checked at the end of the two-minute period. **If it were I:**

hat	man	pencil	dog
bee	broom	cup	eggs

A. I would say the names of the pictures one at a time, repeating each label five times in a row. Rehearsal would sound like this, "Bee, bee, bee, bee, bee, broom, broom, etc."
B. I would say the names of the pictures consecutively from left to right, first while looking at the pictures and then with my eyes turned away. Rehearsal would sound like this, "Bee, broom, cup, eggs, hat, man, etc."
C. I would look carefully at each of the pictures and try not to be distracted from the task during the two-minute period.
D. I would look at the pictures at the start of the study period but get distracted by other things in the room for most of the time.

12. A student is shown a set of pictures of common objects, arranged on cards in a random display like those shown below. The student is told that he or she should learn the names of the cards, in order to repeat them from memory. The cards can be recalled in any order that the student wants to use. The student is given three minutes to study the pictures. How much he or she remembers is checked at the end of the three-minute study period. **If it were I:**

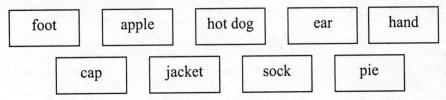

A. I would look at the pictures intently and try not to be distracted from the task during the time period.
B. I would say the names of the pictures over and over to myself, while looking at each in turn.
C. I would sort the items into categories of related things (food, clothing, and body parts) and study them in these sets.
D. I would move some items to put them in pairs with others (grouping, for example, sock and foot, hand and hot dog) but leave others pictures unsorted.

13. Suppose the student received a task just like the last task described above, but with one change in the instructions. Now the student is asked to study the items as long as he or she wants to, and to indicate when he or she knows them by ringing a bell. When the bell is rung, the teacher will ask the student to recall the items seen. **If it were I:**
A. I would look at and say each item just one time and then would ring the bell and say the items as quickly as possible.
B. I would look at some of the items, and then ring the bell.
C. I would say each item to myself a fixed number of times (e.g., three times, five times) and then ring the bell.
D. After studying, I would give myself a little "test" to see if I knew all of the items. When I could say them correctly in practice, I would ring the bell.

III. Monitoring and Self-Awareness

INSTRUCTIONS: Below are some brief descriptions of some kinds of understandings a student might have about memory. Read each description and try to decide if the statement is true or false for you most of the time.

(Examiners should read each statement aloud.)

14. T F   I can tell if one way to study something is better than another way.
15. T F   I usually divide my study time so that easier things are studied
            for a longer time than are harder things.
16. T F   I can tell when I know something and don't need to study it any longer.
17. T F   Sometimes I know I know something, but I just can't think of it
18. T F   I usually cannot tell how well I will do on an exam.
19. T F   I do different things when the teacher says to "remember"
            something than when he or she just says to "look it over".
20. T F   I usually do not know if I've answered a test question correctly or not.
21. T F   When I decide how long to study I think about the kind of stuff
            I have to remember and the kind of test I'm going to have.
22. T F   Sometimes I get the feeling that I don't understand what I am reading.
23. T F   I go over difficult material until I understand it better when
            reading or studying.
24. T F   When I work out math problems, I try to make a good guess at what the
            answer should be, so I can compare my answer after I work the problem.
25. T F   When I study for a test, I never think of questions the teacher might ask.

Class Activity 1.2
METACOGNITIVE INTERVIEW SCORING DIRECTIONS

Use in scoring the <u>Metacognitive Interview</u> to create the <u>Student Profile</u> on the next page.

<u>Descriptors:</u>   <u>Directions for Scoring:</u>

1.   If answers "D" on questions 1 and 2, mark "<u>yes</u>" for #1

                     If answers "D" on only one or answers "A" on question 1 or
                     "C" on question 2, mark "<u>emerging</u>"
                     If answers "B" or "C" on question 1 and "A" or "B" on
                     question 2, mark "<u>no</u>"

2.   If answers "B" on question 3, mark "<u>yes</u>" for #2
                     If answers "A" on question 3, mark "<u>emerging</u>"
                     If answers "C" or "D" on question 3, mark "<u>no</u>"

3.   If answers "C" or "D" on question 4, mark "<u>yes</u>" for #3
                     If answers "B" on question 4, mark "<u>emerging</u>"
                     If answers "A" on question 4, mark "<u>no</u>"

4.   If answers "B" on question 5, mark "<u>yes</u>" for #4
                     If answers "D" on question 5, mark "<u>emerging</u>"
                     If answers "A" or "C" on question 5, mark "<u>no</u>"

5.   If answers "B" on question 6, mark "<u>yes</u>" for #5
                     If answers "C" on question 6, mark "<u>emerging</u>"
                     If answers "A" or "D" on question 6, mark "<u>no</u>"

6.   If answers "A" on question 7, mark "<u>yes</u>" for #6
                     If answers "D" on question 7, mark "<u>emerging</u>"
                     If answers "B" or "C" on question 7, mark "<u>no</u>"

7.   If answers "C" on question 8, mark "<u>yes</u>" for #7
                     If answers "D" on question 8, mark "<u>emerging</u>"
                     If answers "A" or "B" on question 8, mark "<u>no</u>"

8.   If answers "A" or "B" on question 9, mark "<u>yes</u>" for #8
                     If answers "C" or "D" on question 9, mark "<u>no</u>"
                     (There is no emerging answer for this question.)

9.   If answers "D", "B", or "A" on question 9, mark "<u>yes</u>" for #9
                     If answers "C" on question 9, mark "<u>no</u>"
                     (There is no emerging answer for this question.)

10.   If answers "D" on question 10, mark "<u>yes</u>" for #10
                     If answers "A" or "B" on question 10, mark "<u>emerging</u>"
                     If answers "C" on question 10, mark "<u>no</u>"

11.   If answers "B" on question 11, mark "<u>yes</u>" for #11
                     If answers "A" on question 11, mark "<u>emerging</u>"
                     If answers "C" or "D" on question 11, mark "<u>no</u>"

12.   If answers "C" on question 12, mark "<u>yes</u>" for #12
If answers "D" on question 12, mark "<u>emerging</u>"
If answers "A" or "B" on question 12, mark "<u>no</u>"

13.   If answers "D" on question 13, mark "<u>yes</u>" for #13
If answers "C" on question 13, mark "<u>emerging</u>"
If answers "A" or "B" on question 13, mark "<u>no</u>"

14.   If answers "True" on question 14, mark "<u>yes</u>" for #14
If answers "False" on question 14, mark "<u>no</u>"
(There is no emerging answer for this question.)

15.   If answers "False" on question 15 and "True" on question 21, mark "<u>yes</u>" for #15
If answers "True" on both or "False" on both, mark "<u>emerging</u>"
If answers "True" on question 15 and "False" on question 21, mark "<u>no</u>"

16.   If answers "True" on questions 16 and 17, mark "<u>yes</u>" on #16
If answers "True" on only one, mark "<u>emerging</u>"
If answers "False" on both questions 16 and 17, mark "<u>no</u>"

17.   If answers "False" on questions 18 and 20, mark "<u>yes</u>" for #17
If answers "True" on one, mark "<u>emerging</u>"
If answers "True" on both questions 18 and 20, mark "<u>no</u>"

18.   If answers "True" on questions 19 and 21, mark "<u>yes</u>" for #18
If answers "True" on only one, mark "<u>emerging</u>"
If answers "False" on both questions 19 and 21, mark "<u>no</u>"

19.   If answers "True" on questions 22 and 23, mark "<u>yes</u>" for #19
If answers "True" on only one, mark "<u>emerging</u>"
If answers "False" on both questions 22 and 23, mark "<u>no</u>"

20.   If answers "True" on question 24 and "False" on question 25, mark "<u>yes</u>" for #20
If answers "True" on both or "False" on both, mark "<u>emerging</u>"
If answers "False" on question 24 and "True" on question 25, mark "<u>no</u>"

Class Activity 1.2
METACOGNITIVE STUDENT PROFILE

Metacognitive Knowledge:	Yes	Emerging	No
1. Understands interference	____	____	____
2. Knows limits of short term memory	____	____	____
3. Knows effective aids to memorization	____	____	____
4. Understands recall of meaningful material (gist vs. verbatim)	____	____	____
5. Understands that meaning increases ease of rote memory	____	____	____
6. Understands that preview increases comprehension	____	____	____
7. Understands that directing attention to key information increases retention	____	____	____

Metacognitive Skills and Strategies:	Yes	Emerging	No
8. Paraphrases information to aid recall in reading comprehension	____	____	____
9. Uses repetition to aid comprehension and memory	____	____	____
10. Uses notes as external aids for recall	____	____	____
11. Uses rehearsal effectively	____	____	____
12. Uses categorization/chunking strategies	____	____	____
13. Self-tests while studying	____	____	____

Monitoring and Self-Awareness:			
14. Varies study techniques to meet task demands	____	____	____
15. Divides study time effectively	____	____	____
16. Has a sense of metacognitive awareness (knowing you know)	____	____	____
17. Predicts exam grades successfully	____	____	____
18. Directs self to perform learning strategies	____	____	____
19. Senses poor comprehension and reviews material	____	____	____
20. Uses estimation/prediction to monitor performance	____	____	____

Class Activity 1.2
INTERVENTION PLAN

Use the results of the Student Profile to fill in the following form. Use a highlighter or another method to indicate suggested interventions for those answers that fall into the "emerging" or "no" categories.
Areas of weakness for this student, _____ , are indicated with highlighting. Suggestions for intervention follow.

Metacognitive Knowledge
1. *Does not understand interference:*
Explain the concept of interference in memory. Provide examples from the student's classroom that illustrate how interference reduces memory.

2. *Does not know limits of short-term memory:*
Explain that our memory can hold about seven (give or take two) units of meaningful information. Relate this to the seven-digit telephone number, the nine-digit social security number, and the five-digit zip code. There's a reason commonly used numbers fit within this range! Point out that the extended zip code numbers have not caught on because they exceed the limits of short-term memory.

3. *Does not know effective aids to memorization:*
Explain efficient rehearsal techniques (rehearse in the manner in which something is to be recalled, group or chunk material to be rehearsed, make associations with known material and rehearse the association). Provide examples from the student's current classwork that illustrate these points.

4. *Does not understand that remembering the gist is easier than verbatim recall:*
Explain how the brain works naturally to abstract out main ideas and themes from what we see, read, and hear. Provide examples from the student's daily life (using popular movies or recent class discussions, for example). Illustrate your point with a practice exercise asking the student to remember the main idea of a paragraph and then a verbatim recall of another paragraph.

5. *Does not understand that meaning increases ease of rote memory:*
Explain that our brain remembers information by association or linking. We link new information to old information. Thus, information that is naturally related in a meaningful way is automatically and easily remembered. Demonstrate with two work lists--one opposites, the other unrelated. Ask students to remember each list and compare the results.

6. *Does not understand that preview increases comprehension:*
Review the steps to the comprehension process (preview, active reading, summary or paraphrase, and review). Discuss how skimming something before reading is akin to getting to open the lid of a box and looking inside

rather than just making a guess about its contents. Which method is most likely to produce an accurate answer? Previewing increases comprehension by letting you know "what's inside" before you read. You might need to use an actual box!

7. *Does not understand that directing attention to key information increases comprehension:*
Explain that making decisions about whether something is important or not increases remembering. When a reader decides to highlight particular information, that decision helps make that information "stick" in the brain. If you highlight too much, you have made no decisions and memory isn't enhanced. Demonstrate this with two readings about two pages long. Ask the student to highlight key ideas in one, but whole paragraphs in the other. Then, have the student compare recall of both stories.

Metacognitive Skills and Strategies
8. *Does not paraphrase information to increase meaning and retention:*
Explain that meaningfulness controls remembering. If it makes sense to us, we can remember it fairly easily. Demonstrate by comparing understanding and retention for work definitions that are learned verbatim rather than through paraphrase.

9. *Does not use repetition to aid memory or use rehearsal effectively:*
Review effective rehearsal strategies and demonstrate student efficacy of different approaches with actual classroom material.

10. *Does not use notes as external aids for recall:*
Explain that taking notes in your own words increases immediate comprehension and copying information from the board or overhead gives a student material to review later. Demonstrate several note-taking methods-- mapping, outline, or split-page methods--for example. Provide feedback to students on the quality of their notes. Review elaboration of notes and provide feedback to students who have highlighted their notes, made clarifications, or added examples. Partner checks can be utilized to reduce teacher time. Compare test grades with and without appropriate notes to demonstrate efficacy with students.

11. *Does not use categorization or chunking strategies:*
Explain how categorization and chunking enhance memory--have the student test him/herself with and without chunking using actual classroom assignments.

12. *Does not self-test while studying:*
Ask the student how a teacher knows when a student has learned information. Suggest that the student could also give him/herself a little test to know when studying and learning were complete. Discuss how reviewing

something a fixed number of times may cause the student to study too little or more than needed.

Monitoring and Self-Awareness

13. *Does not vary study techniques to meet task demands or divide study time effectively:*
Discuss different approaches for different study tasks. Have student number homework from easiest to hardest and estimate the amount of time and type of approach necessary for each task. Record actual time spent and activity used to study. Compare actual and predicted.

14. *Does not predict exam grades successfully*:
Have the student make a chart for upcoming or regularly occurring tests and quizzes and predict his/her grade prior to each evaluation; record actual grade and compare. Discuss how self-testing can contribute to accurate prediction.

15. *Does not have a sense of metacognitive awareness:*
Discuss the "tip of the tongue" phenomena. Has this ever happened to the student? Rate homework and classwork assignments from hardest to easiest. Discuss why the student judged one class harder than another.

16. *Does not direct self to perform learning strategies:*
Discuss different types of strategies for learning (such as mnemonics and other elaborative strategies, organizational and chunking strategies, affective strategies, and rehearsal). Using the student's classwork, demonstrate a variety of strategies to enhance learning. Ask the student to choose his or her most difficult subject and help them apply strategies. Evaluate their success on the next quiz or test.

17. *Does not sense poor comprehension and reviews material:*
Review the steps in the comprehension process: preview, active reading (do I understand the content?), summary or paraphrase, and review. Practice "comprehension checks" during free reading with a timer. When the timer rings, student should record whether or not he or she understands what's being read. If the answer is no, students should review the material using steps above with a partner.

18. *Does not use estimation or prediction to monitor performance:*
Practice estimation and prediction with actual class material. Show that estimation in math and prediction in reading increase accuracy and comprehension. Students should articulate the common purposes of estimation and prediction.

Class Activity 1.3
What Is Motivation?

1. Write your own definition of motivation:

2. Write a definition of motivation *to learn*:

3. Write a definition of motivation *to achieve*:

4. Contrast motivation to learn with motivation to achieve. What are special benefits of each?

5. Describe something in your past or present that you were (or are) particularly motivated to do. Are you good at it (natural ability)? Have you been rewarded for it in the past (either with praise, awards, prizes or a sense of personal accomplishment and pride)? Is it an individual activity or a group activity?

Class Activity 1.4
Educational Research: Confirming The Obvious?

1. _____ Parent involvement programs have a positive effect on the achievement of low income children.

2. _____ New learning is best remembered when the teacher relates it to old learning.

3. _____ The increase in elective courses in American high schools has improved student learning.

4. _____ Homework assignments that are related to work done in class have a positive effect on student achievement.

5. _____ Elementary school children seem to learn as well from their errors as from their successes.

6. _____ Retention helps failing children to achieve better the next year than passing them on to the next grade.

7. _____ Boys score higher than girls on math achievement tests.

8. _____ In reading groups, calling on children in random order yields higher achievement than calling on them in ordered turns.

9. _____ Very bright or gifted children tend to be less athletic and less social than their more average peers.

Class Activity 1.4 Answer Key
Educational Research: Confirming the Obvious?

1. **TRUE** Head Start Programs that were shown to be the most effective in deterring retention, dropping out, and placement in special education were those that most heavily involved parents in the school program.

2. **TRUE** Research on how the brain works reveals new memories are encoded by their relationship to existing knowledge.

3. **FALSE** After an increase in elective options in the 1970's, research showed decreases in basic skills such as writing.

4. **TRUE** Homework is effective when it serves to reinforce skills or concepts already understood in class.

5. **TRUE** Elementary age children need to explore and interact with the world, actively experimenting, they grow cognitively from their errors according to developmental psychologist, Jean Piaget.

6. **FALSE** Research indicates that children who are retained fall back to the bottom of the class within a few years regarding achievement and are more likely to engage in high-risk activities as adolescents.

7. **TRUE** Boys, on average, score higher than girls on quantitative and spatial tasks. Girls score higher on language tests, again, on average.

8. **FALSE** Although a typical instructional activity for years, this procedure allows students to predict when they'll be called on and "tune out" instruction before and after their turn. Initially, teachers used this "round robin" procedure in order to ensure every student was called on.

9. **FALSE** Lewis Terman's classic longitudinal study of gifted children found that they tended to excel academically, socially, and athletically.

AVAILABLE RESOURCES ON-LINE
National Education Association
www.nea.org
This website reviews current issues and articles, provides quick clicks or links to such things as legislative action, NEA Today, and Read Across America, and also lists the top ten clicks. NEA also contains separate links for teachers, students, and parents. The following links on this page are from NEA on the page www.nea.org/teaching/refs.html.

Ask Eric
http://ericir.syr.edu
This website provides a variety of services and products on a broad range of education-related issues. ERIC is a personalized Internet-based service providing education information to teachers, librarians, counselors, administrators, parents, and others throughout the United States and the world. The main components of Ask ERIC are the Question and Answer Service, the Virtual Library, and the ERIC Database.

Discovery Channel School
www.discovery.com
This website contains ideas to enhance learning for parents, teachers, and students. There is a student channel providing help with homework, a teacher channel presenting creative curriculum resources, and a family learning store offering products to help children achieve.

Education World
www.education-world.com
This website covers current school issues such as technology, teacher lesson plans, and curriculum. Each day it provides new information on the following themes: curriculum, school issues, great teaching sites, site reviews, teaching themes, and a lesson plan of the week.

Electronic Collaboration: A Practical Guide for Educators
www.lab.brown.edu/public/ocsc/collaboration.guide
This website reviews key concepts about electronic collaboration; ways to collaborate through activities; methods to design and implement a collaborative environment; ways to choose tools (technology) for things such as discussion groups and data collection; and extra resources for collaboration.

Federal Resources for Educational Excellence (FREE)
www.ed.gov/free/
This website lists education resources according to subject, and provides new FREE resources and interesting facts. There is a search link to find full-text resources on participating agencies, and also a link to resources created for students.

IBM K-12 Solutions
www.solutions.ibm.com/k12/
This website provides professional development to help teachers integrate technology into the curriculum. IBM e-business products can help improve the quality of education, meet the needs of a diverse and competitive student body, and create a flexible, student-centered environment. IBM technologies and offerings can help with theoretical, experimental, computational, and data assimilation/analysis research needs.

Internet Public Library
www.ipl.org
This website provides a reference center with links to many subjects, including education, social sciences, and arts & humanities. The site also contains current, featured, and permanent exhibitions. There are also links for teens, youth, librarians, and links to newspapers and on-line texts.

Phi Delta Kappa International
www.pdkintl.org
This website provides the organization's purpose statement as well as future directions. The website offers member services, program offerings, publications, and educational activities. Phi Delta Kappa also reviews current and past issues of newsletters, lists contacts to international offices and the staff, and contains web-site links for the center in Washington, D.C.

Teacher's Guide to the U.S. Department of Education
www.ed.gov/pubs/TeachersGuide
This website provides articles on such things as Teaching: A National Priority, Voluntary National Tests in Reading and Math, and Raising Academic Standards. The Teacher's Guide lists services and resources such as On-Line Resources and National Library of Education, and field services and resources such as Special Education Programs, and Tech-Prep Education Contacts. The Teacher's Guide also contains grants, publication, and National Education goals.

U.S. Department of Education
www.ed.gov
This website provides the following: education headlines, funding opportunities, student financial assistance, research & statistics, news & events, programs & services, publications & products, education job openings, and links to other sites.

RECOMMENDED VIDEOS FOR CHAPTER ONE
The Making of a Teacher
Episode #2
Price: $19.95
VHS Video 22 minutes
Published by NEA (1992)
7751-2-00-NET
You'll take a look at teacher preparation in the 1990s and see how it is adapting to meet the needs of a changing society.

Teaching Teachers
Episode #41
Price: $19.95
VHS Video 22 minutes
Published by NEA (1995)
7790-3-00-NET
Exciting things are happening in professional development. Featured: a professional development school (PDS) where university faculty, current teachers, and student teachers all work together in an environment similar to a teaching hospital; and a district where teachers have greater control of their own learning and are becoming generators of new knowledge.

Connecting with Kids
Price: $24.95
VHS Video 45 minutes
Published by NEA (1996)
7606-0-00-NET
This is a tale of two teaching styles. First, meet Mary Beth Blegen, the 1996 National Teacher of the Year, who doesn't let anything get in the way of sparking the imaginations of her high school students. Her formula involves taking extraordinary steps to get to know her students and making learning relevant to their lives. Second, you'll see how John Fuerst manages the emotionally disturbed middle school children known for creating chaos in other classrooms. His carefully structured lessons teach rowdy students how to behave. He believes every child can be reached: "I've never met a kid who didn't want to be a star."

HANDOUTS TO ACCOMPANY YOUR LESSONS:

H 1.1   Triarchic Thinking in the Classroom

H 1.2   Metacognition

H 1.3   Characteristics of Expert and Novice Lesson

H 1.4   Lesson Plan Components

H 1.5   Views of Intelligence

H 1.6   Causes of Intrinsic Motivation

H 1.7   How Do Teachers Allow Expectations To Impact Instruction?

H 1.8   Teacher Expectation Effects

H 1.9   How to Increase Intrinsic Motivation

H 1.10   Two Approaches of Research in Instructional Settings

H 1.11   Recommended Journals in Educational Psychology

H 1.1

Triarchic Thinking in the Classroom

The **Practitioner (Practical)** wants to change the consequences of the situation. If the problem is darkness, the practitioner wants the opposite, the mirror image of that, so the goal is to have light. The goal is to act to help immediately.

The **Problem Solver (Creative)** finds unique ways to solve the problem by using resources in new and different ways. Here the goal is to find ways to solve the problem in the future.

The **Researcher (Analytical)** wants to answer the why question. If the problem is that we don't know why the light went out, the researcher's goal is the mirror image of that, to find a cause and effect relationship which explains why it went out. The goal is to understand the problem.

H 1.2

Metacognition

Metacognition – knowledge about cognitive processes and how they function

(For every aspect of cognition there is a metacognitive aspect as well – thus we can discuss metalinquistics, meta-attention, metacomprehension, and metamemory, for example)

- *Metamemory is very strongly related to our ability to learn.*

- **Metamemory** – knowledge about how memory works and how to remember

- **Metacognitive Processes:**

    1. Metaknowledge – what we know about a particular cognitive process

    2. Metamonitoring – out ability to monitor a particular process

    3. Specific strategies – strategies to enhance a particular process

Types of Strategies

1. Rehearsal

2. Elaboration

3. Organizational

4. Comprehension-monitoring

5. Affective

6. Problem-solving

<u>H 1.3</u>

Characteristics of Expert Lesson Plans

✓ Enables the expert teacher to teach effectively and efficiently.

✓ Maximizes the amount of time that students spend learning.

✓ Includes knowledge that is related to teaching content which enables the teacher to connect student feedback to lesson objectives.

Characteristics of Novice Lesson Plans

✓ Contains less complex and less interconnected lesson plans.

✓ Demonstrates problems generating examples and explanations

✓ Tends to have difficulties relating student questions to lesson objectives.

H 1.4

Lesson Plan Components

Global plans	Local plans	Decision elements
Information not related to specific lesson content or subject matter. - Routines for checking homework - Presenting new material - Supervising guided practice	Information related to lesson content and subject matter. - Routines for presenting particular concepts - Routines for assessing student understand-ing of particular concepts	Information that makes the lesson plan responsive to expected and unexpected events. - Prepares teacher for unexpected circumstances - Use at times when students are not quick to understand material

H 1.5

Views of Intelligence

Incremental view	vs	Entity view
The belief that intelligence can be increased.		**The belief that intelligence is fixed.**
➢ Students see corrective feedback as an indication that more work and effort are needed to remediate the weakness.		➢ Students tend to take negative evaluations of their abilities and performance as signs that they are not intelligent enough to succeed.
➢ Students respond to failure by working harder in the future.		➢ Students tend to avoid situations in which they might get negative feedback, and thus, avoid challenges.
➢ Students seek out challenges because these challenges represent learning experiences.		

H 1.6

Causes of Intrinsic Motivation:

1. Need to develop competency

2. Need to satisfy curiosity

3. Need for autonomy

4. Value system for academic work

Individual differences in Intrinsic Motivation occur because:

*   Competence and degree of challenge varies from individual to individual

*   Environmental effects on competence motivation vary

*   Internalized value systems vary

<u>H 1.7</u>

How do teachers allow expectations to impact instruction?

Proactive teachers: do not allow expectations to affect instruction – they manage to spend more time with low achievers without hurting high achievers.

Reactive teachers: allow existing differences between high and low achievers follow their natural course so differences tend to widen.

Over-reactive teachers: overemphasize student differences and treat and teach high and low achievers differently to the detriment of the low achievers.

(Good & Brophy, 1974)

H 1.8

Teacher Expectation Effects

- Students also affect teacher expectation by reinforcing teacher beliefs through *feedback loops* tending to confirm teacher beliefs.

- Teachers' views on intelligence (whether ability is viewed as a stable trait – *entity theory* – or as a set of skills that can be developed –*instrumental theory*) impact their beliefs in their own efficacy as teachers and their expectations of students.

- Goals related to entity belief systems usually result in behaviors designed to help the individual "look smart". Goals related to instrumental belief systems usually result in behaviors designed to increase skill levels.

- Messages about belief systems can be altered by changes in classroom organization (within versus between class grouping for example) and changes in teacher behavior (altering wait time for example).

- Differences in "wait time" after questions shape students' beliefs about teachers' attitudes. Negative and positive feedback, particularly when given quickly and consistently, can shape student behavior.

- *Self-fulfilling prophecies* can occur when students change behavior to meet perceived expectations.

- *Sustaining low expectation effects* may occur when teachers fail to note change or potential in students.

- Students may resist teacher attempts to change expectation sets once they have integrated a certain trait or performance level into their self-concept.

H 1.9

How to increase intrinsic motivation:

1. Increase feelings of competency

2. Increase level of complexity, novelty, variety

3. Present tasks positively

4. Limit the negative effects of evaluation on challenge seeking

5. Don't "over" help

6. Don't pair external rewards with tasks that already have some intrinsic motivation

7. Provide opportunities for student choice

H 1.10

Two Approaches of Research in Instructional Settings

Descriptive Research	Experimental Research
❖ The scientist observes and describes what is happening in a situation without changing the dynamics of the situation.	❖ The scientist designs a test to answer a question and actually changes what happens to people so that effects can be observed.
❖ Researchers can find a correlation, which is a relationship between two measurements.	❖ Subjects must be chosen at random.
❖ A positive correlation is a relationship where as one-measurement increases, the other also increases.	❖ The groups of people who undergo a change by researchers are called experimental groups.
❖ A negative correlation is a relationship where as one-measurement increases, the other decreases.	❖ The groups of people for whom nothing is changed are called control groups.
❖ Researchers can try to determine whether the results are statistically significant.	❖ The purpose of the research is to compare the outcomes for the people in the experimental groups with the outcomes for people in the control groups.
❖ Research can also take the form of a case study, an in-depth observation of one individual.	

H 1.11

Recommended Journals in Educational Psychology

- Adolescence
- American Educational Research Journal
- American Journal of Education
- American Psychologist
- Child Development
- Childhood Education
- Cognition and Instruction
- Cognitive Psychology
- Computers in Education
- Contemporary Education Review
- Contemporary Educational Psychology
- Educational and Psychological Measurement
- Educational Leadership
- Educational Psychologist
- Educational Psychology Review
- Educational Researcher
- Elementary School Journal
- Exceptional Children
- Instructional Science
- Journal of Applied Behavior Analysis
- Journal of Applied Developmental Psychology
- Journal of Educational Computing Research
- Journal of Educational Research
- Journal of Experimental Child Psychology
- Journal of Experimental Education
- Journal of Learning Disabilities
- Journal of Research and Development
- Journal of School Psychology
- Journal of Teacher Education
- Learning and Instruction
- Learning Disabilities Quarterly
- Monographs of the Society for Research in Child Development
- Phi Delta Kappan
- Review of Education Research
- School Psychology Review
- Teaching and Teacher Education
- Theory into Practice
- Young Children

Chapter Two
Cognitive Development

The instructor's manual for this chapter contains:
- A *Chapter-at-a-Glance* chart that reviews all chapter related material
- A detailed chapter outline to highlight main points of the chapter
- A list of transparencies from Transparencies - Educational Psychology IV that correspond to this chapter
- Several activities to deepen student understanding
- An annotated list of additional resources including internet sites
- Handouts to accompany your lessons

CHAPTER-AT-A-GLANCE

Chapter Outline	Objectives	Instructional Aids
1.0 The Importance of Cognitive Development for Teaching, p. 41	1. Describe the importance to teachers of understanding cognitive development. 2. Compare and contrast maturation, learning and canalization. 3. Describe the differences and similarities between theories classified as continuous versus stagelike. 4. Describe the differences and similarities between theories classified as domain-general versus domain-specific.	- Transparencies T7, T8, T9 - Handout 2.1 - Activity 2.1 - Test Bank Questions 1-13, 73-79, 93, 101
2.0 Piaget's Stage Theory of Cognitive Development p.44	1. Describe the mechanisms of cognitive development according to Piaget's theory. 2. Describe the main characteristics and accomplishments for each of Piaget's stages of cognitive development. 3. Evaluate Piaget's theory according to current research. 4. Understand the similarities and differences in Piaget's theory compared with the neo-Piagetian theories described in the text. 5. Describe some ideas related to, but that go beyond, Piaget on the basis of current information. 6. Give examples of Piagetian or neo-Piagetian ideas for teaching.	- Transparencies T10, T11, T12, T12A, T12B, T13, T14 - Handout 2.2 - Activities 2.2, 2.3, 2.4 - Test Bank Questions 14-45, 80-87, 94-96, 102, 103 - Video Segments 2, 3
3.0 Vygotsky's Sociocultural Theory of Cognitive Development p. 55	1. Describe Vygotsky's sociocultural theory of cognitive development. 2. Give examples of internalization. 3. Describe the zone of proximal development. 4. Describe scaffolding. 5. What are the implications for teaching using Vygotsky's theory?	- Transparencies T15, T16 - Handout 2.3 - Test Bank Questions 46-57, 88, 97 - Video Segment 4
4.0 Information Processing Theories: Examining Learning and Memory Skills, p. 61	1. Describe the information processing approach to cognitive development.	- Activity 2.5 - Test Bank Questions 58-62

5.0 Three Major Approaches to Cognitive Development: A Comparison p. 65	1. Compare and contrast the three major approaches of cognitive development.	- Test Bank Questions 63-64, 100
6.0 Language Development p. 66	1. Describe what makes a language a language. 2. Describe the stages of language acquisition. 3. Compare and contrast the theories of language acquisition. 4. Describe the relationship between language and thought.	- Test Bank Questions 65-72, 89-92, 98-99

DETAILED CHAPTER TWO OUTLINE

I. The Big Picture

- Although Joan had taught math for eight years, she soon became frustrated by her change from elementary school to middle school.

- Joan experienced a classroom containing a mixture of kids at different levels of performance.

- Joan began to gain insight into her problem at an in-service about cognitive readiness.

- The part of educational psychology that deals with the type of class Joan was facing is the study of cognitive development - the changes in mental skills that occur through increasing maturity and experience.

II. The Importance of Cognitive Development to Teaching

- Expert teachers know what level of cognitive development they can expect from most of the students in their classes.
- Expert teachers know how to challenge their students in ways that spur cognitive development rather than frustration.

A. Maturation Versus Learning
- Maturation is any relatively permanent change (cognitive, emotional, or physical) that occurs as a result of biological aging, regardless of personal experience.
  - Maturation is preprogrammed - it occurs regardless of the interactions a child has with the environment.
  - Expert teachers know they cannot force a student to do what he or she is not biologically old enough to do.
- Learning is any relatively permanent change in thought or behavior that occurs as a result of experience.
  - Learning is not preprogrammed - it cannot occur in the absence of stimulation.
  - Learning is what education is all about.
- Knowing what almost all children of a certain age can be expected to do helps a teacher plan good lessons and know when to push.

B. Canalization: A Key to Teaching
- Canalization refers to the extent to which a behavior or an underlying ability develops without respect to the environment.
- High versus weak canalization
  - A highly canalized ability develops in nearly all children.
  - A weakly canalized ability develops only with a supportive environment.
  - The interpersonal skills children use in their interactions with each other and teachers are relatively weakly canalized.
  - Teachers are most easily able to help students develop weakly canalized skills.

- Canalization is key to teaching because children come into classrooms with widely differing experiences.
  - Almost all students can be expected to show highly canalized abilities, but some will be likely to show weakly canalized abilities.
  - Expert teachers match their expectations to what is possible and what is likely for their students to accomplish, while bearing in mind the difference.

D. Cognitive Development: Continuous Versus Stagelike
- Theories suggesting that development proceeds continuously assume cognitive abilities are acquired gradually such that each new accomplishment builds directly on those that came before it.
  - A person's thinking is not fundamentally different at any one age or level of development than it is at any other age.
  - People gradually progress to higher levels of cognitive ability.
- Stage theories provide three major assumptions about development.
  - Each stage is associated with a qualitatively distinct set of cognitive structures or mental patterns of organization that influence our ways of dealing with the world.
  - Behavior unfolds in a one-directional, invariable sequence.
  - Later stages build on earlier stages.

E. Domain-General Versus Domain-Specific Cognitive Development
- Domain-general development occurs more or less simultaneously in multiple areas.
- Domain-specific development occurs at different rates in different areas.
- The domain distinction is very relevant to teachers.
  - According to the domain-specific view, a child can be an expert in one domain of schoolwork and a novice in another.
  - With domain-general development, a child is unlikely to get an A in reading and an F in English.

F. Implications for Teaching
- A number of skills, including many academic and interpersonal skills, develop only with respect to the environment.
- Some expert teachers subscribe to stagelike views of development, in which it is assumed that certain inborn factors determine the unfolding of a child's abilities over time.
- The concept of domains helps expert teachers assess why a student's performance in one area, such as math, is not up to par with that in another area, such as reading.

III. Piaget's Stage Theory of Cognitive Development
- Jean Piaget proposed the most influential single theory of cognitive development to date.
- The theory is based on the premise of "the child as scientist."
  - The child's scientific exploration is limited by cognitive abilities that have yet to develop.
  - At all ages, children actively seek to explore the world and to come to terms with it.
- Piaget's theory is a stage theory of cognitive development specifying qualitative changes in cognitive development with each successive stage.
  - Teachers should expect sudden bursts in the development of cognitive abilities rather than a smooth progression of development over time.
  - Piaget's theory is also domain-general in that it predicts that children who show cognitive development in one area generally should show comparable cognitive development in other areas.
- Piaget proposed that although abilities in all areas generally develop concurrently, the spread of an ability to various areas of performance takes place over time.
  - Horizontal decalage is the temporary difference in levels of performance that a child shows between various cognitive domains or activities within a give stage of development.
  - Development is almost domain-general.

A. Mechanisms of Cognitive Development
- The main mechanism by which cognitive development occurs is called equilibration, which is the balancing of cognitive structures with the needs of the environment.
- The mismatch between the state of the world and one's preconceived notions is the state of disequilibrium.
- Two processes involving changes in the child's cognitive schemas can achieve equilibration.
  - In assimilation, the child attempts to fit new information into the schemas he or she has already formed.
  - In accommodation, the child creates new schemas to organize information that he or she cannot assimilate into existing schemas.

B. Stages of Cognitive Development
- The **Sensorimotor Stage**, occurring between birth and about age 2, is characterized by the development of sensory and motor functions.
  - Sensory input includes seeing and hearing.
  - Motor output includes moving and experimenting with objects in the environment.
  - The two main accomplishments of this stage are object permanence and representational thought:
    - Object permanence is the realization that an object continues to exist even when it is not immediately visible.
    - Representational thought is the well formed mental representations, or ideas, of external stimuli.
- In the **Preoperational Stage**, occurring mostly between 24 months and 7 years of age, the child begins to actively develop the mental representations that were just starting to form near the end of the sensorimotor stage.
  - Children begin to communicate by way of words, both with each other and with parents.
  - The communication is often egocentric, centered on the self without understanding how other people perceive a situation.
  - Children often seem to be unaware of the art of conversation, without taking into account what the other party has said.
- In the **Concrete-Operational Stage**, occurring from about ages 7 to 12 years, children become able to mentally manipulate the internal representations they started to form in the previous stage.
  - Children can think logically as long as the logical thinking applies to concrete objects rather than to abstractions.
  - Children through their development of conservation recognize that even when the physical appearance of something changes, its underlying quantity of it remains the same.
  - The concrete operational child has reached a level at which thinking is reversible, where the child can mentally reverse a physical operation.
- In the **Formal Operational Stage**, occurring from 11 or 12 through adulthood, individuals form and operate on abstract as well as concrete mental representations.
  - Children can see second-order relations, or relations between relations, based on the perception of the similarity of like features of two things.
  - During formal operations, the ability to think abstractly, to think about concepts that do not have any concrete, physical equivalents, develops.
  - Formal operational children can also think systematically.

C. Evaluating Piaget's Theory
- Although Piaget's theory is the most nearly complete theory of cognitive development to date, the extent to which it is accurate in describing children's cognitive development has bee questioned.
- The stagelike nature of development proposed by Piaget has many limitations.
- Piaget has underestimated the ages at which children are really capable of performing various kinds of cognitive tasks.

- There are doubts about whether children's failures to perform certain tasks are actually due to the reasons Piaget gave.
- There are doubts about whether all adults ever do become fully formal-operational.
- There are concerns about whether the theory is cross-culturally generalizable.
  - Sometimes children from diverse cultures do not even understand tests developed in Western cultures.
  - Many adolescents and adults in Western cultures also may not reach formal operations.
  - Piaget eventually modified his theory to recognize that formal operations may be more a function of domain-specific expertise than of general cognitive maturation.

D. Neo-Piagetian Views
- Neo-Piagetians are a group of psychologists and educators who have built on Piaget's theory while disowning the parts of the theory that have not held up to close scrutiny.
- One neo-Piagetian approach is to propose alternative sets of stages.
  - Fischer and Pipp have made the distinction between optimal and typical levels of performance.
  - The optimal level is the best performance an individual is capable of making on a given task.
- Another approach that neo-Piagetians have taken is to propose one or more stages beyond the four originally suggested by Piaget.
  - Theorists are basically suggesting the possibility of postformal thinking, or thinking that goes beyond that of formal operations in some way.
  - Theories suggest that a great deal of cognitive development goes on during adolescence and adulthood.
  - Patricia Arlin has suggested that a fifth stage of cognitive development is one of problem finding, in which an individual becomes able not just to solve problems, but also to identify the important problems to solve.
- Others have proposed a stage beyond formal operations called dialectical thinking.
  - Our thinking about problems evolves so we first propose some kind of thesis as a solution to a problem.
  - Someone else proposes an antithesis that directly contradicts the thesis.
  - Someone proposes a synthesis that somehow integrates what had appeared to be two opposing and even irreconcilable points of view.

E. Teaching Beyond Piaget
- While Piaget defined in his stages what children cannot do, teachers should focus on what children can do, and give the child as many opportunities as possible to strengthen her or his abilities.
- While Piaget was concerned with the desire to hurry along the child's development, children's inability to think may be due to the lack of an experiential knowledge base.
- While Piaget overemphasized the scientific side of development at the expense of other sides of development, a balanced education means teaching children to think in many different modes.

F. Implications for Teaching
- Piaget's Theory
  - Mix assimilations and accommodations.
  - Take into account children's level of cognitive development.
  - Teach children in a way that reflects their nature as natural-born scientists.
  - Pay as much attention to understanding and correcting the bases of children's errors as to rewarding their correct answers.
- Neo-Piagetian Views
  - Problem finding is at least as important as problem solving, and becomes more important in adolescence and beyond.
  - Students, as they become adolescents, need to learn to think dialectically.
- Beyond Piaget

- Expert teachers focus on what children of a given age can do.
- Children can be pushed just a bit beyond their current level of cognitive development.
- Children should be taught as multifaceted human beings, not just as developing scientists.

IV. Vygotsky's Sociocultural Theory of Cognitive Development
- Lev Vygotsky's sociocultural theory focuses on cognitive development from the outside, inward.
- The major premise is that a person's intrapersonal, or internal processes, have their roots in interactions with others.
- Vygotsky's theory dominated the thinking of the field in the 1980s and 1990s due to the recognition that developmental accomplishments depend as much on the influence of the social and other environments as they do on sheer maturation.

A. Internalization
- Internalization is the absorption of knowledge from the social contexts in which it is observed, so that one can use it for oneself.
- Through observation, a child can learn how to argue for her own beliefs, both in the context of discussions with others and in the context of thinking through issues for herself.
- Vygotsky believed language development is key to being able to internalize complex ideas.
- Developing children's language skills helps children develop their thought.

B. The Zone of Proximal Development
- The zone of proximal development (ZPD) is the range between a child's level of independent performance and the level of performance a child can reach with expert guidance.
- Measuring the distance between independent performance and child's guided performance can give educators an idea of the level of performance a child is ready to reach on his or her own.
- ZPD can be assessed by testing children via a dynamic assessment environment, a testing situation in which the examiner not only gives the child problems to solve, but also gives the child a graded series of hints when the child is unable to solve the problems.
- In contrast, a static assessment environment is a testing situation in which the examiner gives the child problems to solve, but provides little or no feedback about the child's performance.

C. Scaffolding
- Reuven Feuerstein has suggested that children learn primarily in two different ways.
  - Direct instruction is the teaching situation in which a teacher, parent, or other authority imparts knowledge to a child by teaching it.
  - A mediated learning experience (MLE) is a learning situation in which an adult or older child indirectly helps a child learn by explaining events in the environment, but without directly teaching some lesson.
  - Mediated learning experience is a form of scaffolding--competent assistance or support, usually provided through mediation of the environment by a parent or teacher, by which cognitive, socioemotional, and behavioral forms of development can occur.
- Importance of scaffolding
  - Cognitive, socioemotional, and behavioral scaffolding adequate for a child's development are significantly associated with subsequent outcomes of cognitive development.
  - Scaffolding is a crucial part in planning intervention, action taken to improve a child's cognitive, socioemotional, or behavioral development.
  - Studies of the long-term effects of intervention indicate that without adequate duration of a program and without adequate scaffolding after the program, cognitive gains tend to disappear.

D. Evaluating Vygotsky's Theory
- Vygotsky's theory seems to deal only with limited aspects of cognitive development.
- The zone of proximal development is difficult to know whether any instrument truly measures it.

E. Implications for Teaching
- Children learn by internalizing external dialogue.
- Children almost never operate at the peak of their capacity.
- Language and thought are intimately and inextricably related.

V. Information-Processing Theories: Examining Learning and Memory Skills
- Information-processing theorists seek to understand cognitive development in terms of how people of various ages process information and represent it mentally.
- Two key processes of cognitive development are used in thinking about both numbers and words.
  - Encoding is the process by which we take in new information and make sense of the world.
  - Combination is the process by which we put together the pieces of information we have encoded.
- Cognitive processes need to be studied in two ways.
  - A domain-general way identifies processes used in a variety of cognitive tasks.
  - A domain-specific way identifies how the processes are used in each kind of task.

A. Verbal Skills
- Verbal comprehension, the ability to understand written and spoken material, has been studied in some detail.
- Researchers have studied verbal comprehension of words in sentences.
  - Researchers suggest that children as well as adults use various cues to figure out word meanings.
  - Sternberg and colleagues found that the amount of difficulty children would have in learning a word could be predicted by the kinds and numbers of cues available for figuring out the word's meaning.
- Ellen Markman has studied verbal comprehension at the level of paragraph understanding.

B. Quantitative Skills
- Brown and Burton have found that children's errors in arithmetic can often be accounted for by buggy algorithms, or erroneous strategies the children consistently use when they add, subtract, multiply, or divide.
- Groen and Parkman found that people tend to count upward from the larger addend the amount of the smaller addend when they add two numbers.
- Siegler and Shrager proposed that when children do arithmetic, they first try to solve the problems by direct retrieval of the correct answer.
- Paige and Simon found that students were surprisingly willing to supply answers to problems that simple made no sense.

C. Memory Skills
- Children's memory skills improve with age.
- Two factors that influence this improvement are knowledge about the domain in which people are learning and remembering and people's understanding of their own memory.
- Memory skills lead to increased knowledge, which in turn leads to better memory.
- The ability of people of any age to remember material depends in part on prior experiences.
- Understanding and control of one's own memory can also affect memory performance.
  - Rehearsal is a memory strategy in which a person, either mentally or aloud, recites information over and over again in order to remember it.
  - Rehearsal allows an individual to gain some control of what information gets stored in memory over the long term.

D. Implications for Teaching
- We need to understand not just the answers children provide, but how they arrived at these answers.

- Teach strategies for learning.
- Knowledge as well as strategy is key to expertise.
- How students represent information can be a key to their learning and problem solving.

VI. Three Major Approaches to Cognitive Development: A Comparison
- Piaget's theory and Neo Piagetian Theory
  - Considers cognitive development to be largely a function of maturation.
  - Does not encourage trying to hurry children through the process of cognitive development.
  - Based on stages of development.
  - Development proceeds at the same rate across cognitive domains.
  - Horizontal decalage allows for differences in the speed at which children show development in different domains.
  - Neo Piagetian theory view development largely as a function of cognitive maturation, rather than as based on learning, propose stages of cognitive development, suggest stages beyond Piaget's final stage of formal operations.

- Lev Vygotsky's theory
  - Proposed that cognitive development results from children's internalization of information from their environment.
  - Children learn from people around them.
  - Views internalization as occurring continuously, without distinct stages in cognitive development.
  - Development can occur at different rates in different cognitive domains.

- Information-processing theory
  - See cognitive development as a result of learning and as a result of the child's level of maturation.
  - Development is viewed as a continuous process with no obvious stages.

VII. Language Development
A. What makes a language a language?
- Communication
- Arbitrariness
- Meaningful structure
- Multiplicity of structure
- Productivity

B. Stages of Language Acquisition
- Prenatal responsivity to the human voice.
- Cooing - the production of sounds by an infant.
- Babbling - an infant's preferential production of sounds that are characteristic of the infant's to-be-learned first language.
- One-word utterances
  - Overextension errors - applications of a word beyond its legitimate use
  - Underextension errors - using words too specifically
- Two-word utterances
- Telegraphic speech - speech that uses simple syntax in utterances of two or three words that impart simple meaning.
- Basic adult sentence structure

C. Theories of Language Acquisition: A Comparison
- One theory, sometimes called a behavioral one, holds that acquisition is largely by imitation.
  - This theory emphasizes the role of nurture in language acquisition.
  - Limitations to this theory:
      Children constantly produce new sentences different from any they have ever heard.

Children frequently overregularize, or use word forms which follow a rule rather than recognize an exception to it.
- Another theory emphasizes nature.
  - Humans possess a language acquisition device (LAS), an innate predisposition or ability to acquire language expertise.
  - Children exhibit critical periods, certain points in their development during which they are particularly tuned for various aspects of language development.
- Both nature and nurture play interactive roles in stages of language development
  - Humans do appear to be preprogrammed to learn their first language during childhood.
  - The stimuli presented in the environment can affect how ell people acquire that language.
  - Children seem to learn language through active hypothesis testing, forming hypotheses about language and linguistic forms and trying them out in their environments.

D. The Relationship Between Language and Thought
- Linguistic determinism is the view where the structure of our language shapes our thought processes.
- Linguistic relativity suggests that language influences but does not determine thought.
- It is important to teach language well because language can facilitate thought.

E. Bilingualism and Education: An Introduction

F. Implications for Teaching
- Ensure that children understand the language in which new material is presented.
- How you say something affects, but does not determine how children think about that thing.
- Show respect for all languages, regardless of the language in which you teach.
- Developing additive bilingualism enriches cognitive skills, whereas developing subtractive bilingualism detracts from them.

TRANSPARENCIES
- T7   Lateralization of Brain Functioning
- T8   Central Issues in Development
- T9   Schemes of Learning
- T10   Piaget's Stages of Cognitive Development
- T11   Piagetian Conservation Tasks
- T12   Reversible Thinking
- T12A The Task of Conservation
- T12B Centration
- T13   A Piagetian Class Inclusion Problem
- T14   A Test of Problem-Solving Abilities: Concrete And Formal Operations
- T15   Teaching Model Based on Vygotsky's Theory
- T16   Learning Activity Based on Vygotsky's Theory

CLASS ACTIVITIES
Activity 2.1 Maturation, Learning, and Instruction Reflection
Use this handout in conjunction with the beginning of the chapter to help students explore their own conceptions of how learning and maturation differ, the nature of development, and the role of instruction in facilitating both processes. The initial handout can be completed as an out-of-class assignment so that student responses can become the base for an opening discussion. The handout can also be used to report the results of small group discussion in-class. Each group's report can be put on the board, overhead, or computer projector and then synthesized. A handout with instructor responses to the questions is also provided. You may want to simply use this as a transparency and review it in class to summarize discussion.

Activity 2.2 Cognitive Development, Language, and Humor Reflection
This activity is designed to help students deepen their understanding of cognitive level by examining how cognitive development affects what students find funny. The universal appeal of humor makes for a lively discussion. In addition, this activity helps students realize how everyday interactions with students can provide insight into children's level of cognitive development.

A two-page handout is provided. Again, the activity can be completed out-of-class or as an in-class activity, individually or in small groups, after initial presentation of Piaget's stage theory. Students examine typical jokes for insight into why children of various ages find them funny. Another good activity is to have students ask children and adolescents for jokes they have recently heard and found funny and to review them in class. This will give you some examples of humor typical of older students that are appropriate for class discussion but not for inclusion in this manual!

Activity 2.3 Piagetian Stages: Self Quiz
Often students feel they have a greater understanding of Piaget's stage theory than they actually do. A self- quiz has been provided to check their understanding. This activity works well as a homework assignment or when students complete it in pairs during class.

Activity 2.4 Applying Piaget to the Classroom
While Piaget's work has been widely applied to the classroom, he actually said very little about formal education. This activity provides a handout with a paraphrase from a 1964 publication when Piaget addressed his view of the goals of education.

Use the quotes as prompts for discussion and have students answer the questions in small groups. After each group reports their findings, summarize the information in large group discussion.

A follow-up activity is to ask students to write an essay reflecting on the relevance of Piaget's comments to today's educational environment and workplace demands. David Elkind's video, *Using What We Know: Applying* Piaget's Developmental Theory, is an excellent adjunct to this discussion (see Video Resources).

Activity 2.5 The Learning Process Activity
This activity helps students understand the core features of the information processing model by presenting a simple schematic and testing their own memory and recall abilities.

This activity is designed to be used after the information processing view of learning has been presented in class. Use the first schematic presented with Activity 5 as an overhead transparency or PowerPoint prompt or distribute it during instruction as a handout.

After your class presentation, distribute the packet of handouts included in Activity 5 (after the initial schematic), adding a blank page behind the list of directions and questions. After students have completed the activities individually (as directed in #1-5 on the question sheet), have them share their responses in small groups. Summarize in a large group discussion emphasizing individual differences in memory and approaches to learning tasks consistent with the triarchic theory of intelligence.

Class Activity 2.1
Maturation, Learning and Instruction Reflection

Discuss the following questions with your group members and try to answer the questions based on your current understanding of development and learning.

What is learning?

What are learning principles?

How do learning principles form theories of learning?

How can we tell if learning has occurred?

What is the difference between maturation and learning?

What is instruction?

Class Activity 2.1 Answer Key
Maturation, Learning, and Instruction Reflection

What is learning?

A complex process (like digestion) that enables organisms to modify their behavior rapidly in a more or less permanent way.

What are learning principles?

The accumulation of knowledge gathered through scientific methods.

How do learning principles form theories of learning?

Learning principles are put together to form a model of the learning process, which is elaborated on to form a particular learning theory.

How can we tell if learning has occurred?

1. Note behavioral change
2. Note persistence of change

What is the difference between maturation and learning?

Maturation occurs when changes result from the growth of internal structures. Learning occurs when changes happen after interaction with the external environment. (Learning can occur internally as capacity for learning increases developmentally and the external world is mentally represented.)

What is instruction?

A set of events designed to initiate, activate, and support learning.

Class Activity 2.2
Cognitive Development, Language, and Humor Reflection

Children's growing cognitive abilities and greater understanding of language are reflected in what they find humorous. While children first enjoy visual puns (e.g. a picture with a man wearing a pair of pants on his head), as they grow cognitively, they begin to appreciate verbal puns. In adolescence, "put down" humor is common.

Read each of these popular jokes with your group members and list the growing cognitive abilities that allow children and adolescents to find the joke "funny."

Elementary   **Cognitive Characteristics**

Q: What did zero say to eight?
A: Nice belt. (0 - 8)

Knock, knock.
Who's there?
Lettuce.
Lettuce who?
Lettuce in and you'll find out.

Q: How can you tell if a cat burglar has been in your house?
A: Your cat is missing.

Knock, knock.
Who's there?
Boo.
Boo who?
Ghosts are nothing to cry about, silly!

A three-legged dog walked into a bar
and said, "I'm looking for the guy who shot my paw."

Older Elementary   Cognitive Characteristics

Three tomatoes were walking down the street,
Mama Tomato, Papa Tomato, and Baby Tomato.
Baby Tomato was lagging behind,
so Papa Tomato turns to him, squishes him,
and says, "Ketchup!"

Q: What is green and sings?
A: Elvis Parsley.

Q: How do you get an elephant up in a tree?
A: Sit him on an acorn and wait.

Junior High

A duck walks into a pharmacy and asks for
some *Chapstick.* The cashier asks, "Is this cash?"
The duck says, "No, put it on my bill."

A cheese sandwich walked into a bar and
ordered a drink. The bartender said,
"Sorry, we don't serve food here."

Q: If Pete and Repete were sitting on a bench
     and Pete left, who would still be there?

A: Repete.

• Repeat the question as often as you like.

High School

There were two atoms taking a walk.
One atom said to the other atom,
 "I think I lost an electron!"
The second atom replied, "Are you sure?"
The first atom replied, "Yes, I'm positive!"

Class Activity 2.3
Piagetian Stages Self-Check

Match the following examples with the appropriate Piagetian stage (sensorimotor, preoperational, concrete, or formal) and cite relevant characteristics of children at that stage to justify your choice.

Examples	Stage/Characteristic
1. Bill puts the apple and orange together because both are round.	
2. A student is able to discuss the question, "What would the world be like if the South had won the Civil War?"	
3. A baby plays "peek-a-boo."	
4. When given 2 kinds of lunchmeat, 2 kinds of cheese, and 3 kinds of dressings, students can make 12 different sandwiches.	
5. A child believes that the sun comes up when she opens her eyes.	
6. A mother divides the ice cream in one bowl into two to satisfy a child who wants more.	
7. A teenager is able to identify examples of hypocrisy.	
8. Ordering steps in a set of directions.	
9. A baby kicks his cradle to make a mobile turn.	
10. Mother: "How do you think Sam feels when you hit him?" Child: "He feels better."	

Class Activity 2.4
Applying Piaget to the Classroom

Answer the following questions keeping in mind the paraphrased quote of
Piaget's printed below:

The two goals of education:

• To prepare students to do things that have never been done before.
(educate people who can invent, discover, and create) and

• To develop students who can think logically and reason.

(Piaget, 1964)

---

1. What are some implications of Piagetian theory to the classroom?

2. What impact might it have on timing or placement of curriculum?

3. What is suggested for classroom organization and activities?

Class Activity 2.5
The Learning Process

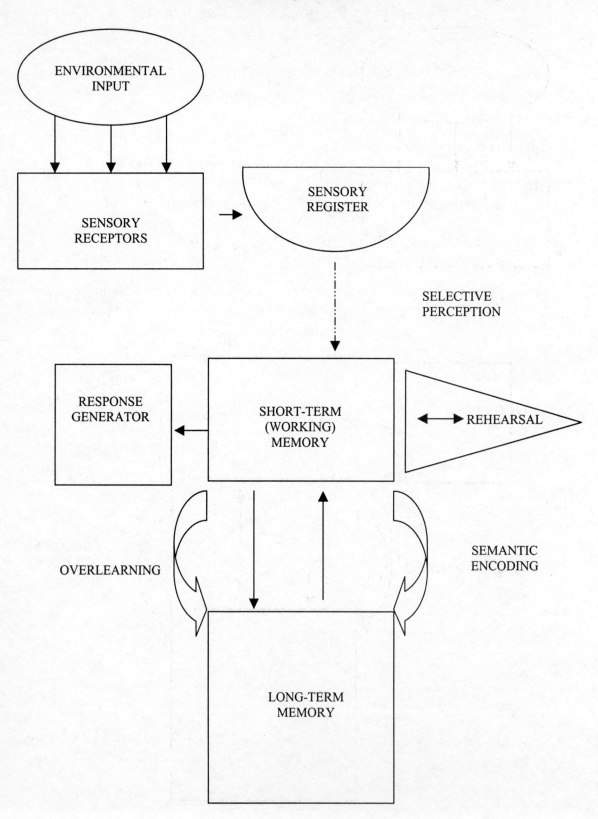

Class Activity 2.5
The Learning Process

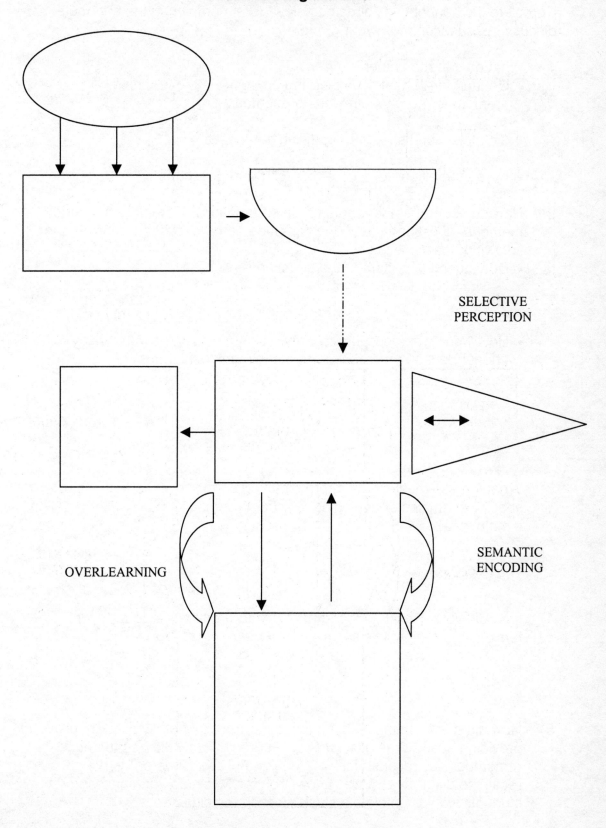

SELECTIVE
PERCEPTION

OVERLEARNING

SEMANTIC
ENCODING

Class Activity 2.5

Complete the handouts as directed below. After completing the handouts, discuss the questions with your group.

1) What do you remember?
    *   On the blank sheet titled learning process write everything you remember from the previous presentation.

    *   On the second sheet - try to "fill in the blanks"

    *   In your small group, answer the following questions.

2) How do you remember and encode information? Complete the "study methods" questionnaire on the last page of the packet and answer the following questions in your small group:
    *   Do you note a pattern in the questions?

    *   How would you describe your style of studying? Are you mostly dependent on rehearsal or on meaningful techniques?

3) What did you recall from the presentation on the "blank sheet" (e.g. specific examples or analogies, a schematic diagram, bits of information, a main idea)

4) How did you recall it (in the form of a diagram or in paragraph/verbal form)? What might this say about your learning style?

5) How did the "fill in the blank" sheet differ from the totally blank page? Did providing specific retrieval cues aid in recall? How did you try to remember - by reconstructing a meaningful sequence or by trying to recall the diagram as it was shown to you? How do you think your students would complete a similar task in the classroom?

Class Activity 2.5

STUDY METHODS QUESTIONNAIRE:

Place an "O" in the blank preceding items that describe study activities that you use VERY OFTEN.

Place an "X" next to those that you use SOME OF THE TIME.

Leave blank all items that are NOT characteristic of your own study activity.

_____ 1. I memorize factual material by looking at it once or twice.

_____ 2. When I study something, I devise a system for recalling it later.

_____ 3. To learn formulas, names, and dates, I say them over and over to myself.

_____ 4. After studying a unit of material, I often summarize it in my own words to see if I have mastered it.

_____ 5. For exams, I memorize the material as given in the text or class notes.

_____ 6. I learn new words or ideas by associating them with words and ideas that I already know.

AVAILABLE RESOURCES ON-LINE
Explorations in Learning & Instruction: The Theory Into Practice Database
gwis.circ.gwu.edu/~tip/index.html
TIP is a tool intended to make learning and instructional theory more accessible to educators. The database contains brief summaries of 50 major theories of learning and instruction. These theories can also be accessed by learning domains and concepts.

Cognitive Development- Piaget, Vygotsky, and Bruner
trackstar.hprtec.org/main/display.php3?option=text&track_id=292
This web site will help you find information on the leading cognitive developmental psychologists, including their biographies, theories, and ideas. There is also a site on a charter school implementing Bruner's ideas, and a site on the Piaget Society.

Vygotsky's Theory of Cognitive Development
csunixl.lvc.edu/~b_rehm/Vygotskyindex.html
This web site provides information about Vygotsky's Theory of Cognitive Development. It begins with some facts about Vygotsky himself and then talks about ideas on social origins of thought, tools for thought, language and development, and the zone of proximal development. The sight then investigates his theory's contribution to education, exploring the role of private speech, the importance of adult guidance, reciprocal teaching, and the role of peer interactions. Finally the site explores contrasts between Piaget's and Vygotsky's Theories.

The Information Processing Approach
chiron.valdosta.edu/whuitt/col/cogsys/infoproc.html
This web site provides background information on Information Processing a stage model of Information Processing, a description of each stage, and ways to apply Information Processing to the classroom. The site also has links to internet resources, electronic files, additional articles, and additional books all related to Information Processing.

Language Learning
www.sil.org/lglearning/
Language learning in SIL focuses on developing the ability to communicate in a second language, with special emphasis on languages for which there are few or no written or recorded resources.

RECOMMENDED VIDEOS FOR CHAPTER TWO
Cognitive Development
Price: $129
VHS Video (60 minutes), Guide
Published by Films for the Humanities & Sciences, Princeton, NJ
Order #ECU6013
Examines Piaget's theory and critically evaluates it in light of current research. The study of child development has revolved around Jean Piaget's theories and the program describes their themes, covering the cognitive stages of development from birth to twelve years old, giving illustrations of children's behavior at each level. Recent research is examined in relation to each stage and comparisons drawn with the theories of Jerome Bruner. Current and future developments such as metacognition and theory of mind are outlined and recent research findings reported.

Cognitive Development: Representation in Three- to Five-Year-Old Children
Price: $129
VHS Video (30 minutes)
Published by Films for the Humanities & Sciences, Princeton, NJ
Order #ECU10222
How do children between the ages of three and five internally represent the complexity of their world? In this program, academic researches from Cambridge University and elsewhere discuss a theory of mind that stems from a child's experiential-based understanding of causal relationships. Observations drawn from experiments employing false belief tasks and analogical reasoning games support their hypothesis as an alternative to the neuro-cognitive module concept. Piaget's theory is also addressed.

The Infant Mind
Price: $139
VHS Video (30 minutes)
Published by Insight Media, New York, NY (1992)
Order #TAA277
Jean Piaget's theories of object performance and sensory-motor development are explained and challenged. Research with newborns has revealed that infants possess a basic perception of cause and effect, number, and object permanence and that memory skills and the capacity to form concepts are present much earlier than formerly believed.

Vygotsky's Developmental Theory: An Introduction
Price: $249
VHS Video (28 minutes)
Published by Insight Media, New York, NY (1994)
Order #TAA1280
This program examines the life and work of Lev Vygotsky and his theory of constructivist education. It illustrates the four principles of Vygotsky's work: children construct knowledge; learning can lead development; development cannot be separated from social context; and language plays a key role in mental development.

Learning in Context: Probing the Theories of Piaget and Vygotsky
Price: $149
VHS Video (30 minutes)
Published by Films for the Humanities & Sciences, Princeton, NJ
Order #ECU10221
This program presents recent work by developmental psychologists that emphasized the influence of contextual factors in learning and performance. Three sets of experiments involving children are examined: tasks in which deliberately gender-biased instructions are provided; tasks requiring cooperation between asymmetrical pairs of peers; and tasks involving training of students by adults and by peers. The intriguing results of these tests shed light on the impact of stereotyping on performance; the effects of self-perception on competence; and the influence of different teaching approaches on learning.

Language and Thinking
Price: $139
VHS Video (30 minutes)
Published by Insight Media, New York, NY (1992)
Order #TAA279
The acquisition of language skills signals a major change in a child's ability to interact with the world. Examining research on language development, this video investigates how the brain facilitates and processes language during early childhood. It examines the beginnings of language in infancy, explains how children learn language from their caregivers, and explores the relationship between language and certain cognitive skills.

HANDOUTS TO ACCOMPANY YOUR LESSONS:

H 2.1   Cognitive Development (Continuous vs. Stagelike)

H 2.2   Four Factors Underlying Development

H 2.3   Piaget's Stages of Cognitive Development

H 2.4   Information Processing Model

H 2.5   The Development of Strategies for Remembering

H 2.6   Classroom Suggestions to Improve Information-Processing in Kindergarten-First Grade

H 2.7   The Zone of Proximal Development

H 2.1

Cognitive Development

Continuous	Stagelike
• Cognitive abilities are acquired gradually such that each new accomplishment builds directly on those that came before it. • A person's thinking is not fundamentally different at any one age or level of development than it is at any other age. • People gradually progress to higher levels of cognitive ability.	• Each stage is associated with a qualitatively distinct set of cognitive structures or mental patterns of organization that influence our ways of dealing with the world. • Behavior unfolds in a one-directional, invariable sequence. • Later stages build on earlier stages.

Domain-General	Domain-Specific
• Development occurs more or less simultaneously in multiple areas • A child is unlikely to get an A in reading and an F in English.	• Development occurs at different rates in different areas • A child can be an expert in one domain of schoolwork and a novice in another.

H 2.2

Four Factors Underlying Development

1. Maturation

Impact of heredity (and environment) on the development of the central nervous system.

2. Experience

Contact with the environment leads to two types of knowledge:
      *physical – knowledge of observables through
          empirical abstraction and later through
          pseudoempirical abstraction

      *logicomathematical – knowledge acquired by
          reflection on one's own
          actions through a process
          called *reflective abstraction*

3. Social transmission

The influence of the culture on the child's thought.

4. Equilibration

A process that integrates the other three and is the self-regulatory process of the mind.

H 2.3

Piaget's Stages of Cognitive Development

Sensorimotor 0-2 years	The child begins to interact with the environment. The child begins to make use of imitation, memory, and thought. The child begins to recognize that objects do not cease to exist when they are hidden. The child moves from reflex actions to goal-directed activity.
Preoperational 2-6 or 7 years	The child begins to represent the world symbolically. There is a gradual increase in language development. The child is able to think operations through logically in one direction. The child has difficulties seeing another person's point of view.
Concrete Operational 7-11 or 12 years	The child learns rules such as conservation. The child is able to solve concrete problems in logical fashion. The child is able to classify and seriate. The child understands reversibility.
Formal Operational 12-adulthood	The adolescent can transcend concrete situations and think about the future. The adolescent is able to solve abstract problems in logical fashion. Thinking becomes more scientific for the child. The child develops concerns about social issues and identity.

H 2.4

INFORMATION PROCESSING MODEL

STIMULI

- Visual
- Auditory
- Tactile
- Kinesthetic
- Olfactory

SENSORY REGISTER

Recognition Selective Perception

- Information retained briefly (1/10 second or less)
- Photographic memory
- Has no way of determining what stimuli will be of value
- Pattern recognition supplied and transferred to short-term memory
- Recognition of important stimuli in a situation increases with age during childhood (processing distracting stimuli decreases with age)
- Capacity of sensory register does NOT appear to increase with age

SHORT-TERM MEMORY

Encoding Recall

- Working memory
- Short duration of 30 seconds or less unless information is actively rehearsed
- Maintenance rehearsal can maintain information in short-term memory for an indefinite period
- Limited capacity
- Pseudo forgetting can occur because information decays within 30 seconds after rehearsal ends (and/or other information bumps material out of short-term memory)
- Capacity of short-term memory increases with age
- Site of learning strategies that process information

LONG-TERM MEMORY

- Permanent record of all we have learned and experienced
- Unlimited capacity
- Appears organized
- Amount of information stored increases with age
- Site of learning strategies
- Efficiency of getting information into and out of long-term memory increases with age during childhood

H 2.5

THE DEVELOPMENT OF
STRATEGIES FOR REMEMBERING

Strategy	Independently Displayed	Example
Preliminary Strategies Simple and direct methods for remembering, such as naming, looking, and pointing	By age 2	Pointing to a toy when asked to remember the toy
Rehearsal Rote repetition of material	By age 6	Writing spelling words five times each
Organization Semantic grouping of material	By fifth grade	Grouping spelling words according to prefix
Self-Testing Methods of knowing when one can terminate studying	By fifth grade	Taking a practice spelling test
Elaboration Creating visual or verbal connections that add meaning to material	Adolescence (or later)	"The meat we eat has the word EAT in it; the other MEET does not."

Strategies for Learning and Remembering, Rafoth, Leal, and DeFabo. Copyright 1993. Washington, DC: National Education Association. Reprinted by permission of the NEA Professional Library.

H 2.6

CLASSROOM SUGGESTIONS TO IMPROVE INFORMATION-PROCESSING IN KINDERGARTEN-FIRST GRADE

INFORMATION PROCESSING SYSTEM	SUGGESTIONS
SENSORY REGISTER	**Use concrete methods** to focus children's attention: use markers for following along and color coding relevant information.
	Reduce visual distractions by displaying only one example at a time.
	Increase the relevance of material by relating it to children's lives.
SHORT-TERM MEMORY	**Carry out learning strategies** for children in order to free up processing space.
	Review previous relevant lessons.
	Preview material.
LONG-TERM MEMORY	**Relate new material** to information already stored in long-term memory.
	Provide activities that promote **visualization** and **organizational** learning strategies.
	Train children to use **rehearsal** strategies.

Strategies for Learning and Remembering, Rafoth, Leal, and DeFabo. Copyright 1993. Washington, DC: National Education Association. Reprinted by permission of the NEA Professional Library.

H 2.7

The Zone of Proximal Development

The distance between the actual developmental level that is reflected in the child's independent problem solving and the problem solving level accomplished with guidance.

It represents the amount of improvement possible through imitative activity

New Tasks
(tasks that students are capable of learning with facilitation)

Unlearned Tasks (tasks students currently do not have the cultural or cognitive tools to master)

Learned Tasks (tasks students already have in their repertoire)

Zone

of

Interaction

Teacher or Peer (scaffolded instruction)

Learner's private speech (assisted learning)

Proximal

Development

Chapter Three
Personal, Gender, Social, and Moral Development

The instructor's manual for this chapter contains:

- A *Chapter-at-a-Glance* chart that reviews all chapter related material
- A detailed chapter outline to highlight main points of the chapter
- A list of transparencies from Transparencies - Educational Psychology IV that correspond to this chapter
- Several activities to deepen student understanding
- An annotated list of additional resources including internet sites
- Handouts to accompany your lessons

CHAPTER-AT-A-GLANCE

Chapter Outline	Objectives	Instructional Aids
1.0 Why Understanding Personal, Gender, Social, and Moral Development is Important to Teachers , p. 80	1. Describe the importance to teachers of understanding personal, gender, social and moral development.	- Test Bank Questions 1-3, 71-74 - Video Segment 5
2.0 Personal Development: Becoming Unique p. 81	1. Describe each of Erikson's eight psychosocial stages of development. 2. Describe Marcia's theory of the achievement of a personal identity, including the four identity statuses. 3. Evaluate the theories of Erikson and Marcia. 4. Describe the implications for teaching of Erikson's and Marcia's theories.	- Transparencies T17, T19 - Handouts 3.1, 3.2 - Activities 3.1, 3.4 - Test Bank Questions 4-22, 75-77, 91-92, 99-100
3.0 Sexual and Gender Development, Acquiring Gender Roles, p. 89	1. Describe the main characteristics of acquiring gender roles. 2. Compare and contrast Freud's theory of sexual development, behaviorism, social learning theory, and schema theory. 3. Describe sexual preferences. 4. Describe the implications for teaching of theories of sexual and gender development.	- Handout 3.3 - Activity 3.3 - Test Bank Questions 23-32, 78-84, 93-94
4.0 Social Development: Learning to Interact with Others, p. 95	1. Describe attachment, and evaluate Ainsworth's three styles of attachment. 2. Describe the importance of friendship and play. 3. Describe Selman's five stages of perspective-taking. 4. Describe the implications for teaching of attachment, play, friendship, and perspective-taking.	- Handout 3.4 - Test Bank Questions 33-47, 85-90, 95, 98, 101
5.0 Moral Development, Acquiring a Sense of Right and Wrong, p. 102	1. Describe Piaget's theory of moral development. 2. Describe Kohlberg's theory of moral development. 3. Describe Gilligan's alternative to Kohlberg's theory of moral development. 4. Evaluate Kohlberg's theory of moral development. 5. Describe the implications for teaching of moral development.	- Transparencies T18, T20 - Handout 3.5 - Activity 3.2 - Test Bank Questions 48-57, 96

6.0 Identifying, Understanding, and Managing Developmental Risks, p. 108	1. Describe how to identify and manage the various risks children and adolescents face today	- Transparency T21 - Test Bank Questions 58-70, 97

DETAILED CHAPTER THREE OUTLINE

I. Why Understanding Personal, Gender, Social, and Moral Development is Important to Teachers

- An expert teacher has to understand the processes of personal, social, and moral development.
  - Personal development is the process of human development in which individuals acquire the set of attributes that makes them unique.
  - Social development is the process of human development in which individuals learn how to interact with others and understand themselves as social beings.
  - Moral development is the process of human development in which individuals acquire a sense of right and wrong, to use in evaluating their own actions and the actions of others.

- Expert teachers use this knowledge to plan developmentally appropriate lessons that challenge but do not frustrate students.

- Expert teachers use this knowledge to help them see when students are having problems in one or more areas.

- In designing lessons, teachers need to keep in mind the overlapping nature of domains of student development.

II. Personal Development: Becoming Unique

A. Erikson's Theory of Psychosocial Development

- Psychosocial theory of personal development is a theory which explicitly acknowledges that individual development takes place in a social context.
- At every stage of psychosocial development comes one issue of developmental crises where an individual has an opportunity to take a significant step in development.
  - Trust versus Mistrust (birth to 1 year) – the outcome of this stage determines in part whether a person will come to view the world as basically supportive and friendly or as basically unsupportive and even hostile.
  - Autonomy versus Shame and Doubt (1 to 3 years) – the outcome of this stage determines in part whether a person has confidence in their ability to succeed in their relationships or doubt themselves in their ability to cope with the environment.
  - Initiative versus Guilt (3 to 6 years) – the outcome of this stage determines in part whether a person feels a sense of purpose in life or finds difficulty taking initiative in one's life endeavors.
  - Industry versus Inferiority (6 to 12 years) – successful passage means the development of a sense of competence, whereas unsuccessful passage results in feelings of inferiority.
  - Identity versus Role Confusion (adolescence) – success in this stage is the development of a sense of fidelity, whereas those who do not remain confused about who they are, what they can become, and what they should do with their lives.
  - Intimacy versus Isolation (early adulthood) – success at this stage results in the person learning nonselfish love, whereas failure results in a sense of isolation and in an inability to achieve intimacy.
  - Generativity versus Stagnation (middle adulthood) – successful adults feel a need to nurture and provide for the generation that follows, whereas unsuccessful adults feel as though they have not made a meaningful contribution to the world through their careers or raising of children.
  - Integrity versus Despair (late adulthood/old age) – those who succeed in this stage gain the wisdom of older age, whereas unsuccessful completion creates a sense of despair over the

mistakes they have made.

B. Marcia's Theory of the Achievement of a Personal Identity
- James Marcia has suggested that four main kinds of statuses can emerge during adolescence from the conflicts faced and the decisions made by adolescents.
- The four kinds of identities are possible combinations of yes-no answers to two questions.
  - Has the person engaged in an active search for identity?
  - Has the person made commitments?
- Identity achievement
  - Answers yes to both questions
  - This individual has searched for his or her identity and has made an educational, vocational, or other personal commitment.
- Identity diffusion
  - Answers no to both of the questions
  - This person has neither engaged in a search for identity nor committed to any significant aspects of an identity.
- Identity moratorium
  - Answers yes to the first question and no to the second
  - He or she has made a search for an identity, but has not yet made commitments.
- Identity foreclosure
  - Answers no to the first question and yes to the second.
  - This person has made commitments to a job, school, or other aspect of his or her identity without first engaging in a search process.

C. Evaluating the Theories of Erikson and Marcia
- Both Erikson and Marcia believe that healthy adolescents can include a moratorium period.
  - A moratorium period is a time of searching for an appropriate identity while avoiding firm commitments.
  - A moratorium period may be important to adolescents in a socially diverse, urbanized society where they must choose from among many options for how to live their lives.
- The goal of an adolescent identity search is that the adolescent emerges with a firm and secure sense of self, and identifies his or her own characteristics, abilities, and behaviors.
  - The adolescent's self-esteem is the value one places on oneself.
  - The adolescent's view of oneself is referred to as one's self-concept.
- One limitation is the lack of solid empirical data supporting them.
- Marcia's theory applies only to a very limited aspect of the life span, thereby not taking fully into account the lifetime process of identity formation.

D. Implications for Teaching
- Erikson's Theory of Psychosocial Development
  - Expert preschool teachers provide young children with opportunities to perform tasks independently.
  - Expert teachers foster children's ability to assert themselves by allowing them to make as many of their own decisions as possible about schoolwork.
  - Expert teachers foster feelings of competence in students by noticing and praising students' successes.
  - Expert teachers of adolescents reassure themselves and students by pointing out examples of the normalcy of identity searches.
- Marcia's Theory of Attachment of a Personal Identity
  - Demonstrate role models for identity achievement.
  - Facilitate exploration of alternative value systems, and the advantages and disadvantages of each.
  - Encourage students to make commitments that are sensible for their age level.
  - Consider cultural differences.
  - Be aware of the ongoing nature of identity formation.

III. Sexual and Gender Development: Acquiring Gender Roles

- Differences exist between sex and gender.
- Sexual development refers to increasing awareness of the characteristics of each of the sexes, of the differences between the sexes, and of changing perceptions of one's own sexuality.
- Gender identification is a person's acquisition of sex-related roles, regardless of whether they correspond to one's physiological sex.
  - The culture in which an individual is raised shapes gender roles:
      The typical feminine gender role is comprised of expressive behavior.
      The typical masculine role is made up of instrumental behavior.
      Many gender roles are actually sex-neutral; they could be performed equally well by males or females.
      Androgyny is a state in which an individual feels comfortable displaying both expressive and instrumental qualities.
  - The distinction between sex and gender is a vital one for teachers to keep in mind:
      Expert teachers do not make assumptions about their students' abilities based on biological sex.
      Many male and female students behave very differently in certain contexts.

A. Theories of Sexual and Gender Development
- Biological Perspectives
  - Boys and girls acquire different gender roles because they are biologically predisposed to do so.
  - Some theorists emphasize the role of evolution in determining sexual behavior.
  - Biological differences between boys and girls may also trigger different treatment from parents and others in their environments.
B. Freud's Theory of Psychosexual Development
  - Gender-role identification arises primarily from psychological crises faced during a stage of development that lasts from about 4 to 7 years of age.
  - Children start to have sexual feelings for the parent of the opposite sex:
      For boys, this conflict is called the Oedipal conflict.
      The comparable reaction in girls is referred to as the Electra conflict.
C. Behaviorism
  - Boys and girls are treated differently from the moment they are born.
  - These differences in treatment can lead to different behavior.
D. Social Learning Theory
  - People come to think and behave as they do by observing others and then by imitating the behavior they have seen.
  - Television provides many children with a way to observe a variety of models.
E. Schema Theory
  - Everyone possesses organized mental systems of information which help people make sense of and organize their experiences.
  - People acquire schemas that guide their interpretations of what are and are not appropriate gender roles.
F. Homosexuality
  - Homosexuality is a person's tendency to direct sexual attention toward members of the same sex.
  - It is a sexual and affectional orientation and identity, probably most rooted in psychosexual development.
  - Bisexual people direct their sexual attention toward members of both sexes.
  - Explanations of homosexuality have been proposed by the biological, clinical, and cognitive theories.

G. Implications for Teaching
- Model and reward gender behavior desired of students.
- Acknowledge and strive to overcome gender stereotypes.

- Check learning materials for damaging gender stereotypes.

IV. Social Development: Learning to Interact with Others
A. Attachment
- Attachment is the strength and kind of emotional bond that exists between two people.
- Mary Ainsworth assesses attachment style through infants' reactions to the strange situation; an experimental procedure in which the attachment of an infant to the parent is observed after the parent has left the infant with a stranger, and has then returned.
  - The avoidant attachment child avoids or ignores the mother when she returns after leaving the child with the stranger.
  - The secure attachment child shows distress when the mother departs.
  - The resistant attachment child is ambivalent toward the mother.
- Patterns of attachment also differ by cultures.
- Attachment styles first formed during infancy may persist in one form or another throughout the life span.

B. Friendship and Play

C. Stages of Play
- In solitary play, the child plays by herself or himself with things that are available in the environment.
- In parallel play, the child plays with the same toys as other children, but the child does not directly interact with the others.
- In associative play, the child shares toys and interacts to some extent with other children, but still basically plays on his or her own.
- In cooperative play, the child fully cooperates with others in join play efforts.

D. Trends in the Development of Friendships
- Play is the most common activity in friendships and is sometimes the basis for friendships.
- During preschool and the primary grades, children generally form friendships based on shared activities.
- In middle childhood, friendships become more stable, and students may have a more or less permanent best friend.
- Children may be neglected or actively rejected by peers for a variety of reasons.
  - Children may lack prosocial, or helpful, skills.
  - Children may behave aggressively.
- Adolescents in middle school and high school rely on their friends for emotional support and intimacy.
- Most children of both sexes prefer friendships with same-sex peers during these periods.
- The friendships of girls pass through three stages.
  - From the ages of about 11 to 13 years, the girls tend to engage in joint activities, where the central theme is to have fun together.
  - From about 14 to 16, there is more emphasis on sharing secrets, especially about other friends.
  - In later adolescence, shared personalities, shared interests, and general compatibility become more important.

E. Development of Perspective-Taking
- Undifferentiated perspective-taking (3-6 years) – children recognize that others may have perspectives which differ from their own.
- Social-informational perspective (5-9 years) – children realize that others may have different perspectives, because these others may have access to different information.
- Self-reflective perspective-taking (7-12 years) – children become able to see themselves as others see them.

- Third-party perspective-taking (10-15 years) – children become able to see themselves as others see them.
- Societal perspective-taking (14 years-adulthood) – individuals come to understand that third-party perspective-taking is influenced by larger systems of societal values.

F. Implications for Teaching: Attachment
    - Students can form attachments to teachers.
    - Students' infantile attachments to their parents can serve as templates for later interactions with teachers and classmates.
    - Children who have experienced attachment difficulties can later experience problems in school.
    - Teachers need to watch for signs of children who are neglected and abused.
    - Monitor patterns of friendship among students, providing help to isolated students if necessary.
    - Children's preferred play styles may be related to their preferred ways of learning.
    - Gender differences in play styles and friendship patterns may affect learning activities.
    - Children's behavior reflects their ability to take perspectives.

G. Play, friendship, and perspective-taking patterns

V. Moral Development: Acquiring a Sense of Right and Wrong

A. Piaget's Theory of Moral Development
- Heteronomous morality, or moral realism
  - Morality that is subject to rules imposed by others.
  - Young children are egocentric and have difficulty taking the perspective of other people until the age of 7.
- Autonomous morality, or morality of cooperation
  - The level at which children understand that people both make up rules and can change the rules.
  - After about age 8, children are able to understand that rules and laws are formed by the agreement of groups of people.

B. Kohlberg's Theory of Moral Development: Levels and Stages
- Level I – Preconventional Morality – a level of moral reasoning based primarily on egocentric concerns.
  - Stage 1 – An individual behaves in one way or another primarily to obtain rewards and to avoid punishments.
  - Stage 2 – Individuals follow rules when they view such behavior as being to their benefit.
- Level II – Conventional Morality – a level of moral reasoning that reflects a person's internalization of social rules.
  - Stage 3 – People's reasoning is guided by mutual interpersonal expectations and interpersonal conformity.
  - Stage 4 – Adolescents realize the importance of conscience and of the social system.
- Level III – Post-Conventional Morality – a level of moral reasoning based primarily on an internal set of moral absolutes, which may or may not agree with social rules.
  - Stage 5 – Individuals recognize the importance of social contracts and individual rights.
  - Stage 6 – Individuals are oriented toward universal principles of justice.

C. Gilligan's Alternative to Kohlberg's Theory
- Carol Gilligan has suggested that women tend to have a different conception of morality than do men.
- Women tend to view morality more in terms of caring and compassion.
- Women seem better able to show empathy, or the ability to understand how another person feels when interacting with others.

D. Evaluating Kohlberg's Theory
*   The scoring of the scenarios is somewhat subjective, and can lead to errors of interpretation.
*   Stages of moral development seem to be less domain-general than Kohlberg's theory suggests.
*   Kohlberg's own finding that people can regress in their behavior points out the weak link which often exists between thought and action.
*   The theory was originally validated on a relatively small sample of white, middle-class American males under 17 years of age.

E. Implications for Teaching
*   Teachers need to expect a level of moral thought and behavior that is appropriate to the child's age.
*   Having classroom discussion of moral dilemmas helps challenge students' moral reasoning.
*   Self-assessment will help teachers assess their own level of moral development to better understand how they perceive the thinking and behavior of their students.
*   Teachers need to realize that no one theory of moral development is universally accepted.
*   Teachers need to encourage and develop thinking that is not just moral, but also, wise.

VI. **Identifying, Understanding, and Managing Developmental Risks**
A. At Risk for Eating Disorder
*   **Anorexia nervosa** – a life-threatening ailment characterized by a distorted self-image and the resulting severe fear of gaining weight.
    - People refuse to eat sufficient food to maintain adequate body weight and nutrition.
    - Anorexia is far more common in women than in men.
    - Ages 15 to 19 are the peak years for anorexia.
    - The self-starving that results from anorexia can bring on irreversible physiological changes, including heart and muscle damage.
*   **Bulimia nervosa** – an eating disorder characterized by food bingeing followed by purging.
    - The disorder is far more common in women than in men.
    - Bulimics may also have dental problems as their teeth become discolored or damaged because of the effects of acid from the purging.
    - Bulimia is more easily treatable than anorexia, usually by a combination of therapy and re-education.

B. At Risk for Major Depression
*   **Depression**
    - Depression is quite common among adolescents.
    - Physical symptoms include loss of appetite, sleep difficulties, fatigue, and somatic complaints such as stomachaches.
    - A person with major depression is affected by feelings of hopelessness that significantly interfere with the person's life.
    - Agitated depression is characterized by a person's being unable to stay still, being constantly on the go, speaking loudly or rapidly, and complaining a lot.
    - Retarded depression is characterized by profound sadness and hopelessness.
    - Depression in children and adolescents is often related to disruptions in the student's life, such as homelessness, child abuse, or parental divorce.
*   **Suicide**
    - The suicide rate for young people ages 15 to 24 has roughly tripled over the past 30 years.
    - Suicide is the second leading cause of death among teenagers.
    - Three times as many females as males attempt suicide, often by overdosing on sleeping pills or other drugs.
    - Eighty percent of people who commit suicide have given some warning beforehand.
    - The death of students by suicide increases the risk of further students' suicides.

C. At Risk for Violent Behavior

- In the past ten years there has been an increase of violence in schools.
- Schools are making schools safer through closed circuit TVs, zero-tolerance policies, safe havens for students, locker searches, metal detectors, phones in the classroom, and security personnel.

D. Drug Use: A Prevalent Problem
- Teachers must become expert at recognizing the effects of drug use in students.
- Indicators include changes in behavior or academic performance, frequent absences, weight loss, unusually lethargic or active behavior, involvement in criminal activities, and possession of drug-using paraphernalia.
- Teachers should encourage students who show signs of drug use to seek help through alcohol and drug abuse prevention programs.

E. Unwanted Consequences of Sexual Activities
- Sexually Transmitted Diseases
  - Three million U.S. teenagers contract a sexually transmitted disease every year.
  - Although many STDs are curable, some are not.
  - About one-fifth of AIDS cases in the United States occur in people between the ages of 20 to 29.
  - Abstinence is the safest course, followed by diligent use of condoms.
- Teen Pregnancy
  - More than a million U.S. teenage girls become pregnant each year.
  - Pregnancy is more prevalent among those who grow up in lower-income homes.
  - One key factor contributing to the high rate of teen pregnancy is ignorance about sexual and reproductive facts.
  - Some teachers and schools are reluctant to provide contraceptive information for fear of encouraging teenage sexual activity.

TRANSPARENCIES
- T17   Erickson's Stages of Psychosocial Development

- T18   Comparing Erickson's and Piaget's Stages

- T19   The Structure of Self-Concept

- T20   Stages of Moral Development: Kohlberg and Gilligan

- T21   Teaching Students to Care for Others

CLASS ACTIVITIES

Activity 3.1 Resolving Erikson's Stages of Developmental Crises: Self-Quiz

A self-quiz has been provided to check students' understanding of Erikson's Stages of Developmental Crises. This activity can be used as a homework assignment or for students to complete in pairs during class.

Activity 3.2 Classroom Exercise: Reflecting on Moral Development and Behavior

Introduce this handout after discussing Kohlberg's theory of moral development to help students apply the different stages to a real life situation. The discussion questions are provided to have students characterize the people in the story according to Kohlberg's stages of moral development. The discussion questions can be completed as an out-of-class assignment, or in small groups during class. As a homework assignment, students could bring their ideas to class and discuss the article in small groups or in class as a whole.

Activity 3.3 Classroom Exercise: Do Schools Increase Gender Differences?

This activity provides students an opportunity to express their experiences in school pertaining to gender issues. The handout can be assigned for homework so they can provide discussion the following class. Students could get into groups to share their experiences, and then share them with the entire class.

Activity 3.4 Classroom Exercise: Impact of Abuse on Self-concept and Identity Formation Reflection

This exercise provides the opportunity for students to reflect on the impact emotional and verbal abuse has on the emotional well-being of a child. The summary of emotional abuse is short enough for students to read in class and provide immediate answers to the discussion questions. Students can share their answers in small groups and then discuss them with the entire class.

Class Activity 3.1
Resolving Erickson's Stages of Developmental Crises: Self Quiz

Match the following types of experiences with the crisis in which they would have the MOST impact.

CRISIS

A. Trust vs. mistrust
B. Autonomy vs. shame and doubt
C. Initiative vs. guilt
D. Industry vs. inferiority
E. Identity vs. role confusion

_____1. When a student finally finishes a difficult and involved paragraph in the book, the teacher criticizes him for taking so much time.

_____2. As Roberta tries to feed herself with a spoon, her father takes the spoon away and tells her how messy she is.

_____3. While playing a computer game, Eric finds his way to the treasure chest before his father does.

_____4. Juanita is concerned with environmental issues, especially recycling. Juanita's teacher helps her find information from local companies.

_____5. As Tommy starts to take his first steps across the room, his grandparents cheer and praise him.

_____6. While the parents are working outside, the baby is left in the playpen all day long.

_____7. When Ricarto comes downstairs in the morning, his mom criticizes the baggy clothes he chose to wear.

_____8. Even though Megan is just learning the rules to Candyland, her mother yells at her for cheating.

_____9. At the end of the school year, Marcie won first place for her science project.

_____10. A baby cries because she is hungry, and the babysitter attends to the child with a bottle.

Class Activity 3.1
Answer Key

__D__ 1. This is an example of industry vs. inferiority because the child may develop feelings of inferiority in not being able to successfully complete a reading passage.

__B__ 2. This is an example of autonomy vs. shame and doubt because Roberta may start to doubt her ability to feed herself properly since her father is unhappy with her attempt.

__C__ 3. This is an example of initiative vs. guilt because Eric will build confidence in his ability to master a computer game without his father's help.

__E__ 4. This is an example of identity vs. role confusion because Juanita is given the opportunity to learn that she has a role in society and is able to make a difference through environmental issues.

__B__ 5. This is an example of autonomy vs. shame and doubt because Tommy will feel an accomplishment about walking on his own through his grandparents' praise.

__A__ 6. This is an example of trust vs. mistrust because the baby will begin to mistrust the environment since nobody comes to his/her attention.

__E__ 7. This is an example of identity vs. role confusion because Ricarto is criticized for choosing to express his own identity and may have problems defining who he wants to be.

__C__ 8. This is an example of initiative vs. guilt because Megan might find it difficult to accomplish certain tasks knowing that she could upset her mother.

__D__ 9. This is an example of industry vs. inferiority because Marcie feels a sense of competence for being successful in her science class.

__A__ 10. This is an example of trust vs. mistrust because the baby will begin to trust the environment for begin feed when hungry.

Class Activity 3.2
Reflecting on Moral Development and Behavior

Samuel Oliner, a professor of sociology at Humboldt State University in California, and his wife Pearl, a professor of education at Humboldt State, studied the selfless acts of some 50,000 to 500,000 non-Jews who risked their lives to save those facing death during the Holocaust. Although helping behavior is more common when the victim is similar to the helper, those being rescued belonged to a despised minority group. In their book, *The Altruistic Personality: Rescuers of Jews in Nazi Europe*, the Oliners revealed similar functions of character and values among the rescuers.

- Rescuers had been raised to be concerned about the needs of other people and to extend themselves to others.
- Rescuers were more likely to apply ethical values to all humans, not just to those who shared similar backgrounds.
- Rescuers often talked of being close to their parents while growing up, and said that discipline was based on reasoning than on physical punishment.
- Feeling a sense of belonging to their community was characteristic of rescuers and non-rescuers alike.

The Oliners also discovered that rescuers were inclined to risk their lives to save others for diverse reasons.

- Eleven percent were motivated by a commitment to the principle of justice, having strong beliefs about how people ought to be treated.
- Fifty-two percent explained their actions by referring to norms that came from the social group they belonged to.
- Thirty-seven percent were empathic rescuers who felt a connection to the victim.

Questions for Discussion

1. Which of Kohlberg's levels and stages would each of the groups of rescuers (those motivated by commitment to a principle, those motivated by the norms of their social group, and those who were empathic rescuers) fall into?
2. What kind of family life and parenting style was characteristic of those who became rescuers?
3. Rescuers were on different levels of moral development according to Kohlberg's theory yet they all performed the same selfless acts - Why?

Information summarized from "Evidence for a moral tradition," printed in <u>Psychology Today</u>, January-February, 1989, pp72-73.

Class Activity 3.3
Do Schools Increase Gender Differences?

Although Congress outlawed sex discrimination in federally aided schools, disparities still exist. A report composed by researchers at the Wellesley College Center for Research on Women indicates that girls are not receiving an equal education. While both boys and girls do equally well in math and science, there is concern about the gap in scores on standardized tests, especially in math and science. On Advanced Placement tests, boys outperform girls in math, physics and biology. On the SAT test, in 1991, boys beat girls by 8 points in the verbal score and 44 points in math. In 1990 the National Center for Education Statistics found that 81.6% of males completed algebra compared to 76.8% of females; 60.1% of males completed trigonometry of geometry compared to 50.3% of females; and 54.2% of males completed chemistry or physics compared to 42.3% of females. Girls are also less likely to consider technological careers, and this may create limitations to their career options and incomes.

Some researchers have suggested that the underlying assumption to these patterns is suggested to be low self-esteem in girls caused by certain occurrences in the classroom. Boys are said to "intimidate girls into silence, monopolize discussions and steal an inordinate amount of teachers' attention." Teachers tend to position themselves to teach more directly to boys, ask them more questions, and ask them questions that involve higher level thinking skills. Teachers also tend to worry about behavior problems, activity level, and attention in boys and focus on them to avoid classroom management problems. The American Association of University Women (A.A.U.W.) proposes improved teacher training to heighten teacher awareness of these behaviors as well as further studies to avoid suggestions of sex-segregated math and science classes.

Information summarized from "Is school unfair to girls?" by Richard Ostling, Time, February 24, 1992.

React to and reflect on the following questions:
1. How do teachers (perhaps unconsciously) communicate differential expectations to girls and boys throughout their school careers?

2. Reflect on your personal experiences in school. Were you a victim of or a witness to gender bias at any time in your educational career?

Class Activity 3.4
Impact of Abuse on Self-concept and Identity Formation
Reflection

Please reflect on and react to the following points after reading the summary of emotional abuse:

The National Committee for the Prevention of Child Abuse (1987) has defined emotional abuse as a pattern of behavior that attacks a child's emotional development and sense of self-worth. Emotional abuse includes excessive, aggressive or unreasonable demands that place expectations on a child beyond his or her capacity. Constant criticizing, belittling, insulting, rejecting and teasing are some of the forms these verbal attacks can take. Emotional abuse also includes failure to provide the psychological nurturing necessary for a child's psychological growth and development, providing no love, support or guidance. The classifications of emotional abuse include rejecting, ignoring, terrorizing, isolating, and corrupting.

1. How can verbal and emotional abuse affect a child's emotional well being? How would it impact each of Erikson's stages of emotional development?

2. What are some reasons as to why an adolescent may be unable to deal successfully with the identity crisis?
    How might delinquency, alcohol abuse, and poor school performance be symptomatic of deeper problems?

3. How might a teacher who was verbally abusive to his/her students affect their emotional development negatively in early childhood, in grade school, and in junior high and high school?

AVAILABLE RESOURCES ON-LINE
Erik Erikson's 8 Stages of Psychosocial Development
Snycorva.cortland.edu/~andersmd/erik/welcome.html
This website provides a summary chart covering Erikson's work, a description of Erikson's 8 stages of Psychosocial Development, a brief biography of Erikson as well as a description of the critiques and controversies of his stages of Psychosocial Development. The site also offers a list of references and other links.

A Look at the Stages of Sexual Development From Infancy to Adulthood
Npin.org/library/1999/n00125/n00125.html
This website explains the "stages of sexual development" and how knowledge of these stages can be used to help children develop. The website also discusses characteristics and behavior, attitudes about sex, and communication issues for parents about children from birth through adulthood.

Lawrence Kohlberg's Stages of Moral Development
Moon.pepperdine.edu/gsep/class/ethics/kohlberg/
This is an introduction to Lawrence Kohlberg and his Theory of Moral Development. The site provides the levels and stages of moral development, pro's and con's to his theory, examples for each stage, and books and sites pertaining to the topic.

Eating Disorders Awareness and Prevention, Inc.
www.edap.org
This website provides information about eating disorders. It has information relating to current research on eating disorders, as well as information regarding treatment of eating disorders and living with eating disorders.

National Institute of Mental Health
www.nimh.nih.gov
This site provides information on a number of mental health issues, including information about eating disorders.

RECOMMENDED VIDEOS FOR CHAPTER THREE
Theories of Development
Price: $139
VHS Video (29 minutes)
Published by Insight Media, New York, NY (1997)
Order # TAA1064
This video presents an overview of the cognitive, psychosexual, psychosocial, behaviorist, social-learning, and sociocultural theories of child development and discusses their contradictions. It profiles the work of Piaget, Freud, Erikson, Gesell, Skinner, and Vygotsky, explains the concept of the "whole child", and shows how most theories focus on one aspect of development.

Erik Erikson: A Life's Work
Price: $250
VHS Video (38 minutes)
Published by Insight Media, New York, NY (1992)
Order # TAA1288
This video combines biographical information and interviews with Erik Erikson with discussion of his theoretical principles. Margaret Brenman-Gibson explains Erikson's biopsychosocial model and describes his Eight Stages of Life, highlighting the unsolvable dichotomies that characterize each stage.

It's elementary
Price: $
VHS Video (77 minutes), Guide, Closed-captioned
Published by New Day Films, New York, NY (1996)
This video is an exploration of what happens when experienced teachers talk to their students about lesbians and gay men. Students are asked to consider issues related to homosexuality at six elementary and middle schools. Footage of classroom activities and discussions are presented with students exploring questions and issues presented to them by teachers and guest lecturers who come into their classes. School-wide presentations, activity-days, and how these events affect faculty, parents and teachers are also discussed.

Sex Roles: Charting the Complexity of Development
Price: $ 139
VHS Video (60 minutes)
Published by Insight Media, New York, NY (1991)
Order # TAA263
This video examines three theories of socialization beginning with the cultural impact of sex roles. Freudian, social-learning, and cognitive-developmental. It analyzes how each theory views the nature versus nurture controversy. It explores the impact of sex-role stereotypes on the developing child, looking at how they affect scholastic achievement, interaction with peers, and expectations for the future.

Self Identity & Sex Role Development
Price: $ 89.95
VHS Video (33 minutes)
Published by Magna Systems, Inc., Barrington, IL (1993)
Order # Mod 23
This video explains the question "Who am I?" The development of self-identity begins in infancy. By middle childhood, a sense of self and self-esteem are well established. The importance of adults in this development is amply demonstrated throughout the video. Through their own observations, and reinforced by others, children acquire ethnic, racial and gender identities. This process is illustrated in the visuals of children at play interacting with parents and other adults, and in scenes of preschoolers at play exploring gender roles. Middle years children are heard grappling with the issue of gender stereotyping.

Play
Price: $ 89.95
VHS Video (29 minutes)
Published by Magna Systems, Inc., Barrington, IL (1993)
Order # Mod 21
This video shows that play is an essential medium for learning and developing. The video explores the significance of play to all areas of development. In real life sequences, the social categories and the content of children's play are demonstrated. The video closes with a description of the adult in facilitating play.

Emotional Development of Children
Price: $ 74
VHS Video (18 minutes)
Published by Films for the Humanities & Sciences, Princeton, NJ
Order # ECU11005
This video shows that parents and caregivers not only need to nurture the physical and intellectual development of young children, but their emotional development as well. Each stage of emotional development provides children with opportunities to explore new feelings as they grow. This timeless program focuses on the importance of emotional education during the various stages of childhood development and explains how caregivers and parents can monitor this vital growth.

Moral Development I - Concept & Theory
Price: $ 89.95
VHS Video (29 minutes)
Published by Magna Systems, Inc., Barrington, IL (1998)
Order # Mod 24A
This video explains the concept of morality and defines key terms such as moral code, moral judgment, and moral intelligence. Using live action video examples and interviews, we help the viewer understand the complexities of helping young people develop a sense of "right" and "wrong." The video presents key values that are fundamental to most moral codes, including empathy, duty, self-reliance, justice and self-control, and helps viewers know how those values are developed throughout childhood and adolescence. The principle theories or moral development are presented, including psychoanalytic, sociobiology, social learning and cognitive learning.

Run Like a Girl
Price: $ 129
VHS Video (57 minutes)
Published by Films for the Humanities & Science, Princeton, NJ
Order # ECU9069
This video in a down-to-earth program, where the unconventional yet extremely demanding sports of rugby, synchronized swimming, and double-Dutch rope jumping provide the context for teenage girls from a cross-section of ethnic backgrounds to probe the issues of adolescence. They discuss their feelings of liberation within the strict regimentation of competitive sports, their search for identity and self-esteem while revolting against the stereotyped expectations of others, body image, dating, and the importance of mothers and coaches as mentors. They also tackle social concerns, including bulimia, self-injury, suicide, broken homes, teen pregnancies, and crime.

Anorexia and Bulimia: The Truth About Eating Disorders
Price: $89.95
VHS Video (30 minutes), Teacher's guide
Published by Edudex, Princeton, NJ (1999)
Order #AAW19883
This video defines anorexia and bulimia, explains how these conditions can begin, and show the damage that is wreaked by these unrealistic quests for "physical perfection." The program also makes the point that men, as well as women, can struggle with eating disorders.

Eating Disorders
Price: $149
VHS Video (28 minutes)
Published by Edudex, Princeton, NJ (2000)
Order #AAW38854
This video profiles four young people who have had eating disorders. Their experiences highlight how this illness is not just about food, but also about struggling with the loss of emotional control. Newer approaches to treatment using cognitive behavioral therapy and antidepressants are explained. Russell Marx, MD, Clinical Director f the Eating Disorders Program at the Medical Center at Princeton, and Marcia Herrin, EdD, MPH, RD at the Dartmouth College Health Service, show what's being done to prevent and treat one of the most lethal categories of mental illness.

Safe at School
Price: $198.95
10 VHS Videos (25 minutes per video)
Published by Teacher's Video Company, Scottsdale, AZ (2001)
Order # SASC Safe at School
This series delves into pressing safety topics and explains proactive techniques for prevention. Developed by skilled administrators, veteran teachers, and police specialists, these videos contain valuable insights, expert interviews, real-life examples, and captivating crisis reenactments. The

videos are designed to be shown at an in-service session or staff meeting, each program encourages teachers and school staff to watch for danger signs and react appropriately.

"I Don't Have a Problem": The Path to Addiction
Price: $109.95
VHS Video (28 minutes), Teacher's guide
Published by Edudex, Princeton, NJ (2000)
Order #AAW30838
This video discusses the typical belief that teenagers hold that they are immune to the problem of serious drug abuse. And that sense of denial is a necessary element in becoming addicted. This video dramatizes the story of one teenager as he progresses from trying his first joint to snorting cocaine, repeatedly denying along the way that he has any problem.. This close-up look at one teen's descent into addiction offers a powerful insight into the nature of the process, and helps students begin to understand their own potential vulnerability.

HANDOUTS TO ACCOMPANY YOUR LESSONS:

H 3.1   Marcia's Theory of the Achievement of a Personal Identity

H 3.2   Erikson's Theory of Psychosocial Development: Implications for Teaching

H 3.3   Theories of Gender and Sexual Development

H 3.4   Robert Selman's Stages of Perspective-Taking

H 3.5   Comparison of Theories of Moral Development

H 3.1

Marcia's Theory of the Achievement of a Personal Identity

James Marcia suggested that four statuses can emerge during adolescence from the conflict faced and the decisions made by adolescents. The four kinds of identities are the result of the combined answers of two questions.

CRISIS? Has the person engaged in an active search for identity?	COMMITMENT? Has the person made commitments? (employment, education, personal values)	STATUS OF IDENTITY
YES	YES	**Identity Achievement** The individual has searched for his or her identity and has made a commitment.
NO	NO	**Identity Diffusion** This person has not engaged in a search for identity and has not committed to any specific aspects of an identity.
YES	NO	**Identity Moratorium** This person has made a search for an identity, but has not made any commitments.
NO	YES	**Identity Foreclosure** This person has made commitments to his or her identity, but did not engage in a search process.

H 3.2

Erikson's Theory of Psychosocial Development
Implications for Teaching

➤ Expert preschool teachers provide young children with opportunities to perform tasks independently.

➤ Expert teachers foster children's ability to assert themselves by allowing them to make as many of their own decisions as possible about schoolwork.

➤ Expert teachers foster feelings of competence in students by noticing and praising students' successes.

➤ Expert teachers of adolescents reassure themselves and students by pointing out examples of the normalcy of identity searches.

H 3.3

Theories of Gender and Sexual Development

Biological Theory	Social Learning Theory
♦ Boys and girls acquire different gender roles because they are biologically predisposed to do so. ♦ Some theorists emphasize the role of evolution in determining sexual behavior and suggest that these differences may be lingering adaptations. ♦ Biological differences between boys and girls may also trigger different treatment form parents and others in their environments.	♦ People come to think and behave as they do by observing others and then by imitating the behavior they have seen being rewarded. ♦ Television provides many children with a way to observe a variety of models. ♦ Television illustrates inaccurate gender stereotypes which are then modeled by children.

H 3.4

Robert Selman's
Stages of Perspective-Taking

Stage 1 Undifferentiated perspective-taking	3 to 6 years	Children recognize that others may have perspectives which differ from their own, but they tend to confuse their own thoughts and feelings with those of other people.	Ex: Ling cannot understand why her mother will not allow her to go out to play at night when she wants to play.
Stage 2 Social-informational perspective	5 to 9 years	Children realize that others may have different perspectives because these others may have access to different information.	Ex: Raul understands why a fireman thinks it is dangerous to play with matches.
Stage 3 Self-reflective perspective-taking	7 to 12 years	Children become able to see themselves as others see them.	Ex: Mimi understands that talking in class is viewed as disruptive by the teacher.
Stage 4 Third-party perspective-taking	10 to 15 years	Children come to understand how their interaction with another person may be viewed by a third party outside their interaction.	Ex: Sally realizes that play punches may be viewed by her teacher as a fight.

H 3.5

Comparison of Theories for Moral Development

Erikson's Theory of Psychosocial Development	Piaget's Theory of Moral Development
Trust versus mistrust (birth to 1 year) **Autonomy versus Shame and Doubt** (1 to 3 years) **Initiative versus Guilt** (3 to 6 years) **Industry versus Inferiority** (6 to 12 years)	**Moral Realism** (Heteronomous morality) ♦ Morality that is subject to rules imposed by others. ♦ Young children are egocentric and have difficulty taking the perspective of other people until the age of 7.
Identity versus Role Confusion (adolescence) **Intimacy versus Isolation** (early adulthood) **Generativity versus Stagnation** (middle adulthood) **Integrity versus Despair** (late adulthood/old age)	**Morality of Cooperation** (Autonomous morality) ♦ The level at which children understand that people both make up rules and can change the rules. ♦ After about age 8, children are able to understand that rules and laws are formed by the agreement of groups of people.

Chapter Four
Individual Differences: Intelligence, Cognitive, and Learning Styles and Creativity

The instructor's manual for this chapter contains:
- A *Chapter-at-a-Glance* chart that reviews all chapter related material
- A detailed chapter outline to highlight main points of the chapter
- A list of transparencies from Transparencies - Educational Psychology IV that correspond to this chapter
- Several activities to deepen student understanding
- An annotated list of additional resources including internet sites
- Handouts to accompany your lessons

CHAPTER-AT-A-GLANCE

Chapter Outline	Objectives	Instructional Aids
1.0 Why Understanding Individual Differences Is Important to Teachers, p. 120	1. Describe the importance to teachers of understanding individual differences.	- Test Bank Question 1
2.0 Understanding Individual Differences in Intelligence, p. 121	1. Describe the beginnings of the modern study of intelligence. 2. Define intelligence as the experts have defined intelligence. 3. Describe the psychometric theories of intelligence. 4. Critique the psychometric theories of intelligence. 5. Describe the contemporary systems theories of intelligence. 6. Critique the contemporary systems theories of intelligence. 7. Compare and contrast the psychometric theories and contemporary systems theories of intelligence, and evaluate them for their implications for teaching.	- Transparencies T24, T25, T26 - Handout 4.2 - Activities 4.1, 4.2, 4.3 - Test Bank Questions 2-28, 61-68, 81-83, 86 - Video Segment 6
3.0 Current Educational Controversies in Intelligence, p. 133	1. Compare the heritability and the modifiability of intelligence. 2. Describe various ability-grouping strategies.	- Transparencies T27, T28, T29 - Handouts 4.3, 4.4 - Test Bank Questions 29-42, 69-71, 84-85, 87-88
4.0 Cognitive Styles, Thinking Styles, and Learning Styles, p. 141	1. Compare cognitive styles with learning styles. 2. Compare and contrast the different cognitive styles (field independence versus field dependence and reflectivity versus impulsivity). 3. Describe the various learning styles discussed in the text	- Transparencies T30, T31 - Handout 4.5 - Test Bank Questions 43-51, 72-77
5.0 Understanding Individual Differences in Creativity, p. 144	1. Describe creativity and the various approaches to understanding creativity	- Handout 4.1 - Activity 4.4 - Test Bank Questions 52-60, 78-80

DETAILED CHAPTER FOUR OUTLINE

I. Why Understanding Individual Differences is Important to Teachers

- Teachers notice that one of the principal differences among students is of intelligence.

- Teachers know that students all have different personalities.

- Teachers notice that students differ in their expressions of creativity.

II. Understanding Individual Differences in Intelligence

   A. What is Intelligence?

- The idea that people vary in intelligence is widely accepted.
- It is difficult to find agreement on just what is meant by intelligence.
- Two groups of experts found common theses in defining intelligence.
  - The ability to learn from experience.
  - The ability to adapt to one's surroundings.
  - Metacognition - people's understanding and control of their own thinking processes.
- The authors define intelligence as the ability to produce goal-directed, adaptive behavior.

   B. Psychometric Theories of Intelligence

- **A General Intelligence Factor**
- Charles Spearman suggested that intelligence can be understood in terms of two kind of underlying mental dimensions.
  - A general factor, g, is a hypothetical single intelligence ability thought to apply to many different tasks.
  - Specific factors, s, are involved in performance on only a single type of mental-ability test.
  - The general factor is relevant to intelligence.
- **Primary Mental Abilities: Many, Not One**
- Louis Thurstone proposed that students' achievement in school can be understood in terms of their amounts of seven basic interrelated factors.
  - Verbal comprehension
  - Verbal fluency
  - Inductive reasoning
  - Spatial visualization
  - Number
  - Memory
  - Perceptual speed
- **Hierarchical Models**
  - The intent of these models was to combine the idea of a general factor with the idea of more narrowly defined subfactors that apply across classes of tasks, which are referred to as group factors.
  - Cattell and Horn suggest that g is the top of the hierarchy and below it are two major subfactors:
    Fluid intelligence is the ability to understand abstract and often novel concepts.
    Crystallized intelligence represents the accumulation of knowledge and is measured by tests of vocabulary and general information.
- Time Constraints: How Fast Is Smart?
  - One element common to many tests of intelligence is the existence of time constraints.
  - Forum: Is Speed of Information Processing Important to Intelligence?

   C. Implications for Teaching

- Accommodate multiple abilities.
- Help students find and use their strengths.

   D. Critique of Psychometric Theories of Intelligence

- The validity of psychometric theories has been questioned.
- Psychometric theories tend to be narrower than contemporary theories in their conception of intelligence.

E. Contemporary Systems Theories of Intelligence
- **Multiple Intelligences**
  - Howard Gardner has proposed a theory of multiple intelligences in which there are eight distinct and relatively independent intelligences:
    - Linguistic intelligence
    - Logical-mathematical intelligence
    - Spatial intelligence
    - Musical intelligence
    - Bodily-kinesthetic intelligence
    - Interpersonal intelligence
    - Intrapersonal intelligence
    - Naturalist intelligence
  - Gardner has speculated on the possibility of two additional intelligences: existential and spiritual.
  - Gardner views each intelligence as modular, or that each intelligence originates from a distinctive portion of the brain.

F. Implications for Teaching
  - take a broad view of what constitutes intelligence.
  - include instruction that addresses underrepresented intelligences.
  - remember, not every topic can be approached through all eight intelligences.
- Focus on the practical as well as the academic aspects of intelligence.
- Consider the various ways students' cultural backgrounds contribute to their definitions and expressions of intelligence.
- Help students capitalize on their strengths.
- The Triarchic Theory of Human Intelligence
  - Robert Sternberg emphasized a set of relatively interdependent processes.
  - There are three related aspects of intelligence, analytical ability, creative ability, and practical ability, each capturing a different "subtheory" of the theory as a whole.
  - The componential subtheory deals with three components underlying intelligent performance:
    - Metacomponents are higher order executive processes used to plan what you are going to do, monitor it while you are doing it, and evaluate it after it is done.
    - Performance components are processes used for implementing the commands of the metacomponents.
    - Knowledge-acquisition components are processes used for learning how to solve problems in the first place.
  - The experiential subtheory suggests that intelligence is related to experience:
    - A task best measures intelligence when the task is either relatively novel or is in the process of being automatized, or becoming more familiar.
    - A novel task is one that is unfamiliar but not totally outside the scope of a person's experience.
    - Automatization is the process by which a task becomes increasingly familiar, requiring less effort in information processing and less explicit consciousness of the way it is performed.
  - The contextual subtheory relates intelligence to the everyday contexts, or settings, in which we live:
    - There are three basic processes of making contact with everyday surroundings.
    - In adaptation, people modify themselves to fit their environment.
    - As people accustom themselves to the environment, they may start to engage in shaping, whereby they modify the environment to fit themselves.
    - In some situations shaping may not work, so you may simply have to select another environment.

G. Critique of Contemporary Systems Theories of Intelligence
•   There have been no published empirical tests of the contemporary systems theory since Gardner's theory.
•   The claim that the multiple intelligences are independent is suspect because so many studies have found intercorrelations among abilities.
•   Contemporary theories have advanced educators' thinking about intelligence.

III. Current Educational Controversies in Intelligence
A. Heritability and Modifiability of Intelligence/To What Extent Are Differences Determined by Genes?
    - Heritability refers to the extent to which individual differences in an attribute are genetically determined independently of any environmental influences.
    - Heritability coefficient is a number on a 0 to 1 scale expressing heritability:
        A coefficient of 0 indicates that heredity has no influence at all on variation among people.
        A coefficient of 1 means that only heredity has an influence on such variation.
    - Heritability measures the extent to which individual differences in intelligence are inherited, not the extent to which intelligence itself is inherited.
    - Heritability of intelligence is measured in many patterns:
        One method involves the study of identical twins separated at or shortly after birth.
        A second method involves comparing identical twins with fraternal twins who are raised in strictly comparable environments.
    - Since early theorists assumed that intelligence was entirely genetically determined, intelligence tests were thought by many to measure a largely inborn trait.
    - Expert teaching does make a difference for intelligence.

B. Can Intelligence Be Modified?
•   Modifiability is the extent to which an attribute is susceptible to change.
•   As environmental factors can have a large effect on development, they can also apply to intelligence.
•   Gene-environment interaction is the idea that genetic and environmental influences can combine to produce results that might be unexpected on the basis of either factor alone.
    - A reaction range is a spectrum of ways that an attribute can be expressed in the environment, bounded by genetic possibilities.
    - A reaction range suggests that the upper and lower limits of a person's intellectual abilities are determined by genetics, and within that range environmental forces determine exactly what level of intelligence the person will attain.

C. How Environmental Influences Make a Difference: Lessons for Teachers
•   A child's home environment during the preschool years is crucial to intellectual development, implying a need for structured preschools.
•   Head Start was designed to provide preschoolers with an advantage both in their intellectual abilities and in their school achievements when they started school:
    - Research reveals that children in the program score higher on achievement tests and show fewer behavioral problems.
    - Some analysts believe that this improvement is only temporary.
•   Instrumental Enrichment is a program designed to remedy deficiencies in cognitive processing and to increase students' internal motivation and feelings of self-worth.
•   Practical Intelligence for School is a program that combines aspects of the theory of multiple intelligences with aspects of the triarchic theory of intelligence.

D. Implications for Teaching
•   Allow children to play and learn without too many limitations.
•   Focus on each student's potential for improvement.
•   Provide opportunities to practice skills that are part of intelligent behavior.
•   Help students link skills to real-world needs.

E. Teaching Students of Varying Levels: Ability Grouping
- **Methods of Ability Grouping**
  - Within-class grouping is where a single class of students is divided into two or three groups for instruction in certain subjects.
  - Between-class grouping is where students are assigned to separate classes according to ability: Assignments are often made on the basis of standardized intelligence or achievement tests.
  - This method can also be expanded into a practice known as tracking, where assignments are made based on variations in ability levels and interests.
  - Regrouping is a method where students are members of two or more classes or groups at once:
    - Students are assigned to a general, mixed-ability class for most of the day, but switch to ability-based groups for certain subjects.
    - Groups can be made up of children who are all at the same age or grade level, or they can be composed of students from a range of ages and grade levels.
    - A regrouping plan in which students of various ages are assigned to the same ability based group is known as the Joplin Plan.
F. Advantages and Disadvantages of Ability Grouping
- The practice can help teachers adjust teaching techniques to the varying levels of their students.
- Adjusting instruction to groups of students helps teachers make effective use of their limited time.
  - Often, between-class groups are "trapped" in their assigned group for an entire school year.
  - Students from lower socioeconomic levels and ethnic minority groups tend to be overrepresented in lower-ability groups.
  - Students in the lower-ability classes often receive lower-quality instruction.
  - Placement in a low-ability group can stigmatize students socially and lower their self-esteem.
  - Between-class grouping may not be effective.

G. Implications for Teaching
- Target ability grouping carefully.
- Assess student progress frequently and adjust group assignments according to progress.
- Avoid comparisons between groups.
- Keep quality of instruction high for all students.

IV. **Cognitive Styles, Thinking Styles, and Learning Styles**
A. Cognitive Styles
- **Field-Independence versus Field-Dependence**
  - A field-independent person is able to separate from the surrounding context.
  - A field-dependent person has trouble separating self from the surrounding field.
  - Field-dependent students tend to be more attuned to the social aspects of school situations, and may perform better at group tasks.
  - Field-independent students may need help seeing how their actions affect the group as a whole.
- **Reflectivity versus Impulsivity**
  - A reflective person tends to consider alternative solutions before reaching a decision.
  - An impulsive person tends to produce quick answers without carefully thinking about them first.
  - Impulsive children tend to make more errors in reading and memory tasks.
  - During individual tasks, encourage impulsive students to talk to themselves mentally as they are working on problems.
- **Mental Self-Government**
  - Sternberg's theory of mental self-government proposes that people need to organize and govern themselves.
  - A Legislative student enjoys creating, formulating, and planning problem solutions and likes to do things his or her own way.
  - An Executive student likes to implement plans, follow rules, and choose from established options.
  - A Judicial student enjoys evaluating rules, procedures, or products.
  - Teachers should include activities that appeal to a broader variety of self-government styles.

B. Learning Styles
- Students vary in preferences for aspects of the classroom environment such as lighting, hard or soft seating, or level of noise.
- Some of the styles expressed as physical preferences may actually be culturally-related differences in learning.
- Individual differences in personality can affect the way different students approach the same learning task.
  - A deep-processing approach seeks the underlying concepts of activities or lessons.
  - A surface processing approach focuses on memorization rather than analysis and understanding.

V. **Understanding Individual Differences in Creativity**
  A. The Mystical Approach
- Creativity is seen as the result either of divine intervention or of other unexplainable forces.
- The problem with this approach is that it lends itself neither to scientific investigation nor to educational interventions.

  B. The Psychometric Approach
- The emphasis is on measuring creative abilities in much the same way as other abilities are measured.
- J. P. Guilford emphasized divergent thinking, or the ability to generate many different ideas in response to a problem.
- The opposite of divergent thinking is convergent thinking, or the process of finding a single correct answer.

  C. Social-Psychological Approaches
- This approach to creativity focuses on environmental variables that influence creative thinking.
- Creative thinking may be caused by intrinsic motivation, or a desire to do something because you really want to do it, not for the sake of any external rewards.
- Extrinsic motivation signifies doing something in order to achieve rewards from an external source.

  D. A Confluence Approach
- The investment theory of creativity describes creative people as good investors who find an idea that is undervalued by contemporaries, then develops that idea into a meaningful contribution.
- This theory represents a coming together, or confluence, of a number of research and theoretical strands.
- Characteristics of creative people
  - Do not accept traditional ways of seeing problems, but try to see problems in new ways.
  - Know something about the field to which they wish to contribute, but do not allow their knowledge to interfere with their seeing things in new ways.
  - Like begin creative.
  - Persevere in the face of obstacles.
  - Are open to new experiences.
  - Are willing to take sensible risks.
  - Are intrinsically motivated.
  - Find environments that support and reward their creative work.

  E. Implications for Teaching
- Model creativity
- Encourage students to question assumptions.
- Encourage sensible risk-taking.
- Promote persistence.
- Allow mistakes.
- Model and encourage divergent thinking.

- Allow time and opportunities for creative thinking.
- Reward creativity.

TRANSPARENCIES
- T24   Eight Intelligences
- T25   An Example of a Lesson Plan on Solving Algebraic
         Equations Incorporating Multiple Intelligences in Planning
- T26   Sternberg's Triarchic Theory of Intelligence
- T27   Illustration of Items Used in Intelligence Testing
- T28   The Modern Stanford-Binet Intelligence Scale
- T29   Characteristics of Giftedness
- T30   Examples of Instructional Enrichment
- T31   A Test of Cognitive Style

CLASS ACTIVITIES
Activity 4.1 Gardner's Multiple Intelligence Self-Rating Scale
Use this activity when discussing intelligence theories to help students explore their own range of intelligence. This activity is a self-rating scale in which students can rate their seperate intellectual abilities. Students reflect about the types of intelligences that they excel in. The activity can then be discussed to see if students have excelled in tasks that required those intelligences. Also, students can be asked to see if they have chosen a career path in tune with those intelligences.

Activity 4.2 Sternberg's Triarchic Theory of Intelligence
Use this activity when discussing intelligence theories to help students recognize examples of the Triarchic Theory. This activity is a quiz that will require students to recognize the Triarchic Theory components within examples. The activity includes examples of people doing various tasks. The students have to determine the correct subtheories and the processes for each example. The activity will help students relate to the concepts within the theory.

Activity 4.3 Gardner's Multiple Intelligence Examples
Use this activity when discussing intelligence theories to help students recognize examples of the Multiple Intelligence Theory. This activity is a quiz that will require students to recognize the various intelligences within examples. The activity includes examples of people doing various tasks. The students have to determine the correct intelligence used in each task. The activity will help students relate to the concepts within the theory.

Activity 4.4 Methods of Encouraging Creativity in the Classroom
This activity will get students thinking about how to promote creativity and divergent thinking in the classroom. The activity requires students to give specific examples about the grades or subjects they will be teaching. The examples will be ways to model or promote creativity or divergent thinking in the classroom. This is a good activity to get students thinking about how they will manage their classrooms to promote both learning and creativity.

Class Activity 4.1
Gardner's Multiple Intelligence Self-Rating Scale

Please rate your ability for each intelligence.
Circle the corresponding number.

Intelligence	Low	Below Average	Average	Above Average	High
1. Linguistic – used in reading, writing, speaking coherently, and understanding lectures.	1	2	3	4	5
2. Logical / Mathematical – used in solving mathematical problems, balancing a checkbook, and doing mathematical or logical proofs.	1	2	3	4	5
3. Spatial – used in walking, driving, reading a map, and packing a suitcase in a trunk of a car so they will all fit.	1	2	3	4	5
4. Musical – used in singing, playing an instrument, composing, and understanding and appreciating the structure of a symphony.	1	2	3	4	5
5. Bodily-kinesthetic – used in playing football, dancing, running, or bowling.	1	2	3	4	5
6. Interpersonal – used in understanding and responding appropriately to others personalities, moods, temperaments, and desires.	1	2	3	4	5
7. Intrapersonal – used in understanding ourselves, why we think, feel, and act the way we do, and knowing our strengths and limitations.	1	2	3	4	5
8. Naturalistic – used in discerning patterns in nature and being able to discern what kinds of weather you can expect on different days.	1	2	3	4	5

Class Activity 4.2
Sternberg's Triarchic Theory of Intelligence

Match the following examples with the appropriate subtheory and relevant processes.

1. Abby has become so good at playing video games that she does not have to think about the controls anymore.
   Subtheory _____Processes_____

2. Bill feels his current job is no longer rewarding and wants to look for a new place to work.
   Subtheory _____Processes_____

3. While at the library, Arlene learns to use the Internet for her class project.
   Subtheory _____Processes_____

4. Jose, a seven year old, is being tested with addition and subtraction tasks.
   Subtheory _____Processes_____

5. Bruce has learned to be more cooperative in order to avoid fights with his sister.
   Subtheory _____Processes_____

6. Alice is reading a book on quantum mechanics.
   Subtheory _____Processes_____

7. Pat is slowly changing his job duties to create a position he will enjoy more.
   Subtheory _____Processes_____

8. Isabella is planning a strategy to complete her upcoming research paper.
   Subtheory _____Processes_____

Subtheory

A. Componential
B. Experiential
C. Contextual

Processes

a. Metacomponent
b. Performance component
c. Knowledge-acquisition component
d. Measure with a novel task
e. Automatization
f. Adaptation
g. Shaping
h. Selection

Class Activity 4.2
Sternberg's Triarchic Theory of Intelligence
Answer Key

1. Abby has become so good at playing video games that she does not have to think about the controls anymore.
    Subtheory _____B_____ Processes _____e_____
    Reasoning: The task of playing a video game has become so familiar that less effort and consciousness is needed to perform the skill.

2. Bill feels his current job is no longer rewarding and wants to look for a new place to work.
    Subtheory _____C_____ Processes _____h_____
    Reasoning: Bill's current position does not satisfy him and he feels that he must select another environment in order to get satisfaction.

3. While at the library, Arlene learns to use the Internet for her class project.
    Subtheory _____A_____ Processes _____c_____
    Reasoning: Arlene learns how to solve a problem for the first time.

4. Jose, a seven year old, is being tested with addition and subtraction tasks.
    Subtheory _____B_____ Processes _____d_____
    Reasoning: Testing is being done within the scope of Jose's experience.

5. Bruce has learned to be more cooperative in order to avoid fights with his sister.
    Subtheory _____C_____ Processes _____f_____
    Reasoning: Bruce is adapting to his environment to provide a more peaceful situation.

6. Alice is reading a book on quantum mechanics.
    Subtheory _____A_____ Processes _____b_____
    Reasoning: Alice is doing the actual task of reading.

7. Pat is slowly changing his job duties to create a position he will enjoy more.
    Subtheory _____C_____ Processes _____g_____
    Reasoning: Pat is modifying the environment to fit himself.

8. Isabella is planning a strategy to complete her upcoming research paper.
    Subtheory _____A_____ Processes _____a_____
    Reasoning: Isabella is using her higher-order processes to plan her paper.

Class Activity 4.3
Gardner's Multiple Intelligence Examples

Match the following examples with the appropriate intelligence.
Examples may use more than one intelligence.

1. _____ Mark is looking at a map to see where Spain is in relation to Africa.

2. _____ Jerry is listening and helping Tammy with a personal problem.

3. _____ Greg is writing a speech he has to give tonight.

4. _____ Olga is singing in the choir.

5. _____ Jeannie is figuring out the distance between Chicago and Philadelphia.

6. _____ Frank and Erin are organizing their closet so everything will fit.

7. _____ Ted is observing how geese migrate.

8. _____ Kelly is playing a song on her guitar.

9. _____ Albert and Pedro are playing a tennis match.

10. _____ Rachael is counseling a family concerning their child's drug addiction.

11. _____ Pete is creating a budget for his household expenses.

12. _____ Juanita is reading a book.

13. _____ Suzanne is doing a career inventory to figure out what she does well.

14. _____ While camping, John observes that it is going to rain soon.

15. _____ Margaret is taking her weekly ballet lesson.

Intelligences

A. Linguistic
B. Logical / Mathematical
C. Spatial
D. Musical
E. Bodily-kinesthetic
F. Interpersonal
G. Intrapersonal
H. Naturalistic

Class Activity 4.3
Gardner's Multiple Intelligence Examples
Answer Key

16. __C__ Mark is looking at a map to see where Spain is in relation to Africa.
Reasoning: Mark is judging spatial relationship between Spain and Africa.

17. __F__ Jerry is listening to and helping Tammy with a personal problem.
Reasoning: Jerry is trying to understand and provide feedback to Tammy.

18. __A__ Greg is writing a speech he has to give tonight.
Reasoning: The task requires linguistic skills.

19. __D__ Olga is singing in the choir.
Reasoning: Olga is using her voice to accompany music.

20. B & C Jeannie is figuring out the distance between Chicago and Philadelphia.
Reasoning: Jeannie is solving a math problem of distance and using spatial skills to relate the cities.

21. __C__ Frank and Erin are organizing their closet so everything will fit.
Reasoning: Frank and Erin are using spatial skills to arrange items so they fit.

22. __H__ Ted is observing how geese migrate.
Reasoning: Ted is observing patterns in nature.

23. D & E Kelly is playing a song on her guitar.
Reasoning: Kelly is playing a musical instrument that requires musical skill and physical skill to manipulate the guitar.

24. E & C Albert and Pedro are playing a tennis match.
Reasoning: Albert and Pedro are using their bodies to play tennis and their spatial skills to maneuver around the court.

25. __F__ Rachael is counseling a family concerning their child's drug addiction.
Reasoning: Rachael is using interpersonal skills to relate to and help a family.

25. __B__ Pete is creating a budget for his household expenses.
Reasoning: The task requires math problem solving skills.

26. __A__ Juanita is reading a book.
Reasoning: Juanita's reading requires linguistic skills.

27. __G__ Suzanne is doing a career inventory to figure out what she does well.
Reasoning: Suzanne is gaining insight into herself to help her choose a career.

28. __H__ While camping, Malik observes that it is going to rain soon.
Reasoning: Malik is observing patterns in nature.

29. __E__ Margaret is taking her weekly ballet lesson.
Reasoning: Margaret is utilizing her body to dance.

Class Activity 4.4
Methods of Encouraging Creativity in the Classroom

1. Using the list below provide three examples that will model or promote creativity in the classroom for the grade levels and/or content areas you plan to teach.

   - Provide profiles of creative individuals
   - Ask questions that require students to take someone else's viewpoint
   - Encourage sensible risk-taking

2. Using the list below provide three examples that will model or encourage divergent thinking in the classroom for the grade levels and/or content areas you plan to teach.

   - Brainstorm ideas for alternative conclusions
   - Predict results of an experiment
   - Experiment with materials in novel ways

AVAILABLE RESOURCES ON-LINE
Intelligence Tests and Trivia Games
www.puzz.com
This website is the largest resource for IQ tests, puzzles, trivia, games & contests for entertainment & education. It contains tests, puzzles, contests and games that teachers could use for their students to experience. These activities can exercise your students' minds & expand their knowledge with trivia, tests, riddles, brainteasers, contests, games, & many different types of puzzles. Books, games, IQ tests, software, magazines, educational & test preparation materials, and puzzles can be purchased on-line.

History of Influences in the Development of Intelligence Theory and Testing
www.indiana.edu/~intell/map.html
This website provides an interactive map with links to all of the theorists that have influenced intelligence theory and testing from historical foundations of 1690 to the current efforts of present day theorists. Each link provides information on their individual contributions to the study of intelligence.

Howard Gardner's Multiple Intelligence Theory
edweb.gsn.org/edref.mi.th.html
This website provides information on Howard Gardner's multiple intelligence theory. There are links to each of the seven faculties of intellect providing examples of people who have exceptional qualities in that particular faculty. Recently added to the original list of seven multiple intelligences, naturalist intelligence is a person's ability to identify and classify patterns in nature. This site also answers questions concerning how this theory has impacted schools, how multiple intelligences would affect the implementation of traditional education, and what the traditional view of intelligence is.

Howard Gardner's Theory of Multiple Intelligences
Surfaquarium.com/im.htm
This website provides information on Gardner's Theory of Multiple Intelligences and the eight criteria for identifying an intelligence. It also provides a ready to print and use multiple intelligence inventory that teachers could use as a classroom activity. This website also provides links to EdWeb's multiple intelligence overview listed above, Dee Dickinson's multiple intelligence overview, and an interview with Howard Gardner on the NEA website.

Creative Thinking Tools
www.jpb.com/creative/indexhttp://www.jpb.com/creative/index
This website provides information on creative thinking tools and advice to help you think more creatively. Teachers can use the ten steps for boosting creativity in the classroom and use some of the creative exercises as activities. This site also provides a complete step by step guide to effective brainstorming.

Creativity Web: Resources for Creativity and Innovation
www.ozemail.com.au/~caveman/Creative/index2.html
This website is a resource center providing information to help one become more creative. This site provides various models of the brain and the creative processes involved. It also provides challenging problems, including lateral thinking puzzles, crossword puzzle, and number puzzles. This website also provides links to books, software, web sites, and people and organizations associated with creativity.

RECOMMENDED VIDEOS FOR CHAPTER FOUR
Intelligence, Creativity, and Thinking Styles
Price: $149
VHS Video (30 minutes)
Published by Insight Media, New York, NY (1996)
Order #TAA1269
Robert Sternberg discusses the "single trait" notion of intelligence and questions the fundamental role of IQ testing in American education. The video also examines the components of intelligence.

Growing Minds: Cognitive Development in Early Childhood
Price: $250
VHS Video (25 minutes), Teacher's guide
Published by Edudex, Princeton, NJ (1996)
Order #AAW32270
This program examines the work of Lev Vygotsky and Jean Piaget, illuminating the similarities and differences of their contributions to our understanding of the cognitive development of young children. Dr. David Elkind uses their research, and his own work, to look at three aspects of intellectual growth: reasoning, visual perception and the use of language. Children are seen both in interview situations and busily participating in an accredited childcare center to illustrate Dr. Elkind's points about their ever-changing intellectual abilities.

Adolescent Cognition: Thinking in a New Key
Price: $250
VHS Video (20 minutes), Teacher's guide
Published by Edudex, Princeton, NJ (1999)
Order #AAW32277
It is not just teenage bodies that undergo tremendous changes in adolescence; young minds begin working in new ways that sometimes cause awkward situations too. In this program, David Elkind, Ph.D., looks at the intellectual, emotional and social consequences that result from the changes in thinking. Referring to the work of Piaget, Erikson, Goffman and his own studies, Dr. Elkind explains how these changes permit new ways of reasoning and enable students to take on much more challenging materials, but also points out that often, the transition results in inconsistent forms of thinking that create social and emotional difficulties.

Teaching to Multiple Intelligences
Price: $179
VHS Video (60 minutes)
Published by Insight Media, New York, NY (1998)
This two-part set uses classroom scenes to explain how to teach to the diverse talents of all students. It discusses the strengths and interests that characterize various types of intelligence and demonstrates how teaching to multiple intelligences can improve student performance, responsibility, and self-esteem.

Multiple Intelligences: Other Styles of Learning
Price: $129
VHS Video (29 minutes)
Published by Films for the Humanities & Sciences, Princeton, NJ
Order #ECU10266
Historically, student progress has been gauged by success in subjects that tap the verbal/linguistic and logical/mathematical talents of students, inevitably leading to the disenfranchisement of learners weak in these areas. In this timeless program, David Lazier, author of Seven Ways of Knowing and Seven Ways of Teaching and founder of New Dimensions of Learning, contends that educators must ensure the success of all students by teaching for the five nontraditional intelligences as well: visual/spatial, musical/rhythmic, body/kinesthetic, intrapersonal, and interpersonal.

Developing the Gifts and Talents of All Students
Price: $129
VHS Video (40 minutes)
Published by Insight Media, New York, NY (1999)
Order #UAA1615
Hosted by Joseph Renzulli, this video describes the Schoolwide Enrichment Model (SEM), which advocates the use of gifted education teaching practices with all students. It details such major features of the SEM as a total talent portfolio that focuses on a student's range of interests and learning style as well as academic strengths; advanced levels of academic challenge; strategies for modifying and differentiating a curriculum to accommodate individuals; and a hands-on approach that focuses on application rather than just assimilation of knowledge.

Addressing Learner Differences
Price: $119
VHS Video (30 minutes)
Published by Insight Media, New York, NY (1998)
Order #UAA1762
Reviewing a number of learning theories that can help instructors develop teaching methods to address a range of learning styles, this video features the commentary of experts who discuss these theories and select one or two as a main model. The program emphasizes the need to understand preferred learning style and to avoid teaching according to one's own learning style.

HANDOUTS TO ACCOMPANY YOUR LESSON:

H 4.1   Approaches to Creativity

H 4.2   Sternberg's Triarchic Theory of Human Intelligence

H 4.3   Methods of Ability Grouping

H 4.4   Implications for Teaching Ability Theories and Classroom Practice

H 4.5   Field-Independence versus Field-Dependence

Approaches to Creativity

The Mystical Approach

- Creativity is seen as the result either of divine intervention or of other unexplainable forces.
- The oldest approach to creativity.

The Psychometric Approach

- Emphasis is on measuring creative abilities.
- This approach to creativity is best exemplified by the Torrance Tests of Creative Thinking.

Social-Psychological Approaches

- Focus on environmental variables that influence creative thinking.
- Creative thinking is seen as intrinsic motivation, or the desire to do something because you really want to do it.

The Confluence Approach

- Describes creative people as good investors.
- The creative individual finds an idea, then develops that idea into a significant, creative contribution.

Sternberg's Triarchic Theory of Human Intelligence

Componential Subtheory	Experiential Subtheory	Contextual Subtheory
• Ability to think abstractly, process information effectively. • Metacomponents are the higher order executive processes used to plan, monitor, and evaluate what you do. • Performance components are the processes used for implementing the commands of the metacomponents • Knowledge-acquisition components are the processes used for learning how to solve problems in the first place.	• Ability to formulate new ideas, to combine seemingly unrelated facts or information. • A task best measures intelligence when the task is either new (unfamiliar) or being learned. • Automatization is the process by which a task becomes increasingly familiar, requiring less effort in information processing, and less explicit consciousness of the way it is performed.	• Ability to adapt to changing environmental conditions and to shape the environment so as to maximize one's strengths and compensate for one's weaknesses. • Adaptation is the process by which people modify themselves to fit their environment. • Shaping is the process by which people modify the environment to fit themselves.

H 4.3

Methods of Ability Grouping

Within-Class Grouping	Between-Class Grouping	Regrouping
<ul><li>A single class of students is divided into two or three groups for instruction in certain subjects.</li><li>This is most commonly used at the elementary school level.</li></ul>	<ul><li>Students are assigned to separate classes according to ability.</li><li>Assignments are often made on the basis of standardized intelligence or achievement tests.</li><li>This method can also be expanded into a practice known as tracking where assignments are made based on variations in ability levels and interests.</li></ul>	<ul><li>Students are members of two or more classes or groups at once.</li><li>Groups can be made up of children who are all at the same age or grade level, or from a range of ages and grade levels.</li><li>A regrouping plan in which students of various ages are assigned to the same ability based group is known as the Joplin Plan.</li></ul>

Implications for teaching: Increasing children's abilities regardless of grouping procedures

- Allow children to play and learn without too many limitations.

- Focus on each student's potential for improvement.

- Provide opportunities to practice skills that are part of intelligent behavior.

- Help students link skills to real-world needs.

Implications for Teaching
Ability Theories and Classroom Practice

Psychometric Theories of Intelligence

- ➤ Accommodate multiple abilities.

- ➤ Help students find and use their strengths.

Theory of Multiple Intelligences

- ➤ Takes a broad view of what constitutes intelligence.

- ➤ Includes instruction that addresses underrepresented intelligences.

- ➤ Remember, not every topic can be approached through all eight intelligences.

The Triarchic Theory of Intelligence

- ➤ Focuses on the practical as well as the academic aspects of intelligence.

- ➤ Considers the various ways students' cultural backgrounds contribute to their definitions and expressions of intelligence.

- ➤ Helps students capitalize on their strengths.

H 4.5

Field Independence	**versus**	**Field Dependence**

♦ A person who is able to separate self, or objects viewed, from the surrounding context.

♦ Might be able to read text upside-down.

♦ May prefer subjects such as math or science that require their analytical abilities.

♦ Has trouble separating self, or objects, from the surrounding field.

♦ Tend to be more attuned to the social aspects of school situations.

♦ May prefer subjects such as literature and history that require them to perceived broad patterns.

Chapter Five
<u>Individual Differences: Exceptional Children</u>

The instructor's manual for this chapter contains:
- A *Chapter-at-a-Glance* chart that reviews all chapter related material
- A detailed chapter outline to highlight main points of the chapter
- A list of transparencies from Transparencies - Educational Psychology IV that correspond to this chapter
- Several activities to deepen student understanding
- An annotated list of additional resources including internet sites
- Handouts to accompany your lessons

CHAPTER-AT-A-GLANCE

Chapter Outline	Objectives	Instructional Aids
1.0 Why Understanding Exceptional Children is Important to Teachers, p. 156	1. Discuss the importance to teachers of understanding exceptional children.	- Handout 5.2 - Test Bank Questions 1, 2, 64
2.0 Teaching Exceptional Children, p. 157	1. Describe the major laws and legal rights of exceptional children. 2. Describe the special education services available in the U.S. 3. Define the steps for referring students for special education.	- Transparencies T32, T33, T34, T35 - Handout 5.1 - Test Bank Questions 3-11, 65-68, 77, 82 - Video Segment 7
3.0 Extremes of Intellectual Functioning: Giftedness, p. 162	1. Distinguish between different ideas about giftedness. 2. Describe different methods for identifying gifted students. 3. Discuss the complexities of teaching gifted students	- Test Bank Questions 12-22, 69, 78-80
4.0 Extremes of Intellectual Functioning: Mental Retardation, p. 167	1. Define mental retardation. 2. Discuss the causes of mental retardation. 3. Describe the various levels of mental retardation. 4. Discuss how best to characterize mental retardation.	- Test Bank Questions 23-35, 70-73, 83
5.0 Challenges to Learning, p. 171	1. Define and describe the various learning disabilities discussed in your text. 2. Discuss ADHD, and the challenges it brings to the classroom. 3. Describe emotional and behavioral disorders found in the classroom. 4. Describe possible health disorders of students. 5. Describe possible sensory impairments of students. 6. Describe the communication disorders discussed in the text	- Transparencies T36, T37 - Activities 5.1, 5.2 - Test Bank Questions 36-63, 74-76, 81

DETAILED CHAPTER FIVE OUTLINE
I. **Why Understanding Exceptional Children Is Important to Teachers**
   - The trend toward full inclusion of all children in the regular classroom has resulted in almost every teacher becoming a teacher of children with special educational needs.

   - An exceptional child is a child who is unusual in one or more ways, and whose unusual characteristics create special needs with respect to identification, instruction, or assessment.

   - The group of at-risk children includes children with exceptionalities, such as emotional and physical problems, and special forms of learning disabilities.

II. **Teaching Exceptional Children**
   A. Major Laws and Legal Rights
   - Special education refers to any program that provides distinctive services for children identified as having special needs.
   - In 1975, Public Law 94-142, the Education for All Handicapped Children Act, required states to provide appropriate public education for every child between the ages of 3 and 21.
   - In 1986, Public Law 99-457 extended these rights to all children ages 3 to 5, and added programs addressing the needs of infants with serious disabilities.
   - In 1990, Public Law 101-476 changed the name of Public Law 94-142 to the Individuals with Disabilities Education Act, or IDEA.
   - IDEA required that schools plan for the transition of adolescents with disabilities into either further education or employment at age 16.
   - IDEA replaced the term "handicapped" with the term "disabled."

   B. Least Restrictive Placement
   - Least restrictive placement means a child must be placed in a setting that is as normal as possible.
   - Mainstreaming places exceptional students in regular classes as soon as they are able to meet the same requirements as typical students.
   - Full inclusion places students into regular classes, making accommodations as necessary to enable the exceptional students to succeed.

   C. The Individualized Education Program (IEP)
   - The special education laws require that each student with special needs have and IEP which specifies the goals and objectives set to improve the student's level of achievement and how these will be achieved.
   - The IEP is written by a team consisting minimally of the student's teacher or teachers, a qualified school psychologist or special-education supervisor, the parents or guardians, and sometimes the individual student.
   - Included in IEPs
     - The student's current level of achievement.
     - Annual goals and short-term measurable instructional objectives that will result in the attainment of these goals.
     - Specific services to be provided to the student, including when the services will be initiated.
     - A specification of how and how fully the student will participate in the regular instructional program of the school.
     - A description of how long the special services will be needed.
     - A statement of how progress toward objectives will be evaluated for those children age 16 and older.
     - A description of needed services to provide a transition to either further education or to work.

   D. Special Education Services: Where Can You Go for Extra Help?
   - Special education teachers often consult on a one-to-one basis with regular classroom teachers.

- Students with special needs may be assigned fixed times to work with teachers who are subject-matter specialists in a resource room.
- Students may need to attend special education classes for all subjects.

   E. Referring Students for Special Education
- Referrals for diagnosis usually originate with teachers' recognition that the relatively poor performance of a student has no readily apparent explanation.
- Parents may provide information that can help the teacher meet the student's needs.

III. Extremes of Intellectual Functioning: Giftedness
   A. Ideas About Giftedness
- A gifted child is one with exceptional abilities or talents.
- Some scholars differentiate giftedness based on level of intelligence, level of accomplishments, or kind of accomplishments.
- Joseph Renzulli believes there are two traditional notions of giftedness.
  - Schoolhouse giftedness usually has high performance in areas such as language skills and math.
  - Creative-productive giftedness is observed in adults as well as children who actually produce works of art or literature, theater, scientific research, or other accomplishments valued beyond the school.
  - Other experts point out how much sociocultural values shape our conceptions of giftedness.

   B. Identifying Gifted Students
- The methods schools use depend on the ways they conceptualize giftedness.
- One view suggests that intelligence is the central attribute of giftedness.
  - Advocates usually place considerable reliance on the results of conventional intelligence tests.
  - Such identification is based on a fairly narrow view of what it means to be gifted.
- The Marland Report believed that children who are exceptional in one or more of the following areas should be identified and provided with special services.
  - General intellectual ability
  - Specific academic aptitude
  - Creative or productive thinking
  - Leadership ability
  - Visual and performing arts
  - Psychomotor ability
- Today most schools use at least some other kind of assessment in addition to intelligence tests.
  - Howard Gardner's theory of multiple intelligences
  - Sternberg's triarchic theory
- According to the three-ring model of Joseph Renzulli, giftedness occurs at the intersection of three attributes.
  - Above-average ability
  - Creativity
  - Task-commitment
- Gifted children are experts in a number of respects.
  - They have more and better learning strategies, metacognition, knowledge about other people, and motivation to learn and excel.
  - They process information more quickly and efficiently.
  - They have more and better insights during problem solving.
  - They create new problems to solve and ask new types of questions.

   C. Teaching Gifted Students
- There are several types of programs for the gifted and talented.
- The pull-out program places gifted children in a normal classroom but takes them out at regular intervals for special instruction by a teacher.
- Acceleration gives students a normal program, but presents the material at a more rapid rate.

- Curriculum compacting involves teaching a normal course, but deleting redundant material that the student already knows.
- In the enrichment approach, children are taught a normal course, but activities are added to enhance the understanding and application of what they have learned.
  - Type I enrichment involves invitations to more advanced levels of involvement in a topic, and is designed to interest students in pursuing a topic further.
  - Type II enrichment consists of activities designed to develop higher-level thinking skills, as well as research skills, reference-using skills, and personal and social skills.
  - Type III enrichment involves individual and small-group investigations of real problems drawing on what the students have learned.
- A revolving-door model of identification is where groups are identified as gifted in different areas and are given opportunities to develop the skills in which they have particular gifts.

D. Implications for Teaching
- Reward gifted students' motivation to learn more.
- Help gifted students find problems to solve.
- Keep gifted students challenged.
- Work with families of gifted students.
- Reinforce gifted student's self-esteem.

IV. **Extremes of Intellectual Functioning: Mental Retardation**
   A. Causes of Mental Retardation
   - Familial retardation tends to run in families.
   - Organic cases are associated with traumatic events or abnormalities, and do not run in families.

   B. Levels of Mental Retardation
   - Children with mild retardation have IQs in the 50 to 70 range.
     - These people represent 80 to 85 percent of those with retardation and roughly two percent of the general population.
     - These students may eventually master academic skills at or below the sixth-grade level.
   - Individuals with moderate retardation have IQs in the 35 to 50 range.
     - They represent 10 percent of retarded persons and about 0.1 percent of the general population.
     - With assistance, they may eventually master academic skills at the fourth-grade level.
   - Individuals with severe or profound retardation have IQs below 35.
     - They represent 5 percent of retarded persons.
     - People with severe retardation are unlikely to benefit from vocational training.
     - People with profound retardation are generally able to respond to training only for very limited tasks, such as walking or using a spoon.
   - The AAMR has developed a classification based upon the amount and types of support an individual needs to function.
     - Intermittent support is provided only occasionally during times of stress.
     - Limited support is provided on a regular basis.
     - Extensive support is provided daily to allow the person to function at work, school, or home.
     - Pervasive support is constant help in accomplishing basic tasks, such as eating and toileting.

   C. Characterizations of Mental Retardation
   - Zigler (1982) argues that individuals with familial retardation simply show slower mental growth than do individuals of normal intelligence.
   - One theory suggests that individuals with mental retardation are more rigid in their thinking.
   - Another suggests that they show deficits primarily in learning and memory.

- Sternberg and Spear (1985) find that children with mental retardation show deficits not only in executive processing, but also in coping with novelty and in adaptive competence in everyday life.
- Reuven Feuerstein believes that retardation is a result of lack of mediated learning experience of the environment by parents for children.

D. Implications for Teaching
- Teach learning strategies.
- Divide lessons into small, clearly defined steps.
- Help students learn self-regulation.
- Make lessons concrete and applicable to daily life.
- Help students raise their self-esteem.

V. Challenges to Learning
A. Learning Disabilities
- Some children show high levels of performance at the same time that they show a deficit.
- The classification of learning disabilities was a result of the need to distinguish such children from children whose performance was depressed in all areas of academic and other kinds of functioning.

B. Defining Learning Disabilities
- Learning disabilities (LD) are diagnosed when performance in a specific subject matter is worse than would be expected from a child's overall level of measured intelligence.
- The definition has been problematic in a number of respects.
  - Many educators question whether the tests used really provide an adequate measure.
  - Discrepancy scores do not seem to serve equally well at all points along a continuum of abilities.
  - Differences in scores are plagued by statistical problems.
  - There is sometimes an overlap between the skills required for intelligence tests and the skills required on tests of specific skills.

C. Problems with Special Services
- The criteria used to identify children as having a learning disability can differ from one state to another.
- The special services can create issues of equity.
- Learning disability-related services are not the same for all students.

D. Making Sense of Reading Disabilities
- Several different theories of reading disability have been proposed.
  - Reading disability is due to deficits in visual perception.
  - Individuals with a reading disability have difficulty in phonemic processing in being able to sound out letters and letter combinations.
  - Reading disability is due to problems in automatization.
  - "Reading disability" is a label that society has created in order to explain its own failure in teaching some children to read.
- Evidence suggests that reading disability is not a single phenomenon, but rather one with multiple causes.
- Both biological and environmental factors may play a role in the development of reading disabilities.

E. Implications for Teaching
- Learning disabilities are specific.
- Teach learning strategies, and encourage students to plan and monitor learning.
- Foster self-esteem and provide motivation for learning.
- Help students find their learning strengths and use those strengths to compensate for their weaknesses.

F.   Attention Deficit Hyperactivity Disorder (ADHD)
- ADHD applies to children who show a significant problem with attention, impulsivity of behavior, and hyperactivity.
- Signs of a significant problem are usually identified by age 7 or 8.
- Teachers are often the first to notice signs of ADHD because school requires more focused attention and self-control than many other situations.
- There has been a large increase in the number of children diagnosed with ADHD.
- Treatment may include counseling, special educational assistance, and the drugs Ritalin, Dexedrine, and Cylert.
- The following techniques may help teachers teach students with ADHD.
  - Carefully structure the classroom environment.
  - Structure activities.
  - Help students focus attention.
  - Help students develop awareness of their behavior.
  - Provide opportunities to use excess energy.

G.   Emotional and Behavioral Disorders
- **Defining and Categorizing Behavioral Disorders**
  - IDEA defines emotional and behavioral disorders as problems that adversely affect a child's education performance and cannot be explained by intellectual, sensory, or health factors.
  - The definition is so vague that it describes the behavior of nearly all students at one time or another.
  - Differing definitions of emotional and behavioral disorders are probably the reason for the wide range of children affected.
- Behavioral disorders can be divided into two main categories.
  - An internalizing behavior disorder is characterized by shyness, withdrawal, or depression.
  - The externalizing type tends to be disruptive, to disobey rules, and may be openly defiant:
    Conduct disorder is an externalizing emotional disorder described as antisocial behavior that violates the rights of others.
    Students with conduct disorder are often aggressive and may get into physical fights.
- **Making Sense of Autistic Disorder**
- Autism, or Kanner's syndrome, is a pervasive developmental disorder:
  - Lack of interest in other people accompanied by strong interest in the inanimate environment.
  - Emotional distance and avoidance of eye contact.
  - Failure in the development of peer relationships.
  - Delayed or nonexistent development of language.
  - Repetitive movement.
  - Self-injurious behavior.
  - Often mental retardation.
  - Symptoms usually start to display themselves shortly after birth or at least within the first year of life.

H.   Health Disorders
- Diabetes mellitus is a chronic disease caused by insufficient production of insulin by the body and resulting in abnormal metabolism.
- Spina bifida is a congenital defect in which the spinal column is imperfectly closed and partly protrudes, and can result in various neurological disorders.
- Muscular dystrophy is a group of progressive and chronic muscle disorders caused by a genetic abnormality and resulting in gradual and irreversible wasting of skeletal muscles.
- Cystic fibrosis is a genetically caused disease characterized by the production of abnormally dense mucus in the affected glands, and usually resulting in chronically impaired respiratory and pancreatic functioning.

- Fetal alcohol syndrome is damage caused by parents' addictions to chemical substances.
- **Making Sense of Seizure Disorders**
  - Epilepsy is characterized by abnormal discharges of electrical energy in parts of the brain.
  - Partial seizures are often unnoticeable.
  - A generalized seizure is typified by uncontrolled jerking movements that can last from 2 to 5 minutes, followed by deep sleep, or coma.
  - An absence seizure is very brief, and may appear as daydreaming followed by a period of disorientation and loss of memory for what happened during the time of the seizure.
  - Seizures can be caused by various illnesses, and can be partially controlled through medication.
- **Making Sense of Cerebral Palsy**
  - Cerebral palsy is a motor impairment caused by damage to the brain.
  - The brain damage is a result of oxygen deprivation before, during, or shortly after birth.
  - Cerebral palsy is not progressive, does not continuously get worse, nor is it contagious.

I. Sensory Impairments
- Sensory impairments refer to difficulties in intake of information through the sensory systems of the body.
- **Seeing Problems**
  - About 1 in one-thousand U.S. children has a visual impairment.
  - Large-print and Braille books, keep lectures on audiotape, special calculators and typewriters, and special measurement devices can aide in learning.
  - Teachers need to be aware of possible visual problems:
    - Holding material very close to or very far from the eyes.
    - Failing to pay attention when a chalkboard or other visual aid is used.
    - Frequent questioning about things that have been presented via visual channels.
    - Great sensitivity to glare.
    - Physical problems with the eyes, such as swelling or redness.
- Hearing problems
  - Hearing impairments are often correctable with a hearing aid.
  - Teachers need to be aware of possible hearing problems:
    - Asking the teacher to repeat questions or statements.
    - Asking frequent questions about orally presented material.
    - Straining or frequently cocking their heads so as to improve their hearing.
    - Asking the teacher to speak louder.

J. Communication Disorders
- Communication disorders are problems with speech or with language in general.
- Stuttering is characterized by repetitions, prolongations, or hesitations in articulation that disrupt the flow of speech.
- Articulation disorders involve substituting one sound for another, distorting sounds, adding sounds, or subtracting sounds.
- Voicing problems are characterized by hoarseness, inappropriate pitch, loudness, or intonation.

TRANSPARENCIES

- T32   Percentage of Special Education Students by Disability

- T33   Number of Children with Disabilities Served by Federal Programs as a Percentage of Total Public K-12

- T34   Least Restrictive Environment (LRE)

- T35   Considerations for Individualized Determination of LRE

- T36   Indicators of ADHD: Attention-Deficit/Hyperactivity Disorder

- T37   What IDEA '97 Says About ADHD

CLASS ACTIVITIES

Activity 5.1 Reading Disability Simulation Exercise
Use this activity when discussing learning disabilities. This activity presents an encrypted story that students will find difficult to decode and read. This experience will give students a feeling of what it would be like to have a reading disability. Students will become more empathetic towards students with reading disabilities. Also, students will gain insight on the strategies students with reading disabilities use and how to use strategies in instruction.

Activity 5.2 Treating Attention Deficit Hyperactivity Disorder with Medication: A Continuing Controversy
Attention Deficit Hyperactivity Disorder (ADHD) is a very popular topic within education. There has been a lot of media attention concerning ADHD and the use of medication to treat it. This activity will give students basic facts and statistics regarding stimulant medications used to treat ADHD. It will help students explore their own beliefs and conceptions about the use medication in the treatment of ADHD.

Class Activity 5.1
Reading Disability Simulation Exercise

As a cooperative learning activity, please read this passage to the best of your ability. Try to successfully read this passage by working together as a group. Once you have read the passage, consider the following discussion items.

An Excergt from *The Frop Kinp*
dy the Primm Drothers

Inolb enti mesw he nwish inps t illh elgeb on ethe reli veb ak inpwh ose bau phter swer eal ldeau tiful, du tth eyou npes twa ssod eaut ifu lth atth esunits elfw hic h ha s se ensom uch, wa sasto nish ebwh ene verits hon einhe rfa ce.

Clo sedy th ekin psca stl ela ya pre atbar kfo rest, an bunb eranol blim e-tr eein t hef ore stwa sawe llan bwhe nth ebay wa sver ywar m, t he ki np's ch ilbwe ntou tint oth efor estan bsa tbow ndyt hes ib e oft heco olfo unt ain, anb wh ens hewa sdor ebs he too kapo lben dal l, an b thre wit u gon hip hanb caup ht it, an bthi sdal lwa sher fav or iteg layt hinp.

No witso hag gen eb tha ton on eocca sio nth egrin ces s's pol ben dal l bib n ot fal lint ot he lit tle han bwh ich s he wa shol binp ug f o rit, du ton to t hep roun b dey onb, anb rol leb s tra iph tin to t he wa ter. T h e kin p's bau pht er fol lowebit wi thher eye sdut itvan isheb, an b t he wel lwas be eg, so b eeg tha t t he dot tom cou lb not de see n. Atthis s he dep an to cr y, anb cri eb loub er anb lou ber, anb cou lb not de comf orteb.

1. How much difficulty did you experience while reading this passage?

2. How did you feel when completing this task?

3. What strategies did you use to complete this task?

4. Do you think this activity helped you to "experience a learning disability?" If so, how?

5. Based on this experience, what can a teacher keep in mind when working with a child identified as learning disabled?

Class Activity 5.1
Reading Disability Simulation Exercise
Answer Key

An Excerpt from *The Frog King*
by the Grimm Brothers

In olden times when wishing still helped one, there lived a king whose daughters were all beautiful, but the youngest was so beautiful that the sun itself, which has seen so much, was astonished whenever it shone in her face.

Close by the king's castle lay a great dark forest, and under an old lime-tree in the forest was a well, and when the day was very warm, the king's child went out into the forest and sat down by the side of the cool fountain, and when she was bored she took a golden ball, and threw it up on high and caught it, and this ball was her favorite plaything.

Now it so happened that on one occasion the princess's golden ball did not fall into the little hand which she was holding up for it, but on to the ground beyond, and rolled straight into the water. The king's daughter followed it with her eyes, but it vanished, and the well was deep, so deep that the bottom could not be seen. At this she began to cry, and cried louder and louder, and could not be comforted.

Class Activity 5.2
Treating Attention Deficit Hyperactivity Disorder
with Medication: A Continuing Controversy

An estimated 2 million American children are believed to suffer from Attention Deficit Hyperactivity Disorder (ADHD). Repeated studies have found stimulants, such as Ritalin, Dexedrine, and Adderall, to be an effective treatment for ADHD. An estimated 90 percent of school-age children with ADHD respond well to treatment with these drugs. Despite these findings, many people question the idea of medicating healthy children and focus on the various negative side effects that can occur. They also question the adverse long-term effects that children may suffer later in life. Another long-term concern of parents is the possibility that treatment with stimulants will encourage their children to use illicit drugs during adolescence.

Many people misunderstand the medical reasons for giving a stimulant to a child who is already hyperactive and inattentive. From 1991 to 1995, the number of stimulant prescriptions written for preschoolers (ages 2-4) increased from 200% to 300%. While studies suggest that Ritalin is overprescribed, others suggest that only a small percentage of children with ADHD are receiving medication. Some studies instead focus their research on how parents can effectively use these drugs in combination with successful use of behavioral interventions.

Answer the following questions regarding the controversy summarized above:

1. What do you think are some positive and negative effects of giving children stimulants to treat ADHD?

2. What is your opinion about growing concern that children and adolescents are abusing prescription stimulants?

3. Do you feel that Ritalin and similar stimulant medications are overprescribed in our society? Why or why not?

Information summarized from Chapter 10: Attention/Deficit-Hyperactivity Disorder in Children's Needs II: Development, Problems and Alternatives by Kathy I. Bradley and George J. Dupaul.

AVAILABLE RESOURCES ON-LINE
Education Consulting Service
Susanwinebrenner.com
This website regarding gifted children links to various sites including: Federally funded centers, universities, and other points of interest, which discuss research and programs available for gifted children. Additional resources are available for parents of gifted children including: state and national gifted organizations and summer programs available to students through several universities.

Study Web - Links for Learning
www.studyweb.com/links/727.html
This website provides links to other websites which cover an array of educational issues in educating gifted children. Some issues addressed include: Career planning, reducing redundancy in the classroom, and using computers to supplement the education of gifted students. There are also links to associations and research centers for gifted children.

Autism/PDD Children
www.geocities.com/EnchantedForest/1142/index.html
This website discusses the responsibilities of schools in educating children with Autism. It includes an extensive discussion of how Autistic children are diagnosed and evaluated, as well as an Autism checklist. The site also discusses the TEACCH program and special education laws.

Carol's Web Corner
www.westfieldacademy.org/adhd/
This website offers some favorite tips of a home educator for teaching a child with ADHD. It also provides a list of chapters from her current book, *How to Get Your Child Off the Refrigerator and onto Learning*, and a list of links related to educating children with ADHD.

Dyslexia Awareness and Resource Center
www.dyslexia-center.com
This website is entitled the Dyslexia Awareness and Resource Center. The goal of this site is to raise the awareness of parents and educators regarding ADD and Dyslexia. It provides the characteristics of Dyslexia and resources about the disorder, as well as available reading programs.

RECOMMENDED VIDEOS FOR CHAPTER FIVE
A New I.D.E.A. for Special Education: Understanding the System and the New Law
Price: $109
VHS Video (40 minutes)
Published by Insight Media, New York, NY (1998)
Order #TAA1299
This video examines the recent changes to the Individuals with Disabilities in Education Act (I.D.E.A.), the law governing special education. It explains the new law, the referral process, the evaluation process, placement and related services, and standardized testing.

The Americans with Disabilities Act: Is It Working?
Price: $69.95
VHS Video (11 minutes)
Published by Films for the Humanities and Sciences, Princeton, NY
Order #EIH11299
During the 1980s, a new civil rights movement got underway-for people with disabilities. In this program, Larry Paradis, executive director of Disability Rights Advocates, speaks with NewsHour correspondent Spencer Michels about the importance of litigation in pressuring companies and communities to comply with the 1990 Americans with Disabilities Act. But are such legal actions actually undermining support for the ADA?

Now We're Including Students, But How Do We Assess and Grade Them?
Price: $129
VHS Video (60 minutes)
Published by Insight Media, New York, NY (1995)
Order # UAA1908
In this video, Mary Falvey addresses some of the many complex issues related to grading students with disabilities who are participating in general education classes. She describes alternative methods of assessment and offers suggestions for how to handle the implementation of multiple assessment systems.

Empowering People with Disabilities Through Technology
Price: $129
VHS Video (49 minutes)
Published by Films for the Humanities and Sciences, Princeton, NY
Order #ECU8796
New inventions are opening the doors to greater independence, satisfying careers, and mainstream leisure activities for people with disabilities. In this program, three people determined to be doers, not viewers, demonstrate the adaptive technology that is improving the quality of their lives. For Larry, an adult quadriplegic, mouth-activated remote controls allow him to do high-end computer drafting and even sail a boat. For Carol, born with an underdeveloped visual cortex, an enhanced computer enables her to attend college. And for Matthew, a child born with cerebral palsy, an orthotic walking device has him up and around while helping him condition his bones and muscles. Other innovations discussed include Braille PCs, talking book scanners, and a remarkable hands-free office.

The Gifted Child
Price: $79
VHS Video (24 minutes)
Published by Films for the Humanities and Sciences, Princeton, NY
Order #ECU11160
When a child displays advanced skills in one or more areas of development, a special challenge is set before teachers, parents, and childcare providers alike. This program seeks to foster and understanding of gifted children by identifying their characteristics, addressing their educational needs, and recommending ways to enhance their development.

The Gifted Child
Price: $139
VHS Video (18 minutes)
Published by Insight Media, New York, NY (1997)
Order #TAA1050
Gifted children can cause problems for parents and teachers unable to relate to their special needs. This video analyzes giftedness, discussing methods of deciding who is gifted and recommending ways to enhance the development of gifted children.

Festival of Dreams: Living with Mental Retardation
Price: $129
VHS Video (42 minutes)
Published by Films for the Humanities and Sciences, Princeton, NY
Order #EIH8453
This program presents an inspiring look at the lives of two people with mental retardation and the community of family, educators, employers, and friends who encourage them to achieve their goals. Meet Matt Klemets, 21, and Annalisa Ericson, 28, as they participate in the Special Olympics. Candid interviews with the special-education directors at Staples High School in Westport, Connecticut, Dr. Donald Cohen of the Yale Child Study Center, and others present both the frustrations and the rewards of working with the mentally handicapped. This program is a moving testimony to the special strengths of people with metal handicaps.

Recognizing, Understanding, and Overcoming Learning Disabilities
Price: $129
VHS Video (33 minutes)
Published by Insight Media, New York, NY (1990)
Order #TAA124
This video explains how to recognize learning disabilities and demonstrates practical teaching strategies. Judith Birsh of Columbia Teachers College explores learning problems.

Learning Disabled
Price: $129
VHS Video (30 minutes)
Published by Films for the Humanities and Sciences, Princeton, NY
Order #EIH8452
Meet the students and teacher of Trillijum High School, a school for the learning disabled. Many parents of disabled children face the dilemma of whether to keep their children in schools with a standard curriculum, or to place them in a school that specializes in the learning disabled. During this program, both students and educators discuss the pros and cons of such schools and why this program has been successful.

Classroom Interventions for ADHD
Price: $139
VHS Video (35 minutes)
Published by Insight Media, New York, NY (1998)
Order #TAA1438
This video provides an overview of interventions that can help students with ADHD enhance their school performance without interrupting the classroom environment. It discusses such behavior management activities as peer tutoring, an Attention Training System, and self-management techniques. It also features a panel discussion on the relative benefits of proactive, preventive measures and reactive techniques.

A New Look at ADHD: Inhibition, Time, and Self-Control
Price: $95
VHS Video (30 minutes), Teacher's Guide
Published by Edudex, Princeton, NJ (2000)
Order #AAW49072
This program provides an accessible introduction to Russell A. Barkley's influential theory of the nature and causes of ADHD. Dr. Barkley shares his breakthrough thinking about the roots of many of the most troubling-and perplexing-ADHD symptoms in children and adults. Concrete ways that our new understanding of the disorder might facilitate more effective clinical interventions are shown. Enhanced by specially designed graphics, the video examines how self-regulation develops in normally functioning individuals. Dr. Barkley elucidates the mental processes that underlie willpower, determination, and motivation, and describes how these processes may be disrupted by ADHD.

Understanding the Defiant Child
Price: $139
VHS Video (34 minutes)
Published by Insight Media, New York, NY (1997)
Order #TAA1175
Looking at children who routinely demonstrate negative, hostile, and defiant behavior, this video illuminates the nature and causes of ODD. It describes symptoms of ODD, explains its relationship to ADD, and teaches how to distinguish it from less severe misbehavior.

Autism: A World Apart
Price: $149
VHS Video (52 minutes)
Published by Films for the Humanities and Sciences, Princeton, NY
Order #ECU5309

This documentary features two children, ages four and six, and 18-year old Lee, who are all autistic. The program shows the strain places on their families and how each family has learned to cope. Above all, it shows the enormous difference that special education can make in enabling autistic children to lead happier and more fulfilled lives-and giving their families hope and relief.

Understanding Asperger's
Price: $179
VHS Video (29 minutes)
Published by Insight Media, New York, NY (2000)
Order #TAA1925
Asperger's disorder is a high-functioning form of autism in which children and young adults display some of the characteristics of autism (poor social skills and limited but intensive interests), yet live in mainstreamed settings. Designed for educators and therapists, this video outlines the major characteristics of this disorder and illustrates them with footage of children with Asperger's.

Understanding Hearing Loss
Price: $89.95
VHS Video (17 minutes)
Published by Films for the Humanities and Sciences, Princeton, NY
Order #EIH4362
This program explains sound, hearing, hearing loss, and the relationship between listening to speech and different kinds of hearing loss. It includes realistic simulations of what speech sounds like with different kinds of hearing loss, and useful hints on improving communication.

Signs of Life
Price: $89.95
VHS Video (40 minutes), Open captions
Published by Films for the Humanities and Sciences, Princeton, NY
Order #EIH4363
People with hearing impairments have been a misunderstood minority for too long. This program blows away the stereotypes, and should be required viewing for everyone, including the Deaf and hard-of-hearing.

HANDOUTS TO ACCOMPANY YOUR LESSONS:

H 5.1   Major Laws and Legal Rights Impacting Special Education

H 5.2   Characteristics and Teaching Strategies for Exceptional Children

H 5.1

Major Laws and Legal Rights Impacting Special Education

- **Public Law 92-142 "The Education for All Handicapped Children Act"**

  In 1975, states were required to provide "free, appropriate public education for every child between the ages of 3 and 21 (unless state law does not provide free, public education to children 3 to 5 or 18 to 21 years of age) regardless of how seriously he may handicapped."

- **Public Law 99-457**

  In 1986, these rights were extended to all children ages three to five, regardless of state laws, and added programs addressing the needs of infants with serious disabilities.

- **Public Law 101-476 Individuals with Disabilities Education Act, or IDEA**

  In 1990, schools were required to plan for the transition of adolescents with disabilities into either further education or employment at age 16.

The special education laws included two other important provisions:

- **Least Restrictive Placement**

  A child must be placed in a setting that is as normal as possible.   Two methods used to accomplish this goal include:
  1. Mainstreaming- placing exceptional students in regular classes as soon as they are able to meet the same requirements as typical students.
  2. Full Inclusion- placing students, even those with severe disabilities, into regular classes, making accommodations as necessary to the exceptional students to succeed.

- **Individualized Education Program (IEP)**

  The special education laws require that each student with special needs have an IEP, which specifies the goals and objectives set to improve the student's level of achievement and how these will be achieved. The IEP is written by a multi-disciplinary team and is updated annually.

H 5.2

Characteristics and Teaching Strategies for Exceptional Children

Characteristics	Teaching Strategies
Giftedness • Exceptional abilities or talents, usually in the areas of language skills or math • An estimated 3% to 5% of school students are gifted • Identification of gifted students depends on how giftedness is conceptualized by a school or by state guidelines	**Giftedness** • Invite students to further pursue topics discussed in class • Design activities to help students develop high-level thinking skills such as doing research • Allow individual or small group investigations of real life problems
Mental Retardation • Significantly below-average intellectual functioning • Limitations in two or more areas of adaptive competence including: communication, self-care, home living, social skills, community use, self-direction, health and safety, functional academics, leisure, and work • Difficulties manifest before the age. of 18	**Mental Retardation** • Divide lessons into small, clearly defined steps • Make lessons concrete and applicable to daily life • Help students learn self-regulation • Help students raise their self-esteem
Learning Disabilities • Diagnosed when performance in a specific subject matter is substantially worse than would be expected from a child's overall level of measured intelligence • Disorders typically manifest during childhood, but they can and often do occur throughout the life span	**Learning Disabilities** • Teaching strategies should address the needs of specific disabilities • Teach learning strategies, and encourage students to plan and monitor learning • Help students find their learning strengths and use those strengths to compensate for their weaknesses

Chapter Six
Group Differences: Socioeconomic Status, Ethnicity, Gender, and Language

The instructor's manual for this chapter contains:

- A *Chapter-at-a-Glance* chart that reviews all chapter related material
- A detailed chapter outline to highlight main points of the chapter
- A list of transparencies from Transparencies - Educational Psychology IV that correspond to this chapter
- Several activities to deepen student understanding
- An annotated list of additional resources including internet sites
- Handouts to accompany your lessons

CHAPTER-AT-A-GLANCE

Chapter Outline	Objectives	Instructional Aids
1.0 Why Understanding Group Differences is Important to Teachers, p. 192	1. Discuss the importance to teachers of understanding group differences.	- Transparencies T38, T39 - Test Bank Questions 1-6, 70-73
2.0 Socioeconomic Diversity, p.194	1. Explain what is meant by socioeconomic diversity. 2. Describe how SES affects school achievement. 3. Describe how SES affects students' development. 4. Describe how SES affects parental style and educational performance. 5. Describe how SES affects self-esteem and achievement. 6. Discuss the variability within any SES group, and how that may or may not affect achievement. 7. Explain how ethnic and racial diversity may complicate the SES issues.	- Transparency T40 - Handout 6.1 - Test Bank Questions 7-22, 74-82, 92-93, 98-99
3.0 Ethnic and Racial Diversity, p. 203	1. Describe group differences in test scores. 2. Discuss role of mentoring in school performance.	- Transparency T41 - Test Bank Questions 23-33
4.0 Gender Diversity, p. 208	1. Define gender diversity. 2. Discuss what teachers need to know about sex differences. 3. Describe the evidence for sex differences in cognitive performance. 4. Compare and contrast the biological versus cultural ideas of female-male differences.	- Transparency T42 - Test Bank Questions 34-47, 83-85, 94, 100-101
5.0 Language Diversity, p. 208	1. Discuss the implications of language diversity in the classroom. 2. Describe the various methods of teaching non-native speakers of English. 3. Explain how SES affects language use.	- Transparency T43 - Test Bank Questions 48-57, 86-88, 95, 97
6.0 Multicultural Education, p. 217	1. Define multicultural education. 2. Discuss the rationale for multicultural education. 3. Compare and contrast cultural values with school values. 4. Discuss how to avoid group stereotypes. 5. Describe some multicultural applications in the classroom.	- Transparencies T44, T45, T46 - Handout 6.2 - Activities 6.1, 6.2 - Test Bank Questions 58-69, 89-91, 96

DETAILED CHAPTER SIX OUTLINE
I. Why Understanding Group Differences is Important to Teachers
- Expert teachers know that students differ, and they appreciate how some of these differences can affect how students learn.

- Expert teachers appreciate group differences and know how to adjust their teaching styles to reach students of various groups.

- Definitions
  - Culture is the socially communicated behaviors, beliefs, values, knowledge, and other traits that characterize a particular time period or a particular class, community, or population of people.
  - Race is a local geographic or global human population believed to share genetically transmitted and biologically based traits and physical characteristics.
  - Ethnicity refers to a distinct national, religious, linguistic, or cultural heritage shared by a sizable group of people.
  - Minority group more currently is used to refer to people from traditionally disadvantaged backgrounds.
  - Discrimination is treatment or consideration based on class or category rather than individual merit.

- In roughly 40 years, the combined proportion of African American, Asian American, Hispanic, and Native American students will outnumber Caucasian students.

II. Socioeconomic Diversity
A. Parents' Income and Children's Scholastic Assessment Test (SAT) Scores
- The average SAT verbal and math scores for children of parents earning a combined income of over $70,000 a year are 469 and 531.
- The average verbal and math scores for children of parents earning between $30,000 and $40,000 a year are 416 and 469.
- SAT scores are important in determining access to higher education and jobs.
- Lower-income children lack certain experiences that would help to prepare them for standardized tests.

B. What Determines Children's SES?
- Children's SES is partly determined by general societal trends in marriage, divorce, and single parenthood.
- Children perform differently in school and have different high school graduation rates depending upon their home environments.
- Extra help from a caring teacher can close the gap between what a student *does* accomplish and what a student *can* accomplish.

C. SES and Students' Development
- While the number of children born per family for nonwelfare families has decreased, the family income per child has increased.
- Children who come from poor families will do better in school if they have fewer siblings and consequently have access to greater financial resources.
- Expert teachers who learn that a student is from a large family must recognize cues that a student needs extra encouragement and support.

D. Parental Styles
- Today's middle-class mothers tend to be more responsive to and less directive of their children than are lower-class mothers.
- Expert teachers need to be attentive to the trends of parental styles and their significance for the students' learning, development, and behavior in school.
- Baumrind views parental behavior as fitting within three general types or patterns.

- Authoritarian parents emphasize obedience, respect for authority, hard work, and discourage real communication.
- Permissive parents have a tolerant and accepting attitude toward their children, rarely punish them, make few demands, and place few restrictions on them.
- Authoritative parents set clear standards and expect their children to meet them, treat their children maturely, and use discipline where appropriate to ensure that rules are followed.

E. Parental Styles and Children's Cognitive Performance

- Parents who display an authoritative style of discipline and child rearing tend to raise children who are more cognitively competent.
  - The authoritative style is more effective in the classroom and leads to better learning outcomes.
  - Children of families with a purely authoritative style had the highest average grades.
- The quality of mother-infant interaction is one of the best predictors of IQ and language development.
  - Teacher-student interactions can also be a significant force in the life of a developing child.
  - Emotional relationships influence cognitive development through the parent's willingness to help children solve problems, through the development of children's social competence, and through the encouragement of children's exploratory tendencies.

F. SES, Self-Esteem, and Achievement

- Surveys of low-achieving students have revealed that the self-esteem levels of these students are comparable to those of high-achieving students.
- Sometimes the highest-achieving students have more self-doubts and lower self-esteem.
- Helping raise students' self-esteem may be a worthwhile goal, but real gains in achievement must be targeted.

G. SES Does Not Predetermine Achievement

- Within any single SES group, achievement is extremely variable.
- Expert teachers should not assume that because students are from a poor family that they are incapable of doing well.

H. Implications for Teaching: SES

- Never judge a student's SES on the basis of superficial attributes like clothing; work to develop a deeper understanding of each student's background.
- Recognize that lower-SES students must overcome greater obstacles to achieve equally to middle- and upper-SES students, and provide these lower-SES students with extra support and encouragement.
- Recognize that students from single-parent homes often have a parent who must work long hours and who cannot provide necessary support; provide extra scaffolding for these students.
- Work to develop an authoritative style to optimize interactions with students, especially students whose parents have authoritarian or permissive styles.
- Discourage a focus simply on "feeling good about ourselves;" instead, help students believe in their ability to accomplish meaningful tasks.
- Remember that SES is not destiny.

III. Ethnic and Racial Diversity

A. Group Differences in Test Scores

- Trends in Test Scores
  - The standardized test scores of American students have been headed upward for the past several years.
  - African American and Hispanic students have achieved the biggest gains.
  - Greater educational spending on minority and disadvantaged children.
  - Smaller family sizes and greater resources per child.
  - Increases in the educational levels of parents:
    Parental educational attainment has increased markedly.

B. Trends in Educational Attainment

- All racial groups have made progress in terms of educational attainment.
- The attainment gap experienced by Hispanics and Latinos is of high school graduation.
- Teachers with Hispanic or Latino students should stress the value of completing high school.

C. Trends in Educational Performance
- According to the National Assessment of Educational Progress (NAEP), African Americans made substantial progress in reading in the 1970s, but their progress in this area leveled out by the mid-1980s and has remained there.
- Expert teachers recognize that extra classroom support and increased challenges can enable African American and Hispanic students to score substantially higher on standardized tests.
- Support can include in-depth feedback and assistance, tutoring, extra reading and assignments, after-school programs, test preparation classes, and computer access.

D. The Role of Mentoring in School Performance
- The data clearly shows the importance of education in breaking the cycle of poverty, especially for African Americans and Hispanics.
- The child's knowing one person with an educational focus is essential to the child's outcome.
- An educated adult in a developing child's life means the child has a mentor and role model who represents the door that education can open.
- As an expert teacher, make clear that education and hard work matter to you, stress their values in your own life, and show students how they can benefit as a result of educational success.

E. Implications for Teaching
- Do not assume that lower scores necessarily reflect lower levels of innate ability.
- Recognize that the parents of today's students are dramatically more educated today than they were a generation or two ago.
- Stress to all students, particularly African American and Hispanic students, the lifetime value and rewards associated with completing high school and attending college.
- Never underestimate what one dedicated teacher can mean at a critical time in a student's life.

IV. Gender Diversity
A. What Teachers Need to Know About Sex Differences
- Sex differences are biologically controlled differences.
- Gender differences are psychologically and socially controlled differences.
- Gender bias exists when a person possesses different views of female versus male competencies.
  - Teachers should be aware of their own biases and beliefs about the sexes.
  - With accurate knowledge, the expert teacher can ensure that all students are given the best possible chance to show what they know.

B. The Evidence for Sex Differences in Cognitive Performance

C. Differences are specific, not general.
- Studies find that there is no overall difference in the intelligence of females and males.
- Certain specific differences do exist on different types of performances.
  - Females score higher than males in many aspects of verbal ability.
  - Males are better than females in many visual-spatial tasks.
  - Males particularly outnumber females in the extreme end of high performance in math tests.

D. Male Performance Is More Variable
  - Males' scores are more widely distributed and more different from one another than are females' scores, which are more tightly clustered.
  - Teachers may see more very high-achieving boys than girls, but may also see many more low-achieving boys than girls.

E. Role of Motivation
- When it comes to explaining why males do better at math, motivation, cultural values, and support must be considered.
- Lubinski and Benbow (1992) believe that female motivation to do well in math is less than male motivation.
  - Society may not support the entry of young females into the ranks of professional scientists.
  - Expert teachers should encourage female students to strive for science and math.

F. Are Female-Male Differences Biological, Cultural, or Both?

G. Biological Differences
- Prenatal sex hormones such as testosterone affect the development of gender differences in the brain.
  - Testosterone affects the development of the right and left hemispheres of the brain.
  - Males have more lateralization of their brains than females do. Another factor influencing females' performance is the pattern of hormonal changes during the menstrual cycle:
     When female hormones are at their lowest, women do better on tasks on which males are usually superior.
     When female hormones peak at midcycle, females do even better on tasks on which they are usually superior.
     The corpus callosum is larger in females than in males, meaning that females' brain hemispheres may be better able than males' to communicate back and forth.

H. Cultural Differences
- In North American culture, females have been enculturated to have lowered expectations for scholastic performance and ultimate career success compared with males.
- Boys ask more questions in math and science classes and receive more teacher attention.
- Males dominate interactions with females as well as the decisions that are reached.
- Boys' toys and play activities might place greater developmental influences on spatial skills.
- Boys are more likely than girls to be hyperactive and to show behavior problems.
- Females score higher than males in classroom grades in math.
- For boys, math achievement can be predicted from previous math achievement and expectations of success or failure in math.
- Girls rate their math abilities lower than do boys, expect to do less well in math, and are less likely to attribute success in math to ability and failures to bad luck.

I. Implications for Teaching
- Strive to eliminate gender bias from your thinking and teaching.
- Biologically based sex differences do exist; however you should not judge any individual student because of trends that characterize the entire population.
- Remember that most abilities do not vary between the sexes.
- Cultural messages about gender-appropriate behaviors received by girls and boys can be destructive.
- Expect the same level of performance from girls and boys.

V. **Language Diversity**
   A. Teaching Nonnative Speakers of English
- Bilingual education is education that to a greater or lesser extent takes place in more than one language.
- English as a Second Language (ESL) is the name used for instructional programs that teach English to students who do not speak English as their first language.
- Not only must children learn standard English, they must also learn social studies, math, science, and other courses while at the same time learning English.
  - Children who do not speak Standard English may have had little exposure to formal

schooling and less parental support in the home for helping them with schoolwork.
- Some educators believe the best way to instruct these limited-English students is to teach in their home language.
- In additive bilingualism, a second language is taught in addition to a relatively well-developed first language (Cummins, 1976).
- In subtractive bilingualism, elements of a second language replace elements of the first language.
- Cummins believes that the additive form results in increased cognitive functioning, whereas the subtractive form results in decreased functioning.

B. SES and Language Use
- Lower-class children often use language with a focus on the present, using fewer words overall to express the same things.
- Middle-class children speak in more elaborate sentences, using more words overall.
- The use of language varies among students partly because of the customary ways of using language in the students' homes.

C. Implications for Teaching
- Work on developing a second language if possible.
- Recognize that speaking habits, such as how descriptive students' language can be, are influenced by cultural values in the home.

VI. Multicultural Education
A. The Rationale for Multicultural Education
- Multicultural education exposes students to the values and norms of different cultures in an attempt to show them the diversity of the human experience.
- The idea that underlies the trend toward multicultural education is that children from certain racial and ethnic groups tend to succeed more easily in typical schools than do children from other groups.

B. Compatibility of Cultural and School Values

C. Culture and Classroom Dynamics Sociolinguistics
- As the typical U.S. classroom contains one teacher and many students, children from group-oriented cultures may be uncomfortable with this approach.
- The normal manner of speaking in the classroom is for the teacher to lead and the students to follow, and this may be unfamiliar to some youngsters.
- As most adults talk in terms of stories, and children have to initiate their own participation, this can be problematic for children at school who are taught at home to interrupt into imaginative stories.

D. Culture and Cognition
- As the typical North American classroom requires analytical, abstract thinking and reasoning, teachers must be aware if different cultural, ethnic, or racial groups solve problems differently.
- Tharp believes that white students find it easier to adopt a verbal/analytical thinking approach, whereas some minority group members tend to emphasize nonverbal thinking.
- To reach these students, change your focus to enable them to show in other ways what they know.
- Allow students to do meaningful, practical work to show what they know.

E. Culture and Motivation
- Minority children need more motivation to overcome the cultural obstacles that will restrain them from succeeding in the mainstream culture.

- A teacher must understand and deal with the students' perceptions about what getting a good education is likely to bring them in life.
- Expert teachers are flexible in their approach when dealing with students from different racial and ethnic groups.
  - Use praise in the way that is most motivating for the students.
  - Phrase and present challenges in the way that fits with students' cultural values.
  - Be aware that subtle differences in classroom activities and structure can make a big difference to students.

F. Avoiding Group Stereotypes
- Expert teachers know not to suggest that all members of each group share any characteristics.
- Expert teachers never assume that a given student will behave in a manner expected for her or his culture.
- Expert teachers view each student as a unique individual and use information about group differences to illuminate their thinking and to help explain why students may learn differently in school.

G. Multicultural Applications in the Classroom
- To teach multiculturally, you must first understand your students and their backgrounds.
- Once you possess the information, you can modify the curriculum to include presentations related to the cultures in the classroom.
- Before using any curricular materials, review them to ensure they are free from stereotypes related to race, ethnicity, gender, and disability.
- To help students overcome their stereotypes, discuss openly the current political and social status of different cultures.
- Take pains to avoid using sexist language, and enacting any stereotypes in the class.
- Teaching from a multicultural approach means encouraging all students to have high goals and aspirations for their futures, regardless of ethnicity or gender.

H. Implications for Teaching
- Recognize that multicultural education is a contentious issue that evokes strong responses from people on both sides.
- Accept that, regardless of your personal views, you will probably be expected to teach from a multicultural perspective.
- Work to familiarize yourself with the range of cultures you are likely to encounter in the classroom.
- Adapt instruction and assessment for students of nonmainstream cultures to provide these students with varied opportunities to show what they know.
- Never equate different styles of speaking and interacting with differences in intelligence.
- Avoid judging individuals on the basis of group stereotypes.
- Accept diverse views in the classroom, and encourage students to elaborate on these views so everyone will understand them.

TRANSPARENCIES

- T38   The Dimensions of Multicultural Education

- T39   Individuals Belong to Many Different Groups

- T40   Projected Number of Children in Poverty

- T41   Projections of the Number of Children in the U.S. by Ethnic Group, 1982-2020

- T42   Gender Schema Theory

- T43   Two Approaches to Balanced Bilingual Instruction

- T44   Approaches to Multicultural Curriculum Reform

- T45   The Impact of Stereotype Threat on College Students' Standardized Test Performance

- T46   Student-Teacher Interaction Differences in Diverse Classrooms

CLASS ACTIVITIES

Activity 6.1 Possible Sources of Cultural Conflict in the Classroom: Resolving Differences
Use this activity when discussing Multicultural Education. This activity will help students develop ways to resolve possible cultural conflicts in the classroom. Students are given various educational situations and the expectations of the school and minority students. With the discrepancies of the expectations, students must think of ways to resolve the problems.

Activity 6.2 Stereotypes May Explain Some Black Boys' Emotional Withdrawal from Academics
Use this activity when discussing socioeconomic, ethnic, and racial diversity. This activity describes a study that examines the relationship of grades, standardized test scores, and self-esteem of African-American, Caucasian, and Hispanic students. This activity will help students gain a better understanding of the variability of achievement motivation. Also, students will have to brainstorm ways to encourage student performance in schools.

Class Activity 6.1
Possible Sources of Cultural Conflict
in the Classroom: Resolving Differences

Cultural Difference in What Is Learned	School's Expectation (Majority Culture Belief)	Student's Expectation (Minority Culture Belief)	How to Resolve
Interpersonal relationship	Students will compete and value individual achievement.	Students will help each other; the group, not the individual, is the source of accomplishment (many Native American and Mexican American groups).	
Orientation toward time	Plan for the future, work, and save now for a better future for yourself.	Focus on the present, trust the central group to provide for the future (certain Native American peoples). or Value the past, tradition, and ancestors (certain Asian cultures).	
Valued personal qualities	Busy	Methodical, relaxed, meditative (some Asian and Hispanic cultures).	
Relationship of people to nature	Control nature, use technology to "improve" nature.	Be at one with nature; respect and live with nature (Native Americans traditionally).	
Most cherished values	Individual freedom.	Group loyalty, tradition (certain Asian cultures).	

Examples adapted from Bennett, C.I. (1990). Comprehensive Multicultural Education, Boston: Allyn and Bacon.

Class Activity 6.1
Possible Sources of Cultural Conflict in the Classroom: Resolving Differences
(Key)

Cultural Difference in What Is Learned	School's Expectation (Majority Culture Belief)	Student's Expectation (Minority Culture Belief)	How to Resolve
Interpersonal relationship	Students will compete and value individual achievement.	Students will help each other; the group, not the individual, is the source of accomplishment (many Native American and Mexican American groups).	Teachers will provide opportunities for the reinforcement of group and individual achievement.
Orientation toward time	Plan for the future, work, and save now for a better future for yourself.	Focus on the present, trust the central group to provide for the future (certain Native American peoples). or Value the past, tradition, and ancestors (certain Asian cultures).	Teachers could invite older members of nondominant cultures to speak about past events and relate them to the future.
Valued personal qualities	Busy	Methodical, relaxed, meditative (some Asian and Hispanic cultures).	Teachers could provide flexible deadlines for assignments allowing children to work at their own pace.
Relationship of people to nature	Control nature, use technology to "improve" nature.	Be at one with nature; respect and live with nature (Native Americans traditionally).	Activities and classroom instruction could be geared toward conserving natural resources.
Most cherished values	Individual freedom.	Group loyalty, tradition (certain Asian cultures).	Students could be asked to investigate their family traditions and present them to the class.

Examples adapted from Bennett, C.I. (1990). Comprehensive Multicultural Education,
Boston: Allyn and Bacon.

Class Activity 6.2
Stereotypes May Explain Some Black Boys'
Emotional Withdrawal from Academics

A study by Jason Osborne of the State University of New York at Buffalo investigated African-American, Caucasian, and Hispanic students' grades, standardized test scores, and self-esteem ratings. This data was derived from the ongoing National Education Longitudinal Study, which began tracking students in 1988 during students' eighth, 10th and 12th grade year.

This study found that African-American boys are more likely than white students or Hispanics to lose interest in academics through middle and high school while their self-esteem ratings remain stable. This data indicated that young African-American males are neither inspired nor disheartened by academic success or failure.

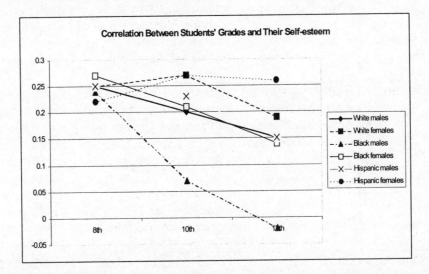

Claude Steele, Ph.D., offered an explanation for this finding. He felt that African-American students withdraw from schoolwork because of stereotypes which devalue their academic abilities. This explanation failed to account for the finding that Hispanic girls became more invested in academics. Additionally, African-American girls', Hispanic boys', and white students' investment in academics dropped only slightly. Osbourne suggested that peer influence may be an important mediator in the decrease in academic investment for African-American boys. He stated that African-American boys derive their self-esteem largely from peer perceptions and athletic success. On a positive note, a weak trend indicated that African-American boys tend to remain interested in science. This may be an area to explore in an effort to promote educational achievement.

1. What issues affect the variability in achievement motivation of different ethnicities in this study?

2. What can teachers do to encourage minority student performance in school?

AVAILABLE RESOURCES ON-LINE
Multicultural Resources and Dialogues for Educators
curry.edschool.virginia.edu/go/multicultural/
This website provides resources for educators to explore and discuss multicultural education, to facilitate opportunities for educators to work toward self-awareness and development, and to provide forums for educators to interact and collaborate toward a critical, transformative approach to multicultural education. This website also provides awareness activities leading to dialogues on multicultural issues, techniques for assessing educational web sites from a multicultural perspective, and lists of songs with identity themes for introducing dialogue.

Diversity Works
www.diversityweb.org
Diversity Works is a family of projects providing resources to colleges and universities that view diversity as a compelling educational priority and institutional commitment, important for every campus, every learner and the wider society. It links thousands of academic and faculty leaders via the World Wide Web and more traditional forms of print communication. Through electronic and print media, Diversity Works also encourages diversity practitioners to effectively communicate the educational value and documented results of their diversity initiatives.

Diversity Information
fisher.osu.edu/diversity/
This website provides tips for teaching diverse classrooms in a global economy, tips for mentoring programs, a collection of online diversity magazines, and links to information concerning gender, disabilities, religious, sexual orientation, African American, as well as other ethnicities.

Center for Applied Linguistics
www.cal.org/crede/
Based at the University of California, Santa Cruz, CREDE assists the nation's population of diverse students, including those at risk of educational failure, to achieve academic excellence. The purpose of CREDE's research is to identify and develop effective educational practices for linguistic and cultural minority students, such as those placed at risk by factors of race, poverty, and geographic location.

Urban Education Web
eric-web.tc.columbia.edu/
UEweb is dedicated to urban students, their families, and the educators who serve them. UEweb offers manuals, brief articles, annotated bibliographies, reviews and summaries of outstanding publications, and conference announcements in urban education.

RECOMMENDED VIDEOS FOR CHAPTER SIX
Respecting Diversity in the Classroom
Price: $285
VHS Video (60 minutes)
Published by Insight Media, New York, NY (1996)
Order #UAA801
This video offers guidelines for developing a multicultural curriculum. It visits multicultural awareness programs and offers commentary from educators and such leaders as Arthur Schlesinger, Jr. Dramatic reenactments illustrate classroom situations that involve diversity of ethnicity, religion, age, gender, and socioeconomic status.

I'm Normal, You're Weird: Understanding Other Cultures
Price: $89.95
VHS Video (23 minutes)
Published by Magna Systems, Inc., Barrington, IL (1998)
Order #Mod 39
Do your students assume they're normal and the guy on the other side of the planet (or city) is weird? Do they figure the world would be a better place if everyone were more like them? This video demonstrates that much human behavior is cultural-how people line up to wait, how they use ice in drinks, cross their legs, use their eyes, eat certain foods at specific times of the day, how they view appointments and time, and even how they define honesty.

Respecting Diversity in the Classroom
Price: $295
VHS Video (60 minutes), Guide, Handouts
Published by Films for the Humanities & Sciences, Princeton, NJ
Order #ECU8639
Too often educators look upon a multicultural classroom as a problem to be dealt with rather than a resource to be developed. Using actual classroom situations, this program is a "how-to" primer offering innovative ideas about exploring the richness of culture and ethnicity. What is the difference between ethnicity and race? When children don't respond, is it because of cultural differences or a teacher's preconceived expectations? What roles can religion and language, both foreign and "street," play in the multicultural framework? What communication strategies best address differences in learning style and social interaction?

The Changing Classroom: Cultural Diversity and Curriculum
Price: $169
VHS Video (30 minutes)
Published by Insight Media, New York, NY (1999)
Order #UAA1784
The first part of this video addresses goal setting and curriculum building for the diverse classroom. The second part features interviews with teachers and students on ten discussion topics and is designed to serve as a resource tool in the development of a school cultural mission statement.

Anything You Can Do, I Can Do Better: Why the Sexes Excel Differently
Price: $89.95
VHS Video (52 minutes)
Published by Films for the Humanities & Sciences, Princeton, NJ
Order #ECU8986
Statistically speaking, why have men and women not proved equally adept at the same things? In this program, researchers debate whether differences in brain architecture lead to a division of talents and aptitudes between the sexes-and draw some startling conclusions. To illustrate these differences, children are observed in classrooms, on the playground, and at home.

He Said, She Said, Gender, Language, & Communication
Price: $275
VHS Video (50 minutes), Teaching Guide
Published by Into the Classroom Media, Los Angeles, CA (2001)
This video takes students on an intellectual journey to the core of how men and women use language, and why communication between the sexes so often goes awry. Deborah Tannen takes a linguistic approach that sheds light on psychology, using everything from scholarly research to familiar examples from everyday life as her canvas. In this illuminating and entertaining presentation, Tannen draws a road map through the complex maze of why we speak the way we do, and why others so frequently don't hear what we mean.

Whisper and Smile: Verbal and Nonverbal Communication Styles
Price: $139
VHS Video (30 minutes)
Published by Insight Media, New York, NY (2000)
Order #UAA1860
This video shows how knowledge of cultural communication styles can facilitate verbal and nonverbal understanding. It considers the nature of communication styles in the United States and discusses how these styles may be understood by other cultures.

Valuing Diversity: Multi-Cultural Communication
Price: $89.95
VHS Video (19 minutes)
Published by Magna Systems, Inc., Barrington, IL (1995)
Order #Mod 40
We often feel comfortable with people like ourselves and awkward when dealing with those who are different. Who's "different?" People from different cultures or social classes, members of older generations, and those with unusual body sizes or visible physical disabilities. This video demonstrates how to overcome this communication barrier.

Bilingualism: A True Advantage
Price: $149
VHS Video (28 minutes)
Published by Films for the Humanities & Sciences, Princeton, NJ
Order #ECU4023
This program looks at the nationally recognized bilingual education program at San Antonio's DeZavala Elementary School, where Spanish-speaking children are developing new skills in English while maintaining their skills in Spanish. The program also follows a group of college students who are realizing the professional and personal benefits of being able to speak two languages. It concludes with a conversation with Cheech Marin, who shares his views on the importance of cultural identity.

Understanding the Similarities and Differences Between Your Culture and Other Cultures
Price: $169
VHS Video (77 minutes)
Published by Insight Media, New York, NY (2000)
Order #UAA2102
Exploring cultural differences in verbal and nonverbal communication, this video offers a comparative summary of cultural value preferences. It includes a cultural genogram activity designed to help faculty reflect upon their personal cultural beliefs and examine how these beliefs impact the classroom.

HANDOUTS TO ACCOMPANY YOUR LESSONS:

H 6.1   Parental Style and School Achievement of Children

H 6.2   Guidelines to Facilitate a Multicultural Education

H 6.1

Parental Style and School Achievement of Children

Parental Style	Characteristics	Effect on School Achievement
Authoritarian	Uses shaping and controlling. Emphasizes obedience, respect for authority, hard work, and traditional values. Discourages real communication.	Associated with lower grades. Negative force in adolescent's life due to lack of school involvement.
Permissive	Gives child considerable freedom. Has a tolerant and accepting attitude, rarely punishes, makes few demands and places few restirctions.	Associated with lower grades.
Authoritative	Sets clear standards. Treats children maturely. Uses discipline where appropriate to ensure rules are followed. Encourages independence and individuality. Practices open communication. Considers child's opinions.	Associated with higher grades. Leads to better school performance and stronger school engagement. Raises children who are more cognitively competent.

H 6.2
Guidelines to Facilitate a Multicultural Education

- Understand your students and their backgrounds.

- Modify the curriculum to include presentations related to the cultures in the classroom.

- Review any curricular materials to ensure they are free from stereotypes related to race, ethnicity, gender, and disability.

- Choose materials depicting both sexes in activities or jobs that are diverse and not associated with stereotypes.

- Discuss openly the current political and social status of different cultures.

- Use high-status individuals from various racial and ethnic groups through the use of case studies and through classroom visits or field trips.

- Avoid using sexist language, and enacting any stereotypes in the class.

- Assign boys and girls to activities without regard to gender, and encourage all children equally.

- Ask members of the class from nondominant cultures to share descriptions of their customs with the class.

- Encourage all students to have high goals and aspirations for their futures, regardless of ethnicity or gender.

Chapter Seven
Behavioral Approaches To Learning

The instructor's manual for this chapter contains:
- A *Chapter-at-a-Glance* chart that reviews all chapter related material
- A detailed chapter outline to highlight main points of the chapter
- A list of transparencies from Transparencies - Educational Psychology IV that correspond to this chapter
- Several activities to deepen student understanding
- An annotated list of additional resources including internet sites
- Handouts to accompany your lessons

CHAPTER-AT-A-GLANCE

Chapter Outline	Objectives	Instructional Aids
1.0 Why Understanding Behavioral Learning is Important to Teachers, p. 233	1. Discuss the importance to teachers of understanding behavioral approaches to learning.	- Transparencies T47, T47A - Test Bank Questions 1-5, 53-54
2.0 Learning by Classical Conditioning, p. 233	1. Describe the basic idea of classical conditioning. 2. Explain how classical conditioning was discovered. 3. Describe the process of classical conditioning.	- Transparencies T48, T49 - Activity 7.1 - Test Bank Questions 6-25, 55-60, 79
3.0 Learning by Operant Conditioning, p. 238	1. Describe the basic idea of operant conditioning. 2. Explain how operant conditioning was discovered. 3. Describe the process of operant conditioning. 4. Discuss changing students' behavior with behavioral modification.	- Transparencies T50, T51, T52, T53, T54, T55 - Handouts 7.1, 7.2, 7.3 - Activities 7.2, 7.3 - Test Bank Questions 26-46, 61-70, 73-75, 77, 80-82 - Video Segment 9
4.0 Social Learning, p. 252	1. Describe the basic idea of social learning 2. Explain how social learning was discovered. 3. Describe the process of social learning.	- Activity 7.4 - Test Bank Questions 47-52, 71, 76
5.0 Cognitive-Behavior Modification, p. 257	1. Discuss cognitive-behavioral modification.	- Handout 7.4 - Test Bank Questions 72, 78

DETAILED CHAPTER SEVEN OUTLINE
I. Why Understanding Behavioral Learning is Important to Teachers
- Every teacher needs to understand behavioral approaches to learning because students' behavior is what teachers deal with every day.

- In a single day in the classroom, you will need most if not all of the principles of behavioral learning to teach effectively.

II. Learning by Classical Conditioning

A. The Discovery of Classical Conditioning
- Classical conditioning is a learning process in which an originally neutral stimulus becomes associated with a particular physiological or emotional response that the stimulus did not originally produce.
- Ivan Pavlov realized that some kind of learning must have taken place for the dogs to salivate before they smelled the meat powder

B. How Does Classical Conditioning Happen?

C. Phases of Classical Conditioning
- The growth of learning through classical conditioning is called the phase of acquisition.
- Extinction phase is the conditioning situation where the level of the CR starts to decline as the CS continues in the absence of the US.
- Spontaneous recovery is where the organism seems to recover some level of response spontaneously during the rest period, even though the US was absent during this period.

D. Generalization and Discrimination
- The mechanism by which stimuli similar to the original CS can elicit the CR is referred to as stimulus generalization.
- Stimulus discrimination is a mechanism by which organisms are able to distinguish between the conditioned stimulus, which elicits a conditioned response, and other stimuli, which do not elicit the conditioned response.

E. How Aversion Occurs in the Classroom
- Classical conditioning can occur whether or not teachers are aware of it.
- The term conditioned emotional response, or CER, is used for emotional responses that have developed from classical conditioning.
- Stimuli that produce negative emotional responses are called aversive stimuli.
- One of the most common conditioned responses teachers will notice is test anxiety, a generalized feeling of dread in response to tests.
- Relaxation training is the basis of the success of many formal programs for reducing test anxiety.

F. Implications for Teaching
- Avoid classically conditioned negative emotions.
- Link learning with positive emotions.
- Teach students to generalize and discriminate appropriately.
- Help students cope with classically conditioned anxiety.

III. Learning By Operant Conditioning

A. The Discovery of Operant Conditioning
- Operant conditioning, or instrumental conditioning, is learning produced by the rewards and punishments of active behavior of a human or other organism interacting with the environment.
- This active behavior, called an operant, is the behavior the organism, or person, uses to "operate" on the environment.
- Scientists who believe that much and possibly all of behavior can be accounted for by operant conditioning are called behaviorists.
- The founding father of behaviorism is John Watson, while the most influential modern behaviorist is B. F. Skinner.
- Edward Lee Thorndike proposed the law of effect which states that those actions that are rewarded will tend to be strengthened and will be more likely to occur in the future, whereas those actions that are punished will be weakened and thus will be less likely to occur in the future.

B. Recognizing Operant Conditioning in the Classroom

- An expert teacher looks for ways to make the subjects that students are less responsive to more interesting, rather than allowing himself to be conditioned.
- Operant conditioning also occurs in interactions among the children you are teaching.

C. How Does Operant Conditioning Happen?

D. Reinforcement
- A reinforcer is a stimulus that increases the probability that the operant associated with it will happen again.
- A positive reinforcer is a reward that follows an operant and increases the likelihood of that operant occurring again.
- A negative reinforcer is an unpleasant stimulus that ceases or is removed following an operant behavior.

E. Choosing Reinforcers
- Primary reinforcers are rewards that provide immediate satisfaction or enjoyment.
- Secondary reinforcers are rewards that gain reinforcement value through their association with primary reinforcers.
- In token economies, students will be rewarded for performing a desired behavior with a token and then exchange them to buy desired rewards.
- Expert teachers realize that what is reinforcing for one person may not be for another.
- The Premack principle states that more preferred activities reinforce those that are less preferred.

F. Schedules of Reinforcement
- A schedule of reinforcement is a certain pattern by which reinforcements follow operants.
- A schedule of continuous reinforcement has the reinforcement following a particular desired behavior.
- In partial reinforcement, or intermittent reinforcement, the desired behavior is reinforced only some of the time.
- In a ratio schedule, a certain number of the desired operants is reinforced, without regard to the passage of time.
- In an interval schedule, reinforcement is a function of the time that has passed, regardless of the number of operants that have occurred.
- In a fixed-ratio reinforcement schedule, reinforcements always occur after a certain number of responses have occurred.
- In a variable-ratio schedule of reinforcement, the individual is rewarded for a certain number of responses, but the exact number of responses needed to gain a reward can vary from one reinforcement to the next.
- In a fixed-interval schedule of reinforcement, individuals are always reinforced after a certain amount of time has passed, as long as there has been at least one successful response.
- In a variable-interval schedule of reinforcement, individuals are rewarded after a certain amount of time has passed, as long as at least one successful response has occurred, but the specific amount of time between reinforcements can change from one reinforcement to the next.

G. Antecedents of Behavior
- Antecedent stimuli, or cues, are events that precede an operant behavior and serve to predict the consequences of that behavior.
- Antecedent stimuli demonstrate the role that cognitive processes can play in operant conditioning.
- A formal method of informing students about the consequences of their behavior is to draw up a contingency contract; a written or oral agreement between student and teacher specifying desired behavior and promised reward.

H. Punishment
- Punishment is the use of a stimulus that decreases the probability of a response.

- A response can be discouraged through presentation punishment, the application of an aversive or unpleasant stimulus.
- A response can also be discouraged through removal punishment, taking away a pleasant stimulus.
- The person administering the punishment should do the following:
  - Provide alternative responses.
  - Couple punishment with positive reinforcement.
  - Explain the problem.
  - Punish immediately.
  - Use appropriate intensity.
  - Punish consistently.
  - Make escape impossible.
  - Use penalties.
  - Ensure appropriateness.
- Timeout, a brief period of social isolation, serves not only as a punishment, but also removes a reward that the student may have been receiving for his or her unacceptable behavior.
- Response cost is a small penalty imposed for each instance of the undesirable behavior.
- Satiation compels students to continue a behavior until they are tired of it.
- Assertive discipline involves carefully stating rules and describing specific reinforcements and punishments that will follow from obedience or disobedience.

D. Behavior Modification: Changing Students' Behavior
- Behavioral modification is changing students' behavior by managing the contingencies, or consequences, of that behavior.

E. Increased Desired Behavior
- Successive approximations involve rewarding behavior that comes closer and closer to the desired behavior.
- Anyone can shape behavior by first rewarding a very crude approximation to the behavior that is desired as the result.
- Teachers' classroom shaping of student behavior includes a number of specific steps.
  - Select the target behavior they wish students eventually to perform.
  - Determine how often the target behavior occurs before shaping.
  - Choose the reinforcers to be used.
  - Reinforce successive approximations of the target behavior on a continuous schedule.
  - Reinforce the target behavior, when it first appears, on a continuous schedule.
  - Switch to variable reinforcement to maintain the target behavior.

F. Implications for Teaching
- First, try to avoid punishment.
- Try ignoring the behavior.
- Provide warning cues before applying punishment.
- Consider appropriate modifications for the environment.

IV. Social Learning
A. The Discovery of Social Learning
- Social learning takes place when we learn from observing the behavior of others and the environmental outcomes of their behavior.
- Albert Bandura studied children who watched films featuring adults interacting with an inflatable toy known as a Bobo doll.
  - Children who had seen the adult rewarded for aggressive behavior were more likely than children in the control group to behave aggressively toward the doll.
  - Children who had seen the adult be punished for the aggressive behavior were less likely than the controls to behave aggressively.
  - Children had learned merely through observation, without any active participation on their own part.

- Strong evidence indicates that exposure to violent activity on television can lead to aggressive behavior on the part of those who watch television.

B. How Does Social Learning Happen?
- Attention
  - Attention refers to information we actively attend to.
  - Expert teachers attempt to reduce distractions in the classroom so each student's attention is focused on the teacher.
  - Teachers sometimes grab students' attention by showing enthusiasm, being passionate about what they teach, and use different activities.
- Retention
  - The individual has to remember what he or she observed when later given the opportunity to act in the same way.
  - Ask students to recall and describe how you handled a certain kind of task for which you served as a role model.
  - Encourage them to figure out why you handled the task as you did.
- Motivation
  - The individual has to be motivated to model the observed behavior.
  - Students can be motivated by being told reasons to behave a certain way, or through reinforcement.
  - Direct reinforcement is when you reward students for behaving the way you wish them to.
  - Vicarious reinforcement occurs when children watch someone else being reinforced.
  - Self-reinforcements are rewards people deliver to themselves for showing desired behavior.
- Potential for modeling
  - The children need to be not only physically, but also mentally and emotionally capable of doing what you wish them to do.
  - The likelihood that a behavior will be modeled is also affected by the nature of the model, or person performing the behavior.
  - The ultimate goal of social learning is to teach students self-regulation, or the ability to control their own behavior.

C. Implications for Teaching
  - Acquire new behavior.
  - Manifest already learned behavior.
  - Strengthen or weaken inhibitions to action.
  - Direct attention toward what is important.
  - Arouse appropriate emotions.

V. Cognitive-Behavior Modification

- Cognitive-behavior modification techniques use a combination of cognitive and behavioral learning principles to shape and encourage desired behavior.

- Donald Meichenbaum has suggested a set of steps that students can use to engage in self-instruction, or teaching themselves.
  - Demonstration by model.
  - Modeling with overt adult guidance.
  - Modeling with overt self-guidance.
  - Modeling with faded self-guidance.
  - Modeling with covert self-guidance.

- Training in self-instruction gives students their own internalized set of rules and procedures to get things done.

TRANSPARENCIES

- T47   Twelve Examples of Learning I

- T47A   Twelve Examples of Learning II

- T48   The Three Stages of Classical Conditioning

- T49   Apparatus Used in Classical Conditioning Experiments

- T50   Kinds of Reinforcement and Punishment

- T51   Schedules of Intermittent Reinforcement

- T52   Written Prompts: A Peer - Tutoring Checklist

- T53   The Effects of Praise

- T54   Example of a Task Analysis

- T55   Group Contingency Program

CLASS ACTIVITIES

Activity 7.1 Examples of Classical Conditioning in Everyday Life

This activity helps to determine how well the students understand the concept of classical conditioning. Students are to determine how classical conditioning was used to change behavior of the individuals in the short story scenarios. This activity can be used as a group activity or as a homework assignment. Students can get together in small groups and generate ideas together and then share their answers with the entire class. Teachers can also assign this activity as a homework assignment to reinforce the lesson on classical conditioning and have the students talk about their answers the following day in class.

Activity 7.2 Recognizing Operant Conditioning in the Classroom

This activity can be used to determine how well students can recognize the type of conditioning mechanism the teacher uses to respond to the students' behavior. Some conditioning mechanisms are represented more than once. This activity can be used during class as a review or as a homework assignment. The teacher can go over the assignment explaining how the conditioning mechanism was used.

Activity 7.3 Behavioral Techniques in the Classroom

This activity can be used as a group activity to assess students' creativity in providing examples of behavioral techniques that teachers may use to control behavior in the classroom. The teacher may ask one person from the group to write down the examples, and one person to address the class explaining the behavioral techniques and how they will affect the students.

Activity 7.4 Observational Learning and the Media

This activity asks students to watch a television program at home for half an hour. They are to respond to the questions regarding the type of program, what positive and negative features the program showed, and how this program would affect those for whom it is intended. Students are to determine how the media affects the behaviors of others through observational learning. Students can share the television program they watched with the group and collaboratively compare and contrast their findings.

Class Activity 7.1
Examples of Classical Conditioning in Everyday Life

Explain the following behaviors:

1. During lunchtime at school, the children tend to be pretty noisy, and some can even get into mischief. Miss Harvey, the principal, has recently been attending lunchtime and walks up and down the aisles between the tables. The number of incidents of misbehavior have decreased since she has started this behavior. Why are the students behaving more appropriately in the lunchroom?

2. Mr. Pontikos teaches his kindergarten class sign language by using flashcards. A few minutes each day, he holds up different pictures of animals and the children immediately respond. When he holds up a picture of an elephant, the children sign "elephant" without any hesitation. Why do the students respond this way?

3. During playtime in nursery school, Lekeisha and Robert were playing with two different activities. Mrs. Baker complimented Robert on how creative he was with the blocks that he was using. The next day, Lekeisha began playing with the blocks during playtime. How could Lekeisha's behavior be explained?

4. One week, Stacey was feeling very sad and unhappy, so she decided to treat herself by going out to dance at a local club at the end of the week. Stacey has always been a good dancer, and she appreciates other people who dance very well. That night at the club, there was a dancing contest in which guys and girls would be paired up to dance, so she decided to give it a try. The guy that Stacey was paired up with was an excellent dancer and they had to dance to a disco song. As they looked into each other's eyes guessing each other's every move, Stacey felt overwhelmed with emotion. She had a huge smile on her face as this handsome guy twirled her around with excitement. Now whenever Stacey hears that particular disco song she feels overcome with that same emotion of happiness. Why does the music affect Stacey in this manner?

5. Mr. Jones, a fifth grade teacher, felt very unhappy about his "Star Project" he developed in his classroom. During a quiz game, Mr. Jones places a star next to the name of the student who is able to answer a question correctly. For some reason, the children just do not seem so interested in earning stars or answering questions. The same student seems to answer all of the questions. Why have the students become less interested in the stars?

Class Activity 7.2
Recognizing Operant Conditioning in the Classroom

Match the following conditioning mechanisms to the teacher responses to student behaviors.

Teacher Responses to Student Behaviors

___ Teacher gives detention to a student for inappropriate behaviors.

___ Teacher writes "good job" at the top of a homework assignment.

___ Teacher announces that there will be no recess in the afternoon due to bad behavior.

___ Teacher writes an "F" at the top of a quiz.

___ Teacher announces that there will be no homework for those with good behavior.

___ Teacher writes an "A" at the top of a test paper.

___ Teacher writes "poor work" on a student's writing assignment.

___ Teacher draws an unhappy face at the top of a homework assignment.

___ Teacher gives a child a note to "go to the office."

___ Teacher announces that there will be no final for students with an A average.

Conditioning Mechanism

a. positive reinforcement

b. negative reinforcement

c. punishment

d. removal punishment / time out

Class Activity 7.2
Recognizing Operant Conditioning in the Classroom
Answer Key

Teacher Responses to Student Behaviors

_c_ Teacher gives detention to a student for inappropriate behaviors.

_a_ Teacher writes "good job" at the top of a homework assignment.

_d_ Teacher announces that there will be no recess in the afternoon due to bad behavior.

_c_ Teacher writes an "F" at the top of a quiz.

_b_ Teacher announces that there will be no homework for those with good behavior.

_a_ Teacher writes an "A" at the top of a test paper.

_c_ Teacher writes "poor work" on a student's writing assignment.

_c_ Teacher draws an unhappy face at the top of a homework assignment.

_c/d_ Teacher gives a child a note to "go to the office."

_b_ Teacher announces that there will be no final for students with an A average.

Conditioning Mechanism

a. positive reinforcement

b. negative reinforcement

c. punishment

d. removal punishment / time out

Class Activity 7.3
Behavioral Techniques in the Classroom

In your group, provide several examples of how a teacher might use some of the following behavioral techniques to manage children's behavior.

1.   <u>Ignoring</u> Bad Behavior

2.   <u>Praising</u> Good Behavior

3.   Use of <u>soft reprimands</u>

4.   Use of <u>daily report cards</u>

5.   <u>Response Cost Procedures</u>

6.   <u>Modeling</u>

Class Activity 7.4
Observational Learning and the Media

Your assignment is to watch one half hour of television!

Choose programs which you feel are popular with a specific age group (preschool, early elementary, later elementary / early adolescents, older adolescents.)

1. List the program you watch, the date and time you watched it, and the audience you think it would appeal to below:

2. What was the "rating code" for the show? What does this code mean? Is the show specifically made for children or targeted to adolescents?

3. Think about the show in terms of gender or cultural stereotypes. Do you notice anything problematic? What about the language used in the show? Was it appropriate for the audience likely to view it? Did the show contain any violence? Were there allusions to sexual situations or actual sexual situations depicted? Was language sexually suggestive? Was there any profanity?

4. Overall, what would the impact of the show be on the child or adolescent likely to watch it? Give your opinion.

5. Was there anything educational about the show? If so, describe:

6. What was your favorite show (or shows) as a child and/or teen-ager? Compare this show to the one you chose for this assignment.

AVAILABLE RESOURCES ON-LINE

Positive Reinforcement

server.bmod.athabascau.ca/html/prtut/reinpair.htm

This website provides an exercise to teach the concept of positive reinforcement. In the first part of the exercise, the concept of positive reinforcement is defined and illustrated in six examples. An example of positive reinforcement is slightly altered to form a nonexample of positive reinforcement, enabling the student to tell the difference between examples and nonexamples that have similar content. In the second part of the exercise, students identify passages as either being or not being examples of positive reinforcement. The tutorial is intended for students at the university level, and should require from .5 to 1.5 hours to complete.

Cooperative Learning in Higher Education

bestpractice.net

The website provides teaching materials that offer practical examples of how teachers from diverse disciplines approach instructional decisions based on cooperative learning. Cooperative Learning is an instructional approach in which students work together in small groups to accomplish a common learning goal. This website also provides cooperative learning resources and links for teachers.

Classroom Discipline

members.aol.com/churchward/hls/techniques.html

This website offers eleven techniques for better classroom discipline. These techniques are designed to help the teacher achieve effective group management and control. Specifically, this website offers insight on subjects including: Focusing attention, direct instruction, monitoring, modeling, non-cueing, environmental control, low-profile interventions, assertive discipline, I-messages, humanistic I-messages, and positive discipline.

Behavior Management in the Classroom

www.ed.gov/databases/ERIC_Digests/ed371506.html

This website answers questions and offers suggestions regarding ways to manage inappropriate behavior in the classroom. It provides both advantages and disadvantages of using specific techniques such as: token economies, use of rewards, overcorrection, punishment. Also, group methods of classroom management are described and evaluated. A lot of available classroom management resources are provided.

RECOMMENDED VIDEOS FOR CHAPTER SEVEN

Classical and Operant Conditioning

Price: $129

VHS Video (56 minutes)

Published by Films for the Humanities & Sciences; Princeton, NJ

Order #ECU6541

This program explains the nature of Behaviorism, so central to the study of human behavior, and its important applications in clinical therapy, education, and child rearing. The program clearly explains, discusses, and illustrates the complex Classical and Operant conditioning theories of Pavlov and Skinner, and features archival footage of laboratory work with dogs and present-day research using rats in Skinner boxes, as well as numerous examples of conditioning in everyday life.

Behavior Control: Freedom and Morality
Price: $89.95
VHS Video (25 minutes)
Published by Films for the Humanities & Sciences, Princeton, NJ
Order #ECU10666
The work of B. F. Skinner reshaped the field of psychology. This vintage program consists of an archival discussion with Professor Skinner and the University of Oxford's Geoffrey Warnock, in which they engage in a good-natured debate on the presuppositions and morality of behavior control. Free will, operant behavior, contingencies of survival, environment, culture, the human capacity for self-analysis, and other key topics are all scrutinized in their turn.

B. F. Skinner: A Fresh Appraisal
Price: $250
VHS Video (41 minutes), Teacher's guide
Published by Edudex, Princeton, NJ (1999)
Order #AAW32205
The work of Jean Piaget has become the foundation of current developmental psychology and the basis for changes in educational practice. Noted author David Elkind, a former student of Piaget's, explores the roots of Piaget's work and outlines important vocabulary and concepts that structure much of the study of child development. Using archival footage of Dr. Piaget and footage of Dr. Elkind conducting interviews with children of varying ages, this program presents and overview of Piaget's developmental theory, its scope and content.

Further Approaches to Learning
Price: $129
VHS Video (57 minutes)
Published by Films for the Humanities & Sciences, Princeton, NJ
Order #ECU6542
This program explores alternative approaches and explanations of learning, including Latent Learning, Learning Sets, Insight Learning, Ethology, Social Learning, and Neuroscience. The program emphasizes the recent move towards a Cognitive Theory of Learning and examines the current research in this area. The program includes archival film featuring B. F. Skinner and Dr. Robert Epstein, who demonstrated apparent "insight" learning in pigeons using behaviorist techniques. Skinner, speaking just before his death, claims that reinforcement rather than higher mental processes are at work in learning. The cognitive behaviorists think differently.

B. F. Skinner and Behavior Change: Research, Practice, and Promise
Price: $495
VHS Video (45 minutes), Discussion Guide
Published by Research Press, Champaign, IL
Order #1510
This video focuses on the work of B. F. Skinner and addresses the issues and controversies generated by behavioral psychology. The video features discussions by Dr. Skinner and other distinguished professionals including Sidney Bijou, Joseph Cautela, C. B. Ferster, Joseph Fletcher, Fred Keller, Gerald Patterson, and Richard Stuart.

HANDOUTS TO ACCOMPANY YOUR LESSONS:

H 7.1	Types of Reinforcers
H 7.2	Guidelines for Using Punishment
H 7.3	How to Shape Behavior in a Classroom
H 7.4	Using Meichenbaum's Self-Instruction in the Classroom

H 7.1

Types of Reinforcers

Primary reinforcers are rewards that provide immediate satisfaction or enjoyment.

- *Examples include food, shelter*

Secondary reinforcers are rewards that gain reinforcement value through their association with primary reinforcers.

- *Examples include grades, money, clothing or fancy cars*

Token economies are systems in which token-based reinforcement is used to change behavior.

- Tokens are objects that in themselves have no value, such as a certificate or a star, but are exchanged for other things that do have value.

- Students will be rewarded for performing a desired behavior with a token and can exchange them to buy desired rewards.

H 7.2
Guidelines for using Punishment in the Classroom

o Provide alternative responses

o Couple punishment with positive reinforcement

o Explain the problem

o Punish immediately

o Use appropriate intensity

o Punish consistently

o Make escape impossible

o Use penalties

o Ensure appropriateness

H 7.3

How to Shape Behavior in a Classroom

1. Select the target behavior they wish students eventually to perform.

2. Determine how often the target behavior occurs before shaping.

3. Choose the reinforcers to be used.

4. Reinforce successive approximations of the target behavior on a continuous schedule, that is, every time they occur.

5. Reinforce the target behavior, when it first appears, on a continuous schedule.

6. Switch to variable reinforcement to maintain the target behavior.

Four Necessary Conditions for Observational Learning

1. Attention

2. Retention

3. Motivation

4. Potential for modeling

H 7.4

Using Meichenbaum's Self-Instruction in the Classroom

Teacher: Who studied for the spelling test?

Students: (Students raise hands.)

Teacher: How did you know when you knew the words and could stop studying?

Students: (Students shrug shoulders; say they don't know.)

Teacher: How do I know when you know your spelling words?

Students: You give us a test.

Teacher: Right. How could you give yourselves a test so you would know when you knew the words well enough to stop studying?

Students: You could write the words down without looking at them. You could get your mom or dad or brother or sister or friend to give you a test.

Teacher: Good. And what should you do after you or someone else gives a test?

Students: (Students shrug their shoulders.)

Teacher: You should check to see if your answers are correct. If a word is not spelled correctly, you have not learned that word yet and need to study more. How will you know when you can stop studying it?

Students: (Students don't know.)

Teacher: You know you can stop studying when you test yourself and spell all the words correctly. By doing this, you will be sure you know all the spelling words and you will earn a good grade. Let me demonstrate how you can test yourself. (Teacher demonstrates, students practice, and teacher gives corrective feedback.)

Strategies for Learning and Remembering: Study Skills Across the Curriculum" by Rafoth, Leal, and DeFabo. Copyright 1993. Washington, DC: National Education Association. Reprinted by permission of the NEA Professional Library.

Chapter Eight
Cognitive Approaches to Learning

The instructor's manual for this chapter contains:
- A *Chapter-at-a-Glance* chart that reviews all chapter related material
- A detailed chapter outline to highlight main points of the chapter
- A list of transparencies from Transparencies - Educational Psychology IV that correspond to this chapter
- Several activities to deepen student understanding
- An annotated list of additional resources including internet sites
- Handouts to accompany your lessons

CHAPTER-AT-A-GLANCE

Chapter Outline	Objectives	Instructional Aids
1.0 Why Understanding Cognitive Approaches to Learning is Important to Teachers, p. 268	1. Discuss the importance to teachers of understanding cognitive approaches to learning.	- Test Bank Questions 1, 71-73, 91
2.0 The Standard Memory Model, p. 269	1. Describe the standard memory model. 2. Explain the process of encoding knowledge into three memory stores. 3. Describe the different types of storage in long-term memory.	- Transparencies T56, T57, T58, T59, T60 - Activities 8.1, 8.2 - Test Bank Questions 2-31, 74-80, 92-93, 98-99
3.0 Alternative Models of Memory, p. 281	1. Describe the connectionist models of memory. 2. Describe the working-memory models of memory. 3. Describe the levels-of-processing model of memory.	- Transparencies T61, T62 - Test Bank Questions 32-39, 81-83, 94
4.0 Retrieving Information p. 286	1. Describe the various tasks used to assess students' memories. 2. Discuss how to facilitate students' retrieval. 3. Describe retrieval failure, and the theories associated with forgetting.	- Transparencies T63, T64, T65, T66 - Handout 8.1 - Test Bank Questions 40-61, 84-88, 95-96, 100 - Video Segment 10
5.0 Constructivist Approaches, p. 294	1. Describe the constructivist approach to memory. 2. Describe the constructivist approach to learning.	- Transparencies T67, T68, T69, T70, T71, T72, T73 - Handout 8.2 - Test Bank Questions 62-70, 89-90, 97

DETAILED CHAPTER EIGHT OUTLINE
I. Why Understanding Cognitive Approaches to Learning is Important to Teachers
- Cognitive approaches to learning have become popular among educators because they can be directly applied to help students learn.

- Teachers want students not only to remember the material they are taught but also to be able to use that material later.

C. Expert teachers know that understanding what is known about the workings of memory can help them create memorable lessons that will be the foundation of complete learning.

II. The Standard Memory Model

A. Encoding Knowledge into Three Memory Stores
B. The Sensory Register
- The sensory register is where information is first stored when it is sensed.
- It holds information for only a very brief time.
- Visual sensory memory lasts for only about one second, and it can hold only about nine items in memory.
C. Short-Term Memory
- Short-term memory is capable of holding relatively limited amounts of information for a matter of seconds, and in some cases, up to two minutes.
- Information will disappear rapidly from short-term memory unless some type of action, like rehearsal, is taken.
- Rehearsal is the way in which people can transfer information from short-term memory to a more nearly permanent form of storage.
- Research suggests that short-term memory holds roughly seven items, plus or minus two.
- Chunking, or grouping items of information, expands the amount of information you can store in short-term memory.
D. Long-Term Memory
- Long-term memory is capable of storing information for very long periods of time, possibly indefinitely.
- The total-time hypothesis suggests that how much you learn typically depends on how much time you spend studying.
- There are three constraints on the total-time hypothesis:
    Use the full amount of time allotted for study to actually study.
    Encode the information in a way that is consistent with the way in which you are tested.
    Elaborate the information as much as possible, thinking about it carefully and associating it with other things you know.
- Learning psychologists distinguish between two kinds of rehearsal strategies:
    Maintenance rehearsal, or rote learning, is simply repetition of items to be learned.
    Elaborative rehearsal involves taking the information to be learned and trying to associate it with other things you know.
- Distributed learning is learning spaced out over several learning sessions.
- Massed learning is learning that is crammed, occurring all at one time.

E. Types of Storage in Long-Term Memory
F. Declarative knowledge
- Declarative knowledge comprises knowledge of facts stored in semantic or episodic memory.
- Semantic memory comprises long-term memories that hold our general knowledge.
- Episodic memory comprises long-term memories that hold knowledge of personally experienced events, or episodes.
- Declarative knowledge is represented in memory in two main ways:
    Analogical representations are declarative memories that preserve many of the aspects of the original stimulus, whether object or event.
    Symbolic representations are declarative memories that rely on arbitrary symbols that bear no obvious relation to whatever is being represented.
- The dual-trace theory suggests that people can represent information both in the form of mental images and in the form of mental propositions.
- Propositions are combined through propositional networks, or schematic integrations of interrelated propositions.
G. Procedural Knowledge
- Procedural knowledge, or "knowing how," is knowledge of how to do certain things.

- Procedural memory holds our knowledge of how to do things and is remarkably long lasting.
- Procedural knowledge appears to be represented in the form of what are called productions, or condition-action sequences.
- Productions are integrated through production systems, which are ordered sequences of productions.
H. Conditional Knowledge
- Conditional knowledge is knowing when and how to apply the declarative and procedural knowledge you have learned.
- Such information might be stored as cognitive strategies, or information about the conditions under which declarative and procedural knowledge is useful.
- Some students experience low levels of success in school because they fail to apply useful study strategies to the information they need to remember.

I. Implications for Teaching
- The Three Memory Stores
  - Get students' attention.
  - Help students develop metamemory.
  - Allow time for rehearsal.
  - Help students elaborate.
  - Schedule frequent practices of new information.
- Long-Term Memory
  - Arrange memorable learning experiences.
  - Use pictures.
  - Organize information.
  - Teach conditional knowledge.
  - Encourage "learning by doing."

III. Alternative Models of Memory
A. Connectionist Models
- Parallel distributed processing (PDP) model, or connectionist model, focuses on the ways declarative and procedural knowledge are combined via a series of connections among elements.
- In a network representation, information is stored via a series of interconnected nodes, or slots in the network.
- The key to knowledge representation lies in the connections among nodes, not in the nodes themselves.
- Activation of one node may prompt activation of another connected node, a phenomenon called spreading activation.
- A node that activates a connected node is termed a prime, and the resulting activation is termed a priming effect.
- Activation spreads simultaneously across many interconnections in the network.

B. The Working-Memory Model
- Working memory is an active part of long-term memory that also includes short-term memory.
- Working memory holds the most recently activated portion of long-term memory, and it moves these activated elements into and out of brief, temporary memory storage.
- Whereas the standard model of memory reflects a more passive receptacle of information, working memory is an active form of storage.
- The concept of working memory reinforces the implication for teachers that activating, or getting students to recall knowledge they already have helps the students integrate new knowledge into their long-term memories.
- The working-memory model further suggests the importance of integrating new, incoming information with information already stored in long-term memory.

C. The Levels-of-Processing Model
- According to the levels-of-processing model, there are infinite number of levels of processing (LOP) at which items can be encoded, with no distinct boundaries between one level and the next.
- The deeper the level at which an item is processed, the higher the probability that the item will be retrieved.
- Teachers should help their students encode information at the deepest level possible.
- The self-reference effect is where people show very high levels of recall when asked to relate words meaningfully to themselves by determining whether the words describe themselves.
  - The best recall results when the words actually do describe the person who evaluates them.
  - The self-reference effect suggests that students better recall information to the extent that they can see its relevance to themselves.
  - Teachers should encourage students to think actively about how new information relates to them personally.

D. Implications for Teaching
- Use the ideas of priming and spreading activation to help students learn.
- Help your students encode information at the deepest level possible.

IV. Retrieving Information
A. Tasks Used to Assess Students' Memories
- Recall Tasks
  - The most common way to assess learning and memory is through a recall task, in which a person is asked to produce information from memory.
  - In free recall, students are presented with a list of items and must recite back the items in any order they prefer.
  - In serial recall, students are presented with a list of items, and their task is to repeat the items back in the order they were presented.
  - In paired-associates recall, students are presented with items in pairs, and they must repeat back the item with which the first item was paired.
- Recognition Tasks
  - In a recognition task, students have to select or identify something that they learned previously.
  - A multiple-choice test or a matching test would be examples of a recognition task.

B. Facilitating Students' Retrieval
- Retrieval Cues
  - Retrieval cues are clues or reminders that can enhance the ability to retrieve stored information from memory.
  - Teachers can greatly enhance students' learning of and subsequent memory for information if they provide some way for them to organize the information in advance.
  - This way of organizing information is sometimes called an advance organizer.
  - According to the principle of encoding specificity, what is recalled depends on the context in which it is encoded.
  - Those things we encode during a particular mood are more easily retrieved if they are recalled when we are in the same mood.
- Mnemonic Devices
  - Mnemonic devices are specific techniques for improving learning and memory that you can use or teach your students to use.
  - With categorical clustering, encourage your students to organize a list of items to be remembered into a set of categories.
  - Interactive images link together items that would otherwise be isolated.
  - With pegwords, associate each word to be learned with a word on a list that has previously been memorized and form an interactive image between the two words.
  - Through the method of loci, have a student visualize walking along a familiar path, and link each of the words to be remembered through an interactive image to each of the landmarks.
  - Use acronyms to form a word or expression whose letters each signify some other word or

concept.

- Use acrostics to form a sentence in which the first letter of each word of the sentence is the first letter of one of the words to be remembered.

- With keywords, form an interactive image that links the sound and meaning of a foreign word with the sound and meaning of a familiar word.

- PQ4R, which stands for Preview, Question, Read, Reflect, Recite, and Review, is designed to help you remember what you read:

> **P**review the material to be read by skimming the main chapter headings, summaries, and any other organizing information the authors included.
>
> **W**rite questions about each section of the material that relate the material to your reason for reading it.
>
> **R**ead the material, paying attention to details.
>
> **R**eflect on the material and try to build your understanding by drawing conclusions from it.
>
> **R**ecite to yourself the contents of what you just read, and answer the questions you wrote without looking back at the text.
>
> **R**eview what you read previously to build on it with the new information you have just read.

C. Retrieval Failure

- Decay theory posits that information is forgotten because of the gradual disappearance over time of an unusual memory trace.

- Interference theory asserts that we forget because competing information renders inaccessible the information we want to remember.

  - Retroactive interference, or retroactive inhibition, is forgetting caused by activity following the time something is learned, but before we need to recall that thing.

  - Proactive interference, or proactive inhibition, is forgetting that occurs when the interfering material precedes the to-be-remembered material.

D. Implications for Teaching

- Be aware of the effect of context on your students' learning and make it a point to pay attention not only to the material the students are to learn, but also to the context in which the students are to learn it.

- Make use of mnemonic devices to help your students study.

V. Constructivist Approaches

A. Constructivist Approaches to Memory

- Constructivist approach to memory recognizes that prior experience and context affect the way we encode memories, how we recall things, and what we actually recall.

- One of the first scientists to recognize the importance of a constructivist approach to memory was Frederic Bartlett.

  - Bartlett suggested that people bring into a memory task schemas, or cognitive frameworks for organizing associated concepts, based on previous experience, which affect how we learn and remember.

  - Students' prior knowledge and expectations may cause them to remember information in a distorted way that fits into their existing cognitive frameworks.

- Other research on eyewitness testimony, done by Elizabeth Loftus and colleagues, also suggests that people can be led to distort their memories.

- Roger Schank and Robert Abelson suggest that people develop organized scripts, or stereotypical story outlines for how events typically proceed.

B. Constructivist Approaches to Learning

- Constructivist approaches to education build on the ideas that learners must build their own knowledge and that new knowledge builds on current knowledge.

- Constructivist approaches to education are based on the theories of Lev Vygotsky.

- Vygotsky believed that children internalize what they see in their surroundings or contexts, building up their knowledge from what they observe around them.
- Constructivists believe other people are a part of every learning situation.
- The expert provides the novice student with scaffolding, or gradually decreasing levels of support, as the novice internalizes the task.
- Situated learning is the view in which social factors and specific learning environments form an important part of the context responsible for how well people learn.
  - Knowledge does not exist independently; rather, learning occurs as people engage in activities.
  - Situated learning suggests that a major part of learning information is achieved through "learning the situation" in a culturally relative context, or enculturation.
- The program called Practical Intelligence for School, or PIFS was developed with the aim of helping students learn to succeed in the culture of school.
  - It emphasizes the understanding and control of one's cognition, or metacognition.
  - Practical intelligence for school has five key components: knowing why, knowing self, knowing differences, knowing process, and reworking.

TRANSPARENCIES

- T56 Kinds of Knowledge

- T57 The Information Processing System

- T58 Display Used in Sensory Register Experiments

- T59 Examples of Gestalt Principles

- T60 Examples of Top-Down Processing

- T61 Working Memory

- T62 Model for Sensory/Working/Long Term Memory

- T63 A Propositional Network

- T64 Schema for the Word "Bison"

- T65 Example of the Use of Images to Aid Recall

- T66 Schemas and Memory Distortions

- T67 Three Types of Memory

- T68 Long-Term Memory

- T69 Example of a Knowledge Structure Arranged as a Hierarchy

- T70 The Hierarchical Structure for Minerals

- T71 Metacognitive Strategies

- T72 Events of Learning and Instruction

- T73 Working and Long-Term Memory

CLASS ACTIVITIES
Activity 8.1 Recall Tasks: The Limits of Short Term Memory
This activity includes the entire class in experiencing the limits of short-term memory. Place the following lists of words individually on the board or on an overhead projector, and allow the students 60 seconds to view each list, and then remove them. Ask the students to write down as many words as they can remember. Take a class average as to how many words were remembered in each list.

Point out the differences between each list: the first being nonsense syllables, the second meaningful words, the third related words, and the fourth forming a sentence. In the first list, you may want to call attention to a word and then find out how many remembered that particular word. Use the first list to demonstrate serial order (primacy and recency) and distinctiveness effects. The other lists demonstrate the meaningfulness effect.

Activity 8.2 Components of Metamemory
This activity can be used when covering the components of metamemory. It defines the three major factors of metamemory and provides several examples of each. The students are then asked to rate themselves in the person, task, and strategy categories. The person category will ask the students to rate their knowledge of their memory abilities. The task category will ask the students to rate their knowledge of memory tasks. The strategy category will ask the students to rate their knowledge of techniques that aid learning and remembering.

After the students rate themselves, a discussion of the various facts and strategies about memory would be appropriate. The students could share examples of their various ratings. Recommendations and examples can be used to help explain the components of metamemory.

Class Activity 8.1
Recall Tasks: The Limits of Short Term Memory

Place the following lists of words individually on the board or on an overhead projector, and ask the students to look at each list of words. Allow them 60 seconds to view each list, and then remove them. Ask the students to write down as many words as they can remember. Take a class average as to how many words were remembered in each list.

In the first list, you may want to call attention to a word, if it happens to be darkened or smudged, and then find out how many remembered that particular word. Point out the differences between each list: the first being nonsense syllables, the second meaningful words, the third related words, and the fourth forming a sentence. Use the first list to demonstrate serial order (primacy and recency) and distinctiveness effects. The other lists demonstrate the meaningfulness effect.

List #1

dit	bed
sac	car
bok	jump
wap	milk
nif	lid
dij	dog
jax	sack
bif	rug
ged	walk
hab	big
lev	hat
wib	ran

List #2

cover	Jefferson
page	early
chapter	opposed
heading	all
binding	forms
print	of
glossary	tyranny
paragraph	over
index	man's
preface	mind
title	and
forward	body

Class Activity 8.2
Components of Metamemory

Three Major Factors	Examples	Rate Yourself
Person Everything we know about the memory abilities of ourselves	• Knowing that we sometimes forget • Knowing whether or not we know a certain fact • Knowing that older children know more than younger children	• • •
Task Everything we know about memory tasks	• Knowing that recognition memory task is easier than recall task • Knowing that verbatim recall is more difficult than gist recall • Knowing that relearning something is easier than learning it the first time	• • •
Strategy Everything we know about techniques of learning and remembering	• Knowing about and using mnemonic methods such as rehearsal, organization, self-testing, and elaboration • Knowing that use of a strategy can facilitate performance	• •

AVAILABLE RESOURCES ON-LINE

Exploratorium
www.exploratorium.edu/memory/index.html
This website is part of Exploratorium.edu's home page. It is an online museum of science, art, and human perception. It offers online exhibits, brain dissections, memory and cognition games, articles, lectures, and links to many sites.

NASA's Cognition Lab
olias.arc.nasa.gov/cogntion/tutorials/index.html
This is part of NASA's Cognition Lab website. It offers five games to explore issues in cognitive psychology. The games test memory and provide mnemonic devices.

Mindtools
www.mindtools.com/memory.html
This website provides memory techniques and mnemonics. It provides explanations of various learning styles and memory techniques. It also explains mnemonic strategies. It gives some specific examples and uses of mnemonics.

National Institute of Mental Health
www.nimh.nih.gov/publicat/baschap3.cfm
This website provides information on perception, attention, memory, and learning. It is part of the National Institute of Mental Health's web page. The sites main page provides a search engine that can locate more information on memory.

Learning to Learn
snow.utoronto.ca/Learn2/introll.html
This website has modules and discussions for memory, learning, and metacognition. The site includes interactive activities such as the Tower of Hanoi game. The site has many links and resources for memory and metacognition.

RECOMMENDED VIDEOS FOR CHAPTER EIGHT

The Study of Memory
Price: $129
VHS Video (74 minutes)
Published by Films for the Humanities & Sciences, Princeton, NJ
Order #ECU6014
This program introduces the basic terms used in the study of memory such as encoding and storage and retrieval, and looks briefly at the historical ideas about memory. Modern theories are explained using diagrams and real-life examples, and the program then goes on to discuss current research in the area of Everyday Memory. The Reasons for Forgetting are explored and the biological basis of memory outlined. In addition, the program examines ways of improving memory. The program also includes eight exercises for viewers to take part in.

Cerebral Showcase: Introduction to the Brain and Learning
Price: $99
VHS Video (25 minutes)
Published by Insight Media, New York, NY (1996)
Order #TAA1588
This video introduces the field of brain-compatible learning. It discuses discoveries in neuroscience that may enable the redesign of learning, teaching, and training strategies, and examines the effects of nutrition, emotion, the clock, the calendar, and gender on attention, true learning, memory, and recall.

Memory
Price: $39.95
VHS Video (30 minutes)
Published by Edudex, Princeton, NJ (1990)
Order #AAW45719
This program explores the work of the scientists whose research is revealing the nature and workings of memory. The program examines how the researchers are uncovering the secrets of memory, through their laboratory work and clinical studies. Viewers also witness what real people with memory disturbances experience and see, and what hope the advances in memory research may offer to individuals with amnesia and Alzheimer's disease.

Strategic Learning
Price: $69.95
VHS Video (9 minutes)
Published by Films for the Humanities & Sciences, Princeton, NJ
Order #ECU7079
This program outlines a concise three-step process for understanding and retaining information. The steps include exposure, review, and practice. Class attendance is stressed for maximum exposure to material. Valuable advice is provided on how to distill weekly lecture notes into a meaningful study guide. Methods for retrieving information learned include recitation and group study.

HANDOUTS TO ACCOMPANY YOUR LESSONS:

H 8.1   Using Mnemonics to Improve Memory for Grammar

H 8.2   Constructivist Approach to Memory and Learning Retrieving Information

H 8.1
Using Mnemonics to Improve Memory for Grammar

PERSONALS

WANTED: **Single transitive verb** looking for a young, attractive **direct object** that will follow me anywhere. Will take your **determiner**. To make a hot **predictable verb phrase**, call anytime 555/357-411.

WANTED: I'm in a **conditional mood** and am looking for a **modal** to be **present** with me. We **can** go anywhere. I **shall** take good care of you; you **will** like what I have to offer, and we **may** develop a great relationship. Please **precede** me in our next **sentence**.

WANTED: **Nonrestrictive relative clause** free to move to any location in your **sentence**. Will be equal with you at all times. But I know when I'm in the way and will leave without changing your meaning. Believe me, I won't tie you down like that **restrictive** guy.

WANTED: Recently widowed **linking verb** in search of nice, dependable, sympathetic **noun** or **adjective phrase**. I'm not like those **intransitive verbs** who can stand alone; I need your help. Together we can **rename** our **subject**. There are only a dozen or so of us around, so join me today, and we can make a beautiful **sentence** together.

CLASSIFIED

EMBED ANY PHRASE OR CLAUSE you wish to include in your **complex sentence**. I also take apart the longest of sentences by removing one piece at a time. Call me today for a wide range of **diagrams** explaining my work.

PREPOSITION SERVICE RELATES SENTENCE PARTS. I deliver either one-word or multi-word packages to precede any noun phrase. Note of caution: your new **prepositional phrase** will often act as an **adverb**, so keep its 13 or so functions well in mind when using.

Strategies for Learning and Remembering, Rafoth, Leal, and DeFabo. Copyright 1993. Washington, DC: National Education Association. Reprinted by permission of the NEA Professional Library.

Costructivist Approach to Memory and Learning

Memory
• Prior experience and context affect the way we encode memories. • Schemas are cognitive frameworks that organize associated concepts. They are based on previous experience and affect how we learn and remember. • Distortion occurs when people use cognitive schemas to build rather than merely take out knowledge when they try to recall. • Scripts are stereotypical story outlines for how events typically proceed.

Learning
• Prior experience and context affect the way we learn. • Learners must build their own knowledge. • New knowledge is built upon current knowledge. • There is a social nature to learning. • Situated learning is where social factors and specific learning environments form an important part of the context responsible for how well people learn.

Chapter Nine
Thinking: Concept Formation, Reasoning, and Problem Solving

The instructor's manual for this chapter contains:
- A *Chapter-at-a-Glance* chart that reviews all chapter related material
- A detailed chapter outline to highlight main points of the chapter
- A list of transparencies from Transparencies - Educational Psychology IV that correspond to this chapter
- Several activities to deepen student understanding
- An annotated list of additional resources including internet sites
- Handouts to accompany your lessons

CHAPTER-AT-A-GLANCE

Chapter Outline	Objectives	Instructional Aids
1.0 Why Understanding Thinking is Important to Teachers, p. 309	1. Discuss the importance to teachers of understanding the process of thinking.	- Test Bank Questions 1, 81-82, 91
2.0 Concept Formation p. 310	1. Define "concept." 2. Describe the defining features of concepts. 3. Describe the characteristic features of concepts.	- Transparencies T74, T75, T76, T77 - Activity 9.1 - Test Bank Questions 2-8, 83-84, 92
3.0 Reasoning, p. 314	1. Define "reasoning." 2. Compare and contrast deductive reasoning with inductive reasoning. 3. Discuss how reasoning skills are developed.	- Transparencies T78, T79 - Test Bank Questions 9-33, 85
4.0 Problem Solving, p. 319	1. Describe the problem-solving cycle. 2. Discuss different types of problems. 3. Discuss different strategies for solving problems. 4. Describe the impediments to problem solving. 5. Discuss expertise in problem solving.	- Transparencies T80, T81, T82, T83, T83A - Handout 9.4 - Activity 9.2 - Test Bank Questions 34-64, 86-87, 93-95, 97-98
5.0 Transfer, p. 329	1. Define "transfer." 2. Describe types of transfer. 3. Discuss teaching for transfer.	- Transparencies T84, T85, T86 - Handouts 9.1, 9.2 - Test Bank Questions 65-73, 88-89, 99
6.0 Teaching for Thinking, p. 333	1. Discuss how teachers can teach students to think more effectively. 2. Describe the use of role playing in the classroom. 3. Describe the use of groups to enhance student thinking. 4. Discuss how to model and explicitly teach thinking skills.	- Handout 9.3 - Test Bank Questions 74-80, 90, 96 - Video Segment 11

DETAILED CHAPTER NINE OUTLINE
I. Why Understanding Thinking is Important to Teachers
- One distinction often made in education is that between critical thinking and mindlessness.

- Educators are particularly interested in encouraging critical thinking, in which students consciously and purposefully direct their thoughts to find a solution to a problem.
- In contrast, most teachers work hard to help their students avoid mindless thinking, or routinely and automatically following a customary thought pattern without consciously directing their thoughts.
- Raymond Nickerson suggests three key reasons why effective thinking is so important.
  - Effective thinking is becoming increasingly important for success in school.
  - Independent thinking and problem solving are becoming job requirements for careers that students may pursue after they leave school.
  - A thoughtful populace is better able to solve the complex problems facing society at all levels, from neighborhoods and towns, to nations and even the world community.

A. Metacognition, or the understanding of one's cognitive processing, is as important to thinking as it is to learning and memory.

II. Concept Formation
A. Defining Features of Concepts
- Concepts are mental abstractions or categories of similar objects, people, events, or ideas.
- Concepts are easily understood in terms of defining features, or features necessary and sufficient for defining a concept.
  - If an integer is evenly divisible by two, this feature is a necessary characteristic of an even number.
  - A widow is a woman who previously has been married (a necessary but not sufficient feature) and whose husband has died (a necessary and sufficient feature.)

B. Characteristic Features of Concepts
- A characteristic feature is a property typical of something represented in a concept, but not always associated with it.
  - The ability to fly is a characteristic rather than a defining feature of a bird.
  - Having multiple players is a characteristic feature of games, but not a defining feature.
- Students should learn to understand the difference between characteristic and defining features.
- The most representative example of a given concept is referred to as a prototype.
- Teaching students about the meanings of concepts can involve teaching them about only defining features, about only characteristic features, or about both defining and characteristic features.
- Some researchers have suggested instead that what people store are good exemplars of such concepts, or the highly typical instances.
- Mentioning a larger category may activate students' memories of related information, helping them fit the new concept into their schemas.
- Teachers can draw a concept map, a picture or diagram, to illustrate the relationships between different concepts.

C. Implications for Teaching
- Use a lot of examples.
- Combine examples with definitions to encourage full understanding of a concept.
- Distinguish between defining and characteristic features.
- Help students link new concepts to what they already know.

III. Reasoning
A. Deductive and Inductive Reasoning
- Deductive reasoning is the process of drawing specific, logically valid conclusions from one or more general premises, or of going from the general to the specific.
  - Deductive reasoning leads to conclusions that are logically certain.
  - Some of the material students learn in school is presented first in terms of general concepts, and second in terms of specific points and conclusions that follow from these concepts.

- Most real-world arguments do not involve the kind of certainty possible in deduction.
- Inductive reasoning is the process of drawing reasonable general conclusions from specific facts or observations; of going from the specific to the general.
  - In induction, it is not possible to have logical certainty, because there is always the chance that the next observation you make will disconfirm what all the previous observations have confirmed.
  - Teachers may discuss how inductive reasoning in scientific research is problematic.

B. Developing Reasoning Skills
- **Using Syllogisms**
  - A syllogism is a deductive argument that permits a conclusion from a series of two statements or premises.
  - Linear syllogisms relate terms to one another over a successive sequence expressed in a series of statements called premises.
  - Categorical syllogisms typically involve relations where members of one category belong to another category as well.
  - Conditional syllogisms involve determining the validity of a deduction based on conditions given in the premises of the syllogism:
      - Two errors are commonly made in conditional reasoning.
      - Affirming the consequent assumes that if the conditional is true, the "if " and "then" statements can be reversed and the conditional will still remain true.
      - Denying the antecedent assumes that if a conditional is true, it is also true with its antecedent negated.
- **Encouraging Inductive Reasoning**
  - Students need to be taught that it is important to make inductive inferences, but also important to be looking constantly for disconfirmations of these inferences.
  - Students can sharpen their reasoning skills in everyday life by using inductive reasoning.
- **Repairing Fallacious Reasoning**
- Fallacies tend to result from the incorrect application of heuristics, or informal, intuitive, and often speculative shortcuts in thinking that may solve a problem but are not guaranteed to do so.
- Misuse of the availability heuristic results when people make judgments on the basis of how easily they are able to call to mind what they perceive as relevant instances of a phenomenon.
- Misuse of the representativeness heuristic results when people judge the probability that a particular event or object belongs to a certain category by how obviously it resembles or represents the population from which it comes.
- Overconfidence, another common heuristic, is an overestimate of the likelihood of the correctness of a judgment.
- Underconfidence is an equally unsuccessful thought pattern in which people believe they are less likely to be correct than they actually are.

IV. **Problem Solving**
A. The Problem-Solving Cycle
- Problem solving is the process of moving from a situation in need of resolution to a solution, overcoming any obstacles along the way.
- The following steps are useful for characterizing problem solving.
  - Identify the existence of a problem.
  - Define the problem.
  - Represent and organize information about a problem.
  - Create or select a strategy for problem solving.
  - Allocate resources for problem solving.
  - Monitor problem solving.
  - Evaluate the solution to a problem.

B. Types of Problems
- **Well-Structured and Ill-Structured Problems**

- Well-structured problems are problems with clear paths to their solution, often encountered in school by students.
- Ill-structured problems, are problems with no clear paths to a solution.
- **Insight Problems**
  - Insight problems are problems that require the problem solver to think in novel ways that are not obvious from the way in which the problem is presented.
  - Janet Davidson and Robert Sternberg have suggested three processes that are key to insightful thinking:
    - Selective encoding is used to distinguish relevant from irrelevant information.
    - Selective combination is used to put together information that is sometimes related in nonobvious ways.
    - Selective comparison is used to relate new information to old information already stored in memory.

C.   Strategies for Problem Solving
- **Algorithms and Heuristics**
  - An algorithm is a clear and fixed set of steps that guarantee a solution to a problem.
  - A heuristic is an informal, intuitive, and often speculative strategy that might solve a problem but is not guaranteed to do so:
    - Means-ends analysis is where the problem solver analyzes the problem by viewing the goal and then tries to decrease the distance between the current state and the goal.
    - Working forward is where the problem solver begins with an analysis of the current state and tries to solve the problem from start to finish.
    - Working backward is where the problem solver starts at the end, or goal, and tries to work backward from there.
    - Generate and test (trial and error) is where the problem solver simply generates alternative courses of action, and then considers whether each course of action works
- **Problem Isomorphs**
  - Problem isomorphs are problems that have the same formal structure, but different ways of expressing this structure.
  - By showing a student how to represent a problem in different isomorphic ways, you can help that student find a representation that works well.
  - Expert teachers may express the instructions in different isomorphic ways in order to help students better understand that tasks they must do.
- **Incubation**
  - Incubation involves temporarily ceasing to work actively on a problem.
  - Psychologists have found that incubating on a problem often helps us solve it.
  - Hard-working students who become frustrated in their problem-solving efforts may believe that incubation means giving up.

D.   Impediments to Problem Solving
- By becoming aware of the reasons we sometimes get blocked during the problem-solving process, we can consciously overcome maladaptive thought processes and reach a solution.
- A predisposition to think about a problem in a particular way is referred to as having a mental set.
- A particular kind of mental set in which a person is unable to invent a specific new use for something because the person is so used to seeing a conventional use for that thing is called functional fixedness.

E.   Expertise in Problem Solving
- A study of the advantages experts have over novices concludes they have five primary advantages.
  - They perceive large, meaningful patterns of information more readily than novices.
  - They perform tasks more quickly and with fewer errors than novices.
  - They deal with problems at a deeper level than novices.
  - Their memory for information in their domain is superior to that of novices because of their

ability to draw on more and better organized prior knowledge about their domain of expertise.
- They take more time to analyze a problem before undertaking it, allowing them then to solve it more efficiently than novices.

- What experts gain from the experience with large numbers of problems in their domain of expertise is automaticity in the solution of domain-relevant problems.

F. Implications for Teaching
- Define problems.
- Teach strategies for insightful problem solving.
- Look for isomorphs.
- Help students overcome impediments to problem solving.

V. **Transfer**
   A. Types of Transfer
   - Transfer means carrying over knowledge from one problem or situation to a new problem.
   - Positive transfer occurs when the solution of an earlier problem facilitates solution of a later problem.
   - Negative transfer occurs when the solution of an earlier problem impedes solution of a later problem.
   - Low-road transfer occurs when a highly practiced skill is carried over from one situation to another, with little or no reflective thinking.
   - High-road transfer occurs when you consciously apply abstract knowledge you have learned in one situation to another situation.
   - In forward-reaching transfer you intend the transfer of knowledge at the time that you are learning.
   - In backward-reaching transfer, you realize the applicability of what you learned in the past only after it becomes relevant.

   B. Teaching for Transfer
   - Meaningfulness
     - The teacher emphasizes tying the lesson to whatever knowledge students already have and use frequently.
     - Students are more likely to learn about the concept of transfer if they see how it can be a key to their own success in school or in life outside school.
   - Encoding specificity
     - Teachers teach new information in a way that will help students retrieve the information more flexibly later on.
     - Expert teachers regularly ask students to suggest their own ideas regarding new contexts in which they can apply information.
   - Organization
     - To help students overcome the limitations of the way they organize information, expert teachers present new information within a coherent, well-organized framework.
     - The expert teacher makes clear to the students the idea that underlies a lesson and also makes clear how the various concepts relate to that idea.
   - Discrimination
     - Expert teachers help students develop discrimination so that students recognize more readily when old information is not relevant in new situations.
     - The teachers may accomplish this goal by stating outright the types of situations to which new information does and does not apply.

VI. **Teaching for Thinking**
   - Approaches to teach thinking
     - Stand-alone program:
        Thinking is taught as a separate unit or even a separate course.
        Students learn and practice specific thinking skills such as classifying items, forming different orders of items, or making comparisons between ideas or things and reasoning skills such as

making inferences.
- Infused instruction:
 Teaching how to think is an integral part of a curriculum.
 The teacher teaches thinking in the course of teaching other subjects, such as history, mathematics, English literature, or science.
- Dialogical thinking involves being able to see not only your own point of view, but also that of others.
- Dialectical thinking is a type of thinking involving someone coming up with a thesis, then an antithesis, and finally an integrating synthesis.

- Guidelines for how teachers can enhance their teaching of thinking in the classroom.
 - Use role playing.
 - Use groups.
 - Model and explicitly teach thinking skills.

TRANSPARENCIES
- T74   Illustrations Help Students to Understand Complex Concepts
- T75   Phases of the Concept Attainment Model
- T76   An Eighth Grader's Concept Map
- T77   A Coding System for Triangles
- T78   The General Inductive Model
- T79   Phases of Expository Teaching
- T80   Four Different Ways to Represent a Problem
- T81   Problem-Solving Process
- T82   Solving Problems Using Algorithms and Heuristics
- T83   Response Set and Insight I: Problems
- T83A   Response Set and Insight II: Solutions
- T84   A Map to Guide Notetaking
- T85   A Map to Organize Studying and Learning
- T86   Kinds of Transfer

CLASS ACTIVITIES
Activity 9.1 Teaching Concepts
This activity can be used as a homework assignment or for students to complete in pairs during class. This activity will help students practice teaching object concepts, defined concepts, and comparative concepts. Students are to come up with examples of each and explain how that concept would be taught to a class.

Activity 9.2 Algorithms & Heuristics
This activity provides students an opportunity to express how they would solve problems using different memory strategies. Students use an algorithm to solve one problem and a heuristic to solve another problem and then compare the processes. Students can do this activity individually and then pair up to share their method of solving the problems.

Class Activity 9.1
Teaching Concepts

A. Identify an <u>object concept</u> you might teach and work through the following directions for teaching object concepts. (Examples: dinosaurs, rainforest, triangles)

    1. List some positive examples of the concept with clear defining attributes.

    2. List some positive examples that contain nondefining attributes.

    3. List some negative examples of the concept.

    4. Juxtapose a wide range of examples of the concept including minimally different examples.

Class Activity 9.1 (continued)

B. Identify a <u>defined concept</u> you might teach and work through the following directions for teaching defined concepts. (Examples: noun, democracy, symbol)

1. Define the concept.

2. Provide some positive examples of the concept.

3. Provide a list containing positive examples and negative examples, as well as minimally different examples.

C. Identify a <u>comparative concept</u> you might teach and work through the following directions for teaching comparative concepts: (Examples: republic, democracy, dictatorship, mammal, fish, amphibian)

1. List several negative examples of the concept.

2. Create a continuum from nonexamples to positive examples with clear defining attributes.

Class Activity 9.2
Algorithms & Heuristics

1. Solve the following problem <u>using an algorithm</u>.
   Identify the type of algorithm.

   Linda went to the store on her bike. She traveled 2 miles per hour. Her brother Jack took his car. He traveled 50 miles per hour. The store is 20 miles from their house. How much longer did it take Linda?

2. Solve the following problem <u>using a heuristic approach</u>.
   Explain the process you use.

   There are ten children playing in the backyard. There are only five cookies. Each child wants a <u>whole</u> cookie.

3. Compare the processes and results in questions one and two.

AVAILABLE RESOURCES ON-LINE

WWW Constructivist Project Design Guide
www.ilt.columbia.edu/k12/livetext-nf/webcurr.htmll
WWW Constructivist Project Design Guide is a website that was created for educators to design learning projects. It provides information on concept formation, exhibitions, and research on constructivist viewpoints. It also provides specific ideas about different subject areas.

The Information Processing Approach
Chiron.Valdosta.edu/whuitt/col/cogsys/infoproc.hmt.
This website provides general information on memory and concept formation. It offers links, articles, electronic files, and books as resources. It also presents information about teaching inductive reasoning.

WWW Cognitive Psychology Tutor
teach.psy/uga.edu/CogPsychTutor/default.htm
The WWW Cognitive Psychology Tutor provides online tutorials about inductive reasoning and problem solving. It also has online quizzes to test knowledge of topics and the application of the knowledge.

Creativity, Problem Solving, Critical Thinking, Lesson Plans, and Resources
www.cloudnet.com/~edrbsass/edcreative.htm
The website offers lesson plans and resources for creativity, problem solving, and critical thinking.

21ˢᵗ Century Problem Solving
www.hawaii.edu/suremath/home.html
21ˢᵗ Century Problem Solving website provides lessons, games, and resources about problem solving. It offers information in many curriculum areas. It caters to teachers, students, parents, and administrators.

RECOMMENDED VIDEOS FOR CHAPTER NINE

Decision Making and Problem Solving
Price: $39.95
VHS Video (30 minutes)
Published by Edudex, Princeton, NJ (1990)
Order #AAW45720
This program focuses on the idea that both rationality and irrationality influence human thought. It defines reasoning, explains the differences between decision making and problem solving, identifies the biases and other factors that limit our ability to make sound judgements. It also describes the problem-solving process.

Problem Solving
Price: $119
VHS Video (30 minutes)
Published by Insight Media, New York, NY (1988)
Order #UAA312
Demonstrating how to teach problem-solving skills, this program visits classrooms to document approaches of different teachers. It discusses how to identify a problem, describe its attributes, and recognize its patterns. Viewers observe elementary school students using computers, fifth-grade students using problems-solving techniques in mathematics, and a high school class studying communication problems.

Role-Playing as a Teaching Alternative: Do I Dare?
Price: $199
VHS Video (30 minutes)
Published by Insight Media, New York, NY (1999)
Order #UAA2112
Role-play can enhance the educational experience of a class while also making it more enjoyable for both students and instructors. This video demonstrates the use of role-play scenarios to dramatize information presented in a class or test, to facilitate understanding through the simulation of real-world situations, and to break up the lecture routine in order to keep students alert throughout a class period.

How to Engage Students in Critical Thinking Skills
Price: $139
VHS Video (15 minutes)
Published by Insight Media, New York, NY (2000)
Order #UAA1983
Students with critical thinking skills are superior learners because of their ability to reason and reflect upon their reasoning. Offering examples from all grade levels and subject areas, this video shows how to interest students in the process and application of critical thinking. It includes interviews with teachers who discuss critical thinking activities and stress the importance of integrating critical thinking into the daily curriculum, rather than teaching it as an isolated skill.

HANDOUTS TO ACCOMPANY YOUR LESSONS:

H 9.1   The Development of Strategies For Remembering

H 9.2   M-I-R-R-O-R-S: Teaching Strategy Use Effectively

H 9.3   Davidson and Sternberg's Three Key Processes to Facilitate Insightful Thinking

H 9.4   Heuristics to Aid Problem Solving

H 9.1

THE DEVELOPMENT OF STRATEGIES FOR REMEMBERING

Strategy	Independently Displayed	Example
Preliminary Strategies Simple and direct methods for remembering, such as naming, looking, and pointing	By age 2	Pointing to a toy when asked to remember the toy
Rehearsal Rote repetition of material	By age 6	Writing spelling words five times each
Organization Semantic grouping of material	By fifth grade	Grouping spelling words according to prefix
Self-Testing Methods of knowing when one can terminate studying	By fifth grade	Taking a practice spelling test
Elaboration Creating visual or verbal connections that add meaning to material	Adolescence (or later)	"The meat we eat has the work EAT in it; the other MEET does not."

Strategies for Learning and Remembering, Rafoth, Leal, and DeFabo. Copyright 1993. Washington, DC: National Education Association. Reprinted by permission of the NEA Professional Library.

H 9.2

M-I-R-R-O-R-S: TEACHING STRATEGY USE EFFECTIVELY

Remember, children's failure to use a study strategy is often due to an instructional failure rather than a learning failure.

GOOD STRATEGY INSTRUCTION INCLUDES:

- Direct **explanation** and **modeling** of the strategy

- Information on **when** and **how** to use it

- **Reminders** to use the strategy

- Repeated use of the **strategy**

- Constant **feedback** about the strategy's usefulness

- Constant **feedback** about the student's improved performance when he or she uses the strategy

- **Generalizing** the **strategy** to other learning tasks

A HELPFUL MNEMONIC: M-I-R-R-O-R-S

M- Model the strategy; explain how to carry it out

I- Inform the strategy about when and how to use it

R- Remind them to use the strategy

R- Repeat the strategy: practice, practice, practice

O- Outline the strategy's usefulness via constant feedback

R- Reassess the student's performance as a result of using the strategy

S- Stress strategy generalization

Strategies for Learning and Remembering, Rafoth, Leal, and DeFabo. Copyright 1993. Washington, DC: National Education Association. Reprinted by permission of the NEA Professional Library.

H 9.3

Davidson and Sternberg's Three Key Processes to Facilitate Insightful Thinking

1. Selective Encoding

- This process is used to distinguish relevant from irrelevant information.
- For example, selecting information to include in notes while listening to a lecture.

2. Selective Combination

- This process is used to put information together that is sometimes related in nonobvious ways.
- For example, when completing a math problem, a student will need to recognize relevant information and how to combine the information to reach a solution.

3. Selective Comparison

- This process is used to relate new information to old information already stored in memory.
- For example, a student may understand how a concept learned in chemistry relates to a previously learning skill in algebra.

<u>H 9.4</u>

Heuristics to Aid Problem Solving

Means-ends analysis

- The problem solver analyzes the problem by viewing the goal and then attempts to decrease the distance between the current state and the goal. For example, a student may choose to divide a term paper into sections and work on each section as a subgoal.

Working forward

- The problem solver begins with an analysis of the current state and tries to solve the problem from start to finish. For example, a student could create an outline of concepts to be covered before beginning assignment.

Working backward

- The problem solver begins at the end, or goal, and tries to work backward from there. For example, a student may use the solution to a math problem to discover what operations were necessary to solve the equation.

Generate and test

- The problem solver simply generates alternative courses of action, not necessarily in a systematic way, and then considers whether each course of action works. This heuristic is generally regarded as ineffective; however, in new situations it may be useful to gather data. For example, a student may write the introduction to a term paper before realizing that he or she needs to do research on the topic.

Chapter Ten
Motivating Students

The instructor's manual for this chapter contains:
- A *Chapter-at-a-Glance* chart that reviews all chapter related material
- A detailed chapter outline to highlight main points of the chapter
- A list of transparencies from Transparencies - Educational Psychology IV that correspond to this chapter
- Several activities to deepen student understanding
- An annotated list of additional resources including internet sites
- Handouts to accompany your lessons

CHAPTER-AT-A-GLANCE

Chapter Outline	Objectives	Instructional Aids
1.0 Why Understanding Motivation is Important to Teachers, p. 345	1. Discuss the importance to teachers of understanding motivation.	- Test Bank Questions 1-5, 71-72
2.0 Intrinsic and Extrinsic Motivation, p. 347	1. Compare and contrast intrinsic motivation with extrinsic motivation. 2. Describe the research on intrinsic and extrinsic motivation.	- Activity 10.2 - Test Bank Questions 6-16, 73-76, 91-92
3.0 Four Ways to Understand Motivation, p. 353	1. Discuss how motivation affects the development of exceptional abilities. 2. Discuss how extrinsic rewards may undermine motivation. 3. Describe the behavioral view of motivation. 4. Describe the cognitive view of motivation. 5. Describe the social learning view of motivation. 6. Describe the humanistic view of motivation.	- Transparency T95 - Test Bank Questions 17-33, 77-79, 93, 98-99 - Video Segment 12
4.0 The Role of Arousal Level, p. 358	1. Discuss how arousal level affects performance. 2. Explain how teachers can create the optimal arousal levels in the classroom.	- Test Bank Questions 34-40, 80
5.0 The Role of Student Goals, p. 361	1. Discuss why and how goals enhance motivation. 2. Describe what makes goals effective. 3. Discuss the importance of teacher feedback and teacher expectations.	- Handouts 10.1, 10.2 - Test Bank Questions 41-52, 81-82, 94-95
6.0 The Role of Student Needs, p. 364	1. Describe Maslow's Hierarchy of Needs. 2. Describe achievement motivation. 3. Discuss self-determination and control.	- Transparency T96 - Activity 10.1 - Test Bank Questions 53-59, 83-86, 96, 100
7.0 The Role of Student Attributions and Beliefs, p. 368	1. Describe attribution theory. 2. Discuss how beliefs about one's abilities affect self-efficacy. 3. Compare and contrast self-esteem and self-efficacy.	- Transparencies T97, T98 - Test Bank Questions 60-69, 87-88, 97
8.0 Motivating Challenging Students, p. 375	1. Describe methods to motivate challenging students.	- Transparencies T99, T100, T101, T102 - Test Bank Questions 70, 89

DETAILED CHAPTER TEN OUTLINE

I. Why Understanding Motivation is Important to Teachers

- Motivation is an internal state that arouses, directs, and maintains behavior.
  - Motivation is important because students who are motivated tend to achieve more in school: they stay in school longer, learn more, and perform better on tests.
  - To understand student motivation, it is essential to remember that motivation is related to context.

- An incentive is an object or event that encourages or discourages behavior.
  - The right incentive for a person is one that is personally meaningful to her or him.
  - Sometimes incentives motivate behavior to meet undesirable goals.
  - Bronfenbrenner showed that girls and boys may need different types of assistance in order to develop motivation.
  - Expert teachers must bear in mind gender and other group differences when they choose the best type of motivating mentorship.
  - Expert teachers also recognize that students' motivational issues and needs change over the years they spend in school.

II. Intrinsic and Extrinsic Motivation

A. Research on Intrinsic and Extrinsic Motivation
- Intrinsic motivation means that an individual has developed an internal desire to do something.
- Extrinsic motivation is the motivation that comes from outside the individual, for example, from gaining the approval of others or performing behaviors valued by the group.
- Extrinsic motivation works particularly well for young students when teachers create systems of rewards to get students excited about learning.
- As students grow older, they must develop intrinsic motivation.
- Expert teachers recognize that motivating students requires the use of both extrinsic and intrinsic motivators.
- Research suggests that extrinsic and intrinsic motivation are not opposite points along the same continuum; they vary independently of one another.

B. Motivation and the Development of Exceptional Abilities
- Intrinsic motivation can empower people to accomplish remarkable tasks.
- Michael Howe has studied the origins of exceptional abilities, and has concluded that intrinsic motivation is often important in the development of exceptional talents.
- Expert teachers understand the importance of motivation in helping children to maximize their potential.

C. Rewards May Undermine Motivation
- Much of our educational system is based on grades, diplomas, and other external manifestations of what a person has accomplished, reflecting how society acknowledges the value of completing an educational program.
- Extrinsic motivators can sometimes undermine intrinsic motivation.
  - Intrinsic motivation produces high achievement, and extrinsic motivation often does not.
  - Researchers identified three facets of people's intrinsic motivation: a quest for master, drive to work, and competitiveness.
  - People driven by a desire for meaningful learning, mastery of skills, and work are sometimes described as mastery-oriented.
- Three factors determine whether an extrinsic motivator will undermine intrinsic motivation.
  - The individual must expect to receive the reward upon completing the task.
  - The reward must be something important to the individual.
  - The reward usually must be tangible (a grade, money, a prize).
- How students perceive their teachers' motivation is also important to student learning.

- Barrett and Boggiano showed that the average parent or college student prefers using controlling strategies with children, and prefers using rewards and other methods for promoting extrinsic motivation.
  - The average individual thought that teachers preferred extrinsically motivated students to intrinsically motivated students, and believed that extrinsically motivated students derive more benefit from feedback.
  - Teachers with an external locus of control preferred to use external motivation in teaching.

D. Implications for Teaching
- Consider student age when choosing motivators.
- Choose from a variety of techniques to motivate students.
- Don't overestimate the substantial value of intrinsic motivation.
- Besides modeling intrinsic motivation, plan classes that stimulate students' curiosity.
- Show your own love and enthusiasm for learning, and try novel methods that reflect your curiosity and interests.

III. Four Ways to Understand Motivation
A. Behavioral Theories
- Behaviorists see motivation as the result of rewards and punishments that serve to mold behavior in the direction of seeking rewards and avoiding punishments.
  - A positive reinforcer is a reward following a behavior that strengthens the behavior.
  - A negative reinforcer is the removal or cessation of an unpleasant stimulus, resulting in an increased probability of response.
  - Punishment is a stimulus that decreases the probability of a response, either through the application of an unpleasant stimulus or through the removal of a pleasant one.
  - Punishment tends to be less effective for achieving behavioral change than does reinforcement.
- Behavioral approaches to understanding motivation are closely linked to extrinsic motivation, because of the reliance on external rewards and incentives in producing certain behaviors.
- One problem with using external rewards to motivate students to learn is that the students may never develop as much intrinsic motivation as they ideally need.
  - Mark Lepper has shown that giving students extrinsic rewards for working on problems they find interesting has the effect of decreasing the students' interest level.
  - External rewards can also focus students on the rewards rather than on learning and growing through the learning experience.
- Another problem with using external rewards to motivate students is that the system becomes less effective as students grow up.
  - More mature students may sometimes perceive attempts to reward them as attempts to bribe them.
  - Offering privileges or time without homework means that older students may not do the work they must do to succeed in school.

B. Cognitive Theories
- Cognitive views of motivation focus on what students think, how they think, and how their thoughts create or reduce motivation to act.
- Cognitive theories of motivation emphasize the importance of intrinsic, as opposed to extrinsic motivation.
- Cognitive theorists explain motivation by pointing to our human need to understand, strive, excel, succeed, advance, and continue to challenge ourselves.

C. Social Learning Theories
- Motivation combines extrinsic and intrinsic motivational factors.
- The scientific name for the combination of internal thoughts and how the environment is perceived is expectancy X value theory.
- According to this theory, people work hard and are motivated when they believe that they have a reasonable chance of succeeding, and when the goal is personally meaningful to them.

   D.   Humanistic Theories
   •   Humanists believe that motivation results from more than just external rewards and internal
        conceptualizations of one's ability and performance.
   •   Humanistic views emphasize a higher order incentive to achieve and excel that comes from within
        the person.
   •   Abraham Maslow believed that humans have an inborn need for self-actualization, or making the
        most of oneself.
   •   The humanistic approach emphasizes the "whole student," or the emotional and social aspects of a
        student's life, in addition to the intellectual aspects that are the focus of most instruction.
   •   This approach assumes students are naturally motivated to learn, provided the educational
        experience is meaningful and the students view themselves as capable of learning.

   E.   Implications for Teaching
   •   Try behavioral motivators, rewards and punishments, when you need motivational techniques that
        work quickly.
   •   Focus on cognitive motivators for the long-term changes in the way students think.
   •   Combine behavioral and cognitive motivators to give students the benefits of each.
   •   Stress the meaningful lifetime rewards and positive feelings of self-actualization that result from
        hard work in the present.

IV. The Role of Arousal Level
   A.   Arousal Level and Performance
   •   Arousal is a state of physical and psychological readiness for action caused by the activity of the
        central nervous system, including the brain.
   •   Too much arousal is often associated with anxiety, a sense of nervousness, worry, and self-doubt.
   •   Yerkes and Dodson showed that very low arousal and very high arousal were both associated with
        poor performance.
   •   People generally also feel their best when their level of arousal is moderate.
   •   In an attempt to preserve discipline in the classroom, beginning teachers sometimes create too
        high a state of arousal and anxiety, thus hindering learning.

   B.   Creating Optimal Arousal Levels
   •   The optimal level of arousal for performance varies with the task as well as with the individual.
        - For simple tasks, moderately high arousal is better, whereas for difficult tasks, moderately low
        arousal is better.
        - Some students work well under deadlines, while other students work best when there are few
        demanding standards.
   •   Curiosity creates a moderate and effective level of arousal in students.
        - Curiosity can be piqued by asking students leading questions and by encouraging students to ask
        themselves these same questions when studying at home.
        - People tend to be curious about things that are moderately novel to them and that are moderately
        complex.
   •   Some teachers and schools have viewed curiosity as disruptive.

   C.   Implications for Teaching
   •   Create optimal arousal levels in students by piquing their curiosity and getting them interested in
        learning.
   •   Work to create optimal arousal.
   •   Learn what works best for each student.

V. The Role of Student Goals
   A.   Why and How Goals Enhance Motivation

- According to Locke and Latham, there are four main reasons why goals are effective as motivators of performance.
  - Goals help focus attention.
  - Goals help mobilize resources.
  - Goals facilitate persistence.
  - Goals facilitate accomplishment.
- Goals can help motivate behavior only if they are accompanied by one or more plans for reaching the goals.
- Having unrealistically high goals can be self-defeating for students.
- Researchers studying the effects of deadlines on students' task performance have found that students given the deadline were less interested in the task than those not given a deadline.
- Goals will not motivate students unless they are accompanied by clear feedback.

B. What Makes Goals Effective?
- Researchers have found that students who emphasize task-mastery goals, which stress working to understand and succeed at a task, report more active engagement in their tasks than students who did not emphasize task-mastery goals.
- Students can have different types of goals: subgoals or portions of the overall task, ultimate goals, and time-oriented goals.
- Teachers should make clear for their students how to use self-monitoring of progress toward subgoals during studying, perhaps by talking students through the teachers' own way of studying with subgoals.

C. The Importance of Teacher Feedback and Teacher Expectations
- Feedback is of central importance in developing expert learners, because it is the vehicle through which students see themselves as others see them and learn to improve.
- Teachers' expectations of students, and the feedback based on these expectations, are extremely important in creating or dampening student enthusiasm.
- The effect of teachers' expectations on student performance was called the "Pygmalion effect."
  - High teacher expectations create better student performance, or at least, the perception of better performance.
  - Research has shown that students praised for effort and for what they succeed at doing perform better overall than students not praised in this way.

D. Implications for Teaching
- Emphasize student goals of mastering tasks and completing meaningful learning.
- Maintain positive expectations of all students.
- Teach students to monitor and control their own rates of progress.

VI. The Role of Student Needs
A. Maslow's Hierarchy of Needs
- Abraham Maslow believed human needs formed a hierarchy in which individuals first need to satisfy needs at lower levels of the hierarchy before they seek satisfaction of higher-level needs.
  - Maslow's first level included basic biological needs such as food, water, and oxygen, which are necessary for continued survival.
  - Maslow's second level addresses needs for safety and security, for shelter, protection, and emotional safety.
  - The third level is the need to belong, to feel that other people love and care about us and to be a part of a meaningful group.
  - The fourth level is the need for self-esteem, or to feel worthwhile as a person.
  - The fifth level is the need to know and understand.
  - The sixth level represents aesthetic needs, or the need for beauty and balance in the physical, intellectual, emotional, and spiritual world one occupies.
  - The highest level, level seven, is the need for self-actualization, or the need to fulfill one's potential as a human being.

- The level that a student occupies in Maslow's hierarchy gives teachers a clue about the motives that will work for the student.

B.   Achievement Motivation
- People who rank high in the need for achievement, or the drive to excel, seek out moderately challenging tasks, persist at them, and are especially likely to pursue success at their occupations.
- Researchers have found that people high in the need for achievement privately set goals for themselves.
- Achievement motivation tends to be domain specific.
- The perception of reality is the more powerful predictor of how people, especially children, react to demands for achievement.
- The motivation to achieve appears to be present in every culture that has been studied.
  - Chinese parents place great emphasis on achievement, but their focus is different from that of American parents.
  - American children are motivated to achieve in order to become independent.

C.   Self-Determination and Control
- Self-determination is the ability to make things happen, and to have control of oneself and one's environments.
- Edward Deci and his colleagues have proposed a theory of self-determination.
  - Humans need to feel competent, related, and autonomous.
  - Intrinsically motivated activities satisfy both people's need for competence and need for autonomy.
  - Many extrinsically motivated activities can undermine people's sense of autonomy because they attribute the control of their behavior to sources outside themselves, rather than to internal ones.
  - Students with self-determined motivation are more likely to stay in school, behave well, show conceptual understanding, and be well adjusted.

D.   Implications for Teaching
- Help students with a need for power and achievement by giving them leadership opportunities and presenting them with challenges.
- Help students with a need for affiliation by being nurturing and providing constructive criticism in a positive environment.
- Motivate students to develop the need for self-determination by allowing them to earn autonomy.
- Ensure that students' basic needs for food, shelter, and security are being met before challenging them to achieve at higher levels.

VII. The Role of Student Attributions and Beliefs
A.   Attribution Theory
- An attribution is an explanation pointing to the cause of a particular behavior.
- Fritz Heider who developed attribution theory, pointed out that people make two basic kinds of attributions.
  - Dispositional attributions are explanations of behavior based on internal characteristics in a person.
  - Situational attributions are caused by external factors such as settings, events, or other people.
- The most important causes of success and failure are people's perceptions of their ability and effort.

B.   Beliefs About Ability and Self-Efficacy
- **How Students Respond to Challenges**
  - Some students, termed "helpless," tend to give up easily or to show poor performance when confronting difficult problems.
  - Other students, called "master-oriented," keep trying just as hard or even harder when problems become more difficult.
  - Helpless students tend to have performance goals, which are related to the judgments others

make of their performance.
- Mastery-oriented children have learning goals; they want to improve their skills and learn new things.

- **Keeping Students Focused on Learning Goals**
  - Expert teachers must maintain a focus on the love of learning and skill-building for their own sake, so as not to allow children to become overly fixated on performance goals at the expense of learning goals.
  - Teachers can encourage learning goals by emphasizing meaningful understanding rather than by simply working through twenty sample problems.
  - Expert teachers should provide instruction that is coupled with meaningful feedback on performance.

- **Perceptions of Ability as Influences on Achievement**
  - Girls and boys tend to have different perceptions about their abilities, with girls believing they are less capable and boys believing they are more capable.
  - Research has shown that students who believe they are quite capable do better than predicted by their ability level, but students who believe they are not capable do less well than predicted by their ability level.
  - Students with higher perceptions of their academic competence and personal control had more intrinsic interest in schoolwork and more preference for challenging school activities.

C. Self-Esteem Versus Self-Efficacy
- Self-Esteem and Motivation
  - Self-esteem refers to the value a person places on himself or herself.
  - People's self-concepts become increasingly differentiated over the course of development.
  - Children's perceptions of their ability become more modest and more accurate as they grow older.
  - Teachers cannot neglect the importance of self-perceptions because inaccurate self-perceptions guide how children handle both schoolwork and life outside of school.
- Self-Efficacy and Motivation
  - Self-efficacy refers to a person's belief in her ability to get things done.
  - Self-efficacy theory emphasizes that one's ability to achieve a goal is based on one's belief as to whether or not one can achieve the goal.
  - Self-efficacy can lead to self-fulfilling prophecies.

D. Implications for Teaching
- Discourage students from blaming their failures on bad luck or other unfortunate situations; instead, encourage students to blame failures on lack of hard work.
- Encourage students to view success in school and in life as a result of hard work, not innate ability.
- Emphasize that students should feel good about themselves as a result of meaningful accomplishments, both within and outside of the traditional school domain.

VIII. Motivating Challenging Students
A. Student Motivation and Achievement
- Students' motivation to plan for the future has declined since 1980.
- This decline has been associated with a widening gap in which students from single-parent families are becoming even less motivated to plan for the future.
- Students with an extrinsic motivational style who earned lower grades were likely to have parents who policed their homework.
- Students with an intrinsic style were likely to have received parental encouragement in response to their grades.

B. Motivating Students from Low-Socioeconomic-Status Backgrounds

- Students from disadvantaged social, ethnic, and racial groups may sometimes benefit from an extra dose of motivation to enable them to overcome obstacles that may keep them from succeeding in the mainstream culture.
- These students must often work harder than their non-disadvantaged counterparts to succeed equally well.

C. Motivating Students in Special Education Programs
- IEPs are used for challenged students not only because they are required by law, but also because they work by focusing students on individual goals that lead to larger goals.
- Motivational orientation is particularly important for challenged populations.

D. Implications for Teaching
- Recognize that students from single-parent homes may need extra encouragement, support, and direction.
- Behavioral motivators are often the best way to start with learning disabled students or students from challenged groups.
- Teachers need to work harder to meet the needs of students from challenged groups.

TRANSPARENCIES
- T95   Four Views of Motivation
- T96   Maslow's Hierarchy of Needs
- T97   Attributions for Successes and Failures
- T98   Weiner's Attribution Theory
- T99   Some Factors Affecting Individual Motivation
- T100   Riskiness in Decision-Making
- T101   Different Goal Structures
- T102   Six Dimensions of Teaching that Can Communicate Expectations

CLASS ACTIVITIES
Activity 10.1 Motivational Factors and Learning
This activity provides the opportunity for students to describe a particularly difficult learning experience. The experience can be at any given age, whether it was learning to tie their shoes, learning the alphabet, or learning calculus.

Activity 10.2 Extrinsic and Intrinsic Motivation
This activity provides a short story explaining the impact of extrinsic rewards on an activity that was already intrinsically motivated. Students are to explain how the story illustrates this point. Describe a similar example that could occur in a school setting.

Class Activity 10.1
Motivational Factors and Learning

1. Please describe in detail some experience you have had, at any point in your life, when you had difficulty learning something. Include your age at the time, any special circumstances, the requirements of the task, and whether or not you eventually succeeded or gave up:

2. Now, speculate as to why you lost the motivation. Were there developmental factors (not mature enough cognitively or physically)? Were there behavioral factors (lack of effective reinforcement, for example)? Were there instructional factors (inadequate teaching or environmental problems)? Were there motivational problems? Were there cognitive limitations (problems in the flow of information, it's retention, it's retrieval)? Try to discover what might have been the source of your problems.

Class Activity 10.2
Extrinsic and Intrinsic Motivation

A group of neighborhood boys decided to play ball at the end of a cul-de-sac. While the boys played, they were very noisy. There was an old man who lived in one of the houses near the cul-de-sac. This old man liked to take a nap at the same time the boys came down to play, and each day they woke him up because they were so noisy. So one day the old man went to the children and told them that he liked them playing down near his house, and he offered to pay them $1 to be noisy. The boys agreed to be noisy, and for the next few days the old man came out and paid them $1 to be noisy. Then the old man told them that he could not afford to pay them $1 anymore, but that he would pay them 50 cents instead. So the boys agreed to be noisy, and the old man paid them 50 cents for the next few days. Then the old man told them that he could not afford to pay them 50 cents anymore, but that he would pay them 25 cents to be noisy. So the boys agreed and continued to be noisy. Then the old man told them that he could not afford to pay them 25 cents anymore, but asked them to be noisy for free. The boys refused to be noisy for free and decided to go elsewhere to play ball.

How does this story illustrate the impact of extrinsic rewards on an activity that was already intrinsically motivated?

Provide a similar example of the relationship between extrinsic and intrinsic motivation in a school setting.

AVAILABLE RESOURCES ON-LINE
Kidsource
www.kidsource.com/kidsource/content2/student_motivation.html
This is part of Kidsource's homepage. It offers information on student motivation. It provides factors that influence student motivation such as intrinsic factors and school settings. It also has related forums and articles.

Education World
db.education-world.com/perl/browse?cat_id=6166
This website provides a list of teacher resources on student motivation. It has articles on student motivation. It also has activities and ideas to increase student motivation.

Peak Performance
www.glencoe.com/ps/peak/index.html
This is part of the Peak Performance website. It provides information about test anxiety. It also provides study and test taking strategies for students. It offers a variety of ways to deal with test anxiety. The site has many links to other test-taking strategy websites.

Valdosta State University - Maslow
teach.valdosta.edu/whuitt/col/regsys/maslow.html
This website is part of Valdosta State University's webpage. It provides detailed information on Abraham Maslow's Hierarchy of Needs. It also provides many examples, visual aids, and references on the Hierarchy of Needs.

RECOMMENDED VIDEOS FOR CHAPTER NINE
Increasing Motivation Through Active-Learning Strategies
Price: $169
VHS Video (80 minutes)
Published by Insight Media, New York, NY (1995)
Order #UAA829
The more students think and respond during instruction, the greater their motivation and retention will be. This video teaches techniques for enlisting students' active participation in learning. It shows how to adapt these techniques to personal teaching styles and how to apply them to various activities.

Motivating Students to Think Critically by Teaching for Discovery
Price: $109
VHS Video (60 minutes)
Published by Insight Media, New York, NY (1993)
Order #UAA699
Designed for teachers of all grade levels, this video demonstrates how to develop "discovery" assignments that encourage students to think critically. Viewers learn what does and does not motivate students, why students remember what they discover themselves, and how to correct misconceptions.

Motivation
Price: $39.95
VHS Video (30 minutes)
Published by Edudex, Princeton, NY (1990)
Order #AAW45723
Several experts clarify why motivation is such a complex process, involving biological, socio-cultural, and personality factors. The program deals with some spectacular extremes in behavior, examining why people are motivated to entertain themselves through thrill seeking or to take high-risks jobs.

HANDOUTS TO ACCOMPANY YOUR LESSONS:
H 10.1   Two Primary Motivators for Students
H 10.2   Performance versus Learning Goals

H 10.1

Two Primary Motivators for Students

Student Goals

1. Goals help focus attention.

2. Goals help mobilize resources by providing a sense of what needs done.

3. Goals facilitate persistence by reminding students of where they want to be versus where they are.

4. Goals facilitate accomplishment by motivating students to continue trying to succeed.

Student Needs

1. Need for Power

- Students try to make the world conform to their image of what it should be
- Students are motivated by leadership and public recognition
- Norm referenced grading conforms to this need

2. Need for Affiliation

- Students like to form close connections with others and be members of groups
- Students tend to avoid competition and feel anxious when being evaluated
- Students are motivated by group activities and nurturing environments which are not evaluative or competitive
- Cooperative learning grading systems conform to this need

3. Need for Achievement

- Students have a drive to excel
- Students seek out moderately challenging tasks and persist at them
- The need tends to be domain specific
- Students are motivated by moderate goals at which they can excel
- Criterion -referenced or "traditional" grading systems conform to this need

H 10.2

Performance vs. Learning Goals

Performance Goals	Learning Goals
• Goals associated with "helpless" students	• Goals associated with mastery-oriented students
• Goals focus on looking smart, earning praise, and avoiding negative judgments	• Goals focus on improving skills and learning new skills
• Students tend to give up easily or show poor performance when given a difficult task	• Students work harder when they encounter problems in obtaining the goal
• Failure to attain goal is attributed to lack of ability	• Failure to attain goal is attributed to lack of effort

Chapter Eleven
Classroom Management

The instructor's manual for this chapter contains:
- A *Chapter-at-a-Glance* chart that reviews all chapter related material
- A detailed chapter outline to highlight main points of the chapter
- A list of transparencies from Transparencies - Educational Psychology IV that correspond to this chapter
- Several activities to deepen student understanding
- An annotated list of additional resources including internet sites
- Handouts to accompany your lessons

CHAPTER-AT-A-GLANCE

Chapter Outline	Objectives	Instructional Aids
1.0 Why Understanding Classroom Management Is Important To Teachers, p. 385	1. Describe the three parts to the "thinking" triangle. 2. Discuss how the knowledge of expert teachers differs from nonexpert teachers. 3. Discuss how expert teachers are efficient.	- Transparencies T103, T105, T106, T107, T108 - Activity 11.1 - Test Bank Questions 1-8, 63-66
2.0 How Effective Teachers Manage Their Students, p. 389	1. Describe what it means to have creative insight. 2. Describe the advantages of expertise. 3. Describe how expert students use effective learning strategies	- Handout 11.1 - Test Bank Questions 9-14, 67-70, 81, 90-91
3.0 Developing and Implementing Rules and Procedures, p. 395	1. Discuss the role of good planning in classroom management. 2. Discuss procedures and rules in classroom management. 3. Discuss how to respond to broken rules. 4. Describe age-related issues in managing students.	- Handout 11.2 - Teat Bank Questions 15-33, 71-74, 82-87, 92 - Video Segment 14
4.0 Maintaining Control and Preventing Problems, p. 406	1. Discuss the importance of good communication in maintaining control and preventing problems. 2. Describe how to respond to student misbehavior. 3. Describe general behavioral influence techniques of classroom management. 4. Discuss how to cope with violence in school.	- Transparency T109 - Activity 11.2 - Test Bank Questions 34-57, 75-78, 88,89
5.0 Special Approaches to Classroom Management, p. 415	1. Describe group consequence systems. 2. Explain the token reinforcement system. 3. Describe contingency contract systems.	- Transparency T104 - Handout 11.3 - Test Bank Questions 58-62, 79, 80

DETAILED CHAPTER ELEVEN OUTLINE

I. **Why Understanding Classroom Management is Important to Teachers**
   A. Changes in Our Society and in Our Schools
   - Changes in Families and Attitudes
     - Most households of today do not stress the same types of values that were seen as important 50 years ago.
     - The United States leads all other developed nations in rates of single parenthood and divorce; more and more children are being raised by one never-married parent.
   - **Increase in Violence**
     - Youth are more likely than adults to be victims of violent crime.
     - School violence is most likely in schools located in high-crime areas, in large schools with large classes, in schools containing a high percentage of male students, and in schools with weak administrators.

   B. Goals of Classroom Management
   - **Allocated Versus Engaged Time**
     - One key way for a teacher to assess the outcome of classroom-management techniques is to evaluate how much time students really have for learning.
     - Allocated time is the time a teacher earmarks and plans to use for learning.
     - Engaged time is the time that students actually spend on learning.
     - A well-managed classroom means more quality learning time, and more quality learning time means more actual learning can take place.
   - **Promoting Self-Management**
     - Other important goals of classroom management are to help students gain in maturity so that they learn how to manage themselves, and to show students how to internalize rules and procedures that enhance learning.
     - By assisting students in developing their ability to understand, control, and evaluate their own learning, teachers help students mature into lifelong learners.

   C. Implications for Teaching
   - Encourage students to reflect about their behaviors and school performance.
   - Recognize and reward meaningful effort.
   - Make an example of successful students' techniques.
   - Provided students are succeeding, allow diversity in methods of self-management.
   - Model good self-management techniques.

II. **How Effective Teachers Manage Their Students**
   A. A Pioneering Study of Classroom Managers
   - **"With-it-ness"**
     - With-it-ness means that teachers are observant and attentive to everything that is going on around the teacher in the classroom.
     - Teachers who show they are "with it" have fewer discipline problems than do teachers who are unaware of or do not react to what is going on.
     - Teachers can become more "with it" by monitoring the entire classroom every minute for signs of disruption or other problems, and by making frequent eye contact with students and calling them by name to show he or she is fully aware of what each student is doing.
     - Teachers can increase their "with-it-ness" by making maximal use of their voice, eyes, and body language to remain simultaneously in contact with different students.
   - **Coping Simultaneously with Numerous Situations**
     - Expert classroom managers must do several things at once.
     - Overlapping is supervising several activities at once.
     - A good way to develop overlapping is to practice it during your student teaching assignment, or to work in another environment that requires coping with simultaneous events.
   - **Creating Momentum and Ensuring Smooth Transitions**

- Interruptions in the classroom detract from meaningful learning.
- Expert classroom managers spend as much uninterrupted time on an activity as is needed before switching children to another activity.
- Expert teachers also keep unnecessary activity changes and interruptions to a minimum.

- **Involving Every Student**
- One way teachers can succeed at involving every student is to call on students using a somewhat unpredictable order.
- Expert classroom managers will engage the entire class in a problem being completed on the board by one student by asking all students to complete the problem in their notebooks.
- Effective teachers call on several students in a row, using a random order to select students, and will get all students to provide answers to the same open-ended problem.
- Expert classroom managers also ask questions in a way that allows all students to display their answers.

- **Generating Enthusiasm and Keeping Lessons Interesting**
- Teachers generate enthusiasm and excitement when they use a variety of approaches and presentation styles.
- Interest levels can be maintained only within the limits of students' attention spans.
- Because children's needs differ as a function of age, techniques for effective classroom management differ for students of different ages.

- **Criticizing Students Constructively**
- Constructive criticism is specific and clear, and it focuses on inappropriate behaviors rather than on the person performing the behavior.
- Constructive criticism is also free of anger, yelling, shouting, sarcasm, or intentional mean-spiritedness.
- Constructive criticism is effective not only for the student to whom the criticism is directed, but also to the other students listening.
- Techniques for responding to misbehavior:
  - A teacher should state the name of the student who is misbehaving and clearly describe what the undesirable behavior was.
  - The teacher should provide a reason why the behavior was undesirable.
  - The teacher should describe the desirable behavior that should replace the undesirable one.
  - The teacher should be firm and in charge, and should not act in an overtly angry or threatening manner.

B. Additional Findings Regarding Classroom Management
- Studies have shown that well-managed classrooms are characterized by students who are actively engaged in lessons being led by their teacher.
- Well-managed classrooms are free of interruptions, confusion, and wasted time.
- Well-managed classrooms are a direct result of teachers' effective use of the management techniques such as the ones just described above.
- The following are general management techniques that apply to students of all ages:
  - Expert classroom managers are well prepared for the first day of class.
  - For the first few weeks of a new school year, effective teachers work with the entire class at once.
  - Once the school year is well under way, the best classroom managers continue to give students clear directions, regardless of the specific activity, and maintain the standards represented by the rules and procedures already announced.

C. Implications for Teaching
- Show students you are "with it."
- Learn how to supervise numerous activities at once.
- Establish and preserve a natural flow of student activities.
- Involve every student in classroom activities and schoolwork.
- Criticize students constructively to help them improve.

III. Developing and Implementing Rules and Procedures

A. The Role of Good Planning

- **Research on Effective Planning**
  - Kounin found that expert and nonexpert teachers did not differ much in their methods for handling student misbehavior.
  - What distinguished these two types of teachers was the expert teachers' use of strategies to prevent classroom disruptions from happening.

- **Students' Developmental Age and Maturity Level**
  - In preparing effective plans, teachers should consider the developmental age and maturity level of the students.
  - The secondary school teacher is more likely to see a wide range of discipline problems and must therefore focus on preventing misbehavior from even developing in the first place.
  - Secondary students often misbehaved because rules and procedures were not clearly understood by the students.
  - Secondary classes sometimes require more elaborate procedures than do elementary school classrooms.

- **The School Environment**
  - Teachers should create rules that are consistent with their overall school environment.
  - Teachers must work within the physical characteristics of the school when developing rules and procedures.
  - Teachers should also consider the school administration's tolerance for new, unusual, or creative rules and procedures.

- Student Characteristics and Histories
  - Teachers must remain sensitive to the needs and expectations of different groups of children, and be cautious when applying rules that worked on one group of children to another group of children from a different socioeconomic background.
  - When teachers change teaching environments, they must take stock of their new situation before creating new rules and new teaching plans.

B. Procedures and Rules

- Procedures
  - Procedures are the methods for accomplishing classroom activities in an orderly manner.
  - Procedures are needed in order to specify how students will get things done and accomplish the activities necessary for learning.
  - The teacher should explain to students the precise steps involved in classroom procedures so that all are equally aware of these procedures.

- Rules
  - Rules are statements that specify acceptable and unacceptable behaviors in the classroom.
  - Effective classroom managers write down the class rules, post them, and hand them out.
  - When setting rules a teacher must be aware of the general school rules.
  - Effective teachers often involve students in creating, reviewing, and reworking classroom rules and consequences for breaking them, while providing these students with input about administrative and general school requirements.
  - Evertson et al. list five types of general rules that are helpful for elementary school:
    - Be polite and helpful.
    - Respect other people's property.
    - Listen quietly while others are speaking.
    - Do not hit, shove, or hurt others.
    - Obey all school rules.
  - Emmer et al. list six general rules that are helpful in managing secondary school students:
    - Bring all needed materials to class.
    - Be in your seat and ready to work when the bell rings.
    - Respect and be polite to everyone.
    - Respect other people's property.
    - Listen and stay seated while someone else is speaking.
    - Obey all school rules.

C. Responding to Broken Rules
- For rules to be effective, broken rules must lead to specific and appropriate consequences.
- For minor rule infractions, students may simply be required to repeat the activity or action, but to do it correctly.
- For more serious infractions, more serious consequences will be necessary in order to uphold the integrity of the rule system with all students.

D. Managing Students from Age 6 to Age 18: Age-Related Issues
- Brophy and Evertson believe that teachers need to use four different approaches to classroom management as a function of the students' age.
- As children begin school and become accustomed to the school environment in kindergarten and grades one and two, they need patient and constant immersion in and reminding of basic classroom rules and procedures.
- By the middle elementary years, teachers must focus on teaching the specific rules that apply to each activity.
- As students finish elementary school and begin adolescence, teachers must concern themselves with motivating students who may be tuning out of school due to puberty pressures, and with handling disruptive and contentious students.
- Once students have reached the last two years of high school, teachers must teach the right material to maximize learning, tailor instruction to life and career goals, and help students to manage their own learning.

E. Implications for Teaching
- Before developing a management plan, consider the developmental age, maturity level, and background of the students.
- Set reasonable procedures and rules and make sure students are familiar with them.
- When drafting the procedures and rules, consider the school's physical and cultural environment, and the advantages and disadvantages of each.
- Review other teachers' rules and procedures before drafting your own; discuss your plans with other teachers for input.
- Tailor punishments to the severity of the misbehaviors that motivated the punishments.

IV. Maintaining Control and Preventing Problems
A. The Importance of Good Communication
- Teachers who communicate effectively with students have better results in managing their students than do less effective communicators who implement the same rules and procedures.
- Communication with parents is also essential.
- Much of being a good communicator consists of being a good listener who is able to empathize with others.
- Another important part of communicating effectively is practicing reflective thinking in which one mulls over situations and works to understand them from each participant's perspective.

B. Responding to Student Misbehavior
- **"I" Messages**
  - An "I" message is a clear, direct, assertive statement explaining exactly what a student did that constitutes misbehaving, how the misbehavior affects the teacher's ability to teach, and how the teacher feels about the misbehavior.
  - The goal of an "I" message is to affect a voluntary change in the student's behavior by appealing to the student's conscience and desire to do the right thing.
  - The premise of the "I" message approach is that the teacher's authority and ability to punish students should be used only when other methods have failed to modify students' behavior.
- **Assertive Discipline**
  - Assertive discipline is a method of responding to misbehavior that is clear, firm, and direct.
  - Teachers who use this style make their expectations clear and firmly state the consequences for misbehavior, and then follow through with these consequences if appropriate.

- Canter believes that teachers who fail at classroom management do so because they have one of two ineffective styles:

    The passive style teacher fails to firmly and directly label the problem behavior and tell the student what should have been done.

    The hostile style teacher pronounces extreme punishments and then attempts to undermine a student's sense of self-worth by telling the student that she seems to be incapable of performing better.

- Canter advocates the assertive discipline approach as an effective method for dealing with student misbehavior:

    The teacher teaches students how to behave.

    The teacher provides positive reinforcement.

    The teacher involves the discipline plan, which consists of the programmatic approach to discipline problems that he or she has developed ahead of time.

- **Deciding Who Owns the Problem**
- Before deciding on a course of action in response to a problem, a teacher must decide who "owns the problem."
- If the teacher owns the problem, the teacher must direct the student to solve the problem.
- If the student owns the problem, the teacher's role becomes one of providing a sympathetic ear and of helping the student find his or her own solution.
- The key is to consider whether the problem obstructs effective teaching and learning.

- **When the Student Owns the Problem: Active Listening**
- Active listening consists of a teacher allotting the time to listen to a student in an active and concerned manner and encouraging the student to state the problem fully.
- This technique involves paraphrasing what the student says and encouraging the student to work through the problem.
- During conversations with students, teachers often find it helpful to implement the paraphrase rule, designed to promote accurate communication.

- When the Teacher Owns the Problem: The No-Lose Method
- The concept behind the no-lose method is that resolving conflicts will be easier and more productive if neither teacher nor student feels that he or she is losing.
- The specific six-step procedure advocated is the following:

    Define the problem.

    Generate possible solutions.

    Evaluate the solutions.

    Decide which solution is best.

    Determine how to implement the solutions.

    Assess the success of the solution.

C. General Behavioral Influence Techniques
- Supporting self-control helps students develop self-control to minimize their misbehavior.
- A teacher can also use proximity with the student as a cue to the student to halt the misbehavior.
- A teacher can also make eye contact with the student or give another nonverbal signal until the student stops the inappropriate behavior.
- During situational assistance, the teacher helps the students over hurdles they are encountering.
- A teacher can give time-out for misbehaving students.
- Reality and value appraisal is designed to redirect students' behavior toward more constructive, useful, and intelligent outcomes.

D. Coping with Violence in School
- School violence is most likely in large schools located in high crime areas, in schools with weak administrators, and in schools with a high percentage of male students.
- Teachers can help direct students' energies more productively onto meaningful achievement.
- Teachers can invite students to participate in developing the rules and procedures that will govern them, as well as in choosing the emphasis of their curriculum.

- Well-managed schools, free of violence, can be of many different types and can cater to diverse types of students.

E. Implications for Teaching
- Cultivate good communication skills that can be applied in diverse educational settings.
- Use "I" messages to explain the consequences of students' misbehaviors in a nonjudgmental manner.
- Be firm, clear, direct, and assertive when dealing with student misbehavior.
- Decide whether a problem is owned by the teacher or the student before taking steps to solve it.
- When the student owns the problem, use active listening to express concern and to give support.
- When the teacher owns the problem, use the no-lose method to achieve a solution.
- Respond immediately to potential threats of violence and involve other teachers, administrators, or other appropriate authorities in solving the problem.

V. Special Approaches to Classroom Management
A. Group Consequence Systems
- In a group consequence system, the teacher keeps track of students' behaviors by adding points to a total, and the class can work toward earning a desired privilege by trying to amass a given number of points.
- The situations in which a group consequence system works best are those in which students are motivated to retain the approval of their peers.
- A teacher must remain alert to the specific class dynamics and ensure that this system is fair and is helping to improve the students' behavior.
- Teachers must also remember that young students have trouble waiting a long time for desired rewards.

B. Token Reinforcement Systems
- In a token reinforcement system, students earn tokens (points, stars) for good behavior or classroom achievement.
- The tokens are collected by the students and can later be exchanged for a reward, such as a gift or privilege.
- To acquaint students with the token system, the teacher should use it aggressively at the start, with tokens being given out often, and then minimize the number of tokens given out later.
- Token economies take a lot of work for the teacher and should therefore be used only in specific and complex situations.

C. Contingency Contract Systems
- A contingency contract is an agreement between the teacher and each individual student regarding the exact goal the student must accomplish in order to earn a reward.
- Both students and teachers can decide on the behaviors to be tallied and on the nature of the rewards to be earned.
- Teachers must be clear about the quality of work that constitutes the successful completion or performance of a task, and such specific criteria should be a part of a contingency contract system.

D. Implications for Teaching
- Try group consequence systems.
- For younger students, and for challenged populations, use token reinforcement systems.
- For older students, use contingency contracts to keep motivation high and attention focused on meaningful learning goals.

TRANSPARENCIES:

- T103   Who Knows Where the Time Goes? Time Available for Academic
         Learning

- T104   A Student Contract Appropriate for Primary Grades

- T105   Elementary Classroom Seating Arrangement

- T106   Secondary Classroom Seating Arrangement

- T107   Initial Kindergarten Room Arrangement

- T108   Improved Kindergarten Arrangement

- T109   Peer Conflict Management

CLASS ACTIVITIES

Activity 11.1 Time Usage in the Classroom Setting

This activity encourages students to think about how the class time is divided between instructional time, engaged time, and academic learning time. Students are to estimate how much time is allotted for each and provide different examples for those times. First students are to apply this to their educational psychology class, and then students are to think back to their elementary or secondary school days and decide how time is divided differently during the day. Students could do this exercise as a take-home assignment and then share their estimations, or could get into pairs and decide between them how class time is divided.

Activity 11.2 Violence in Schools

This activity allows students the opportunity to reflect on issues related to violence in schools. Students are to read the paragraphs regarding bullying, student-teacher ratio, zero tolerance, and gun violence, and respond to related questions. Students can either do this assignment as homework or read the paragraphs in class and respond to the questions in groups.

Class Activity 11.1
Time Usage in the Classroom Setting

For the following questions, estimate the time spent in your educational psychology class and provide examples:

How much time is allocated for the class?

How much time do you estimate is devoted to *instructional time*?

How much time do you estimate is devoted to *engaged time*?

How much time do you estimate is devoted to *academic learning time*?

For the following questions, estimate the time spent in a typical school day in elementary or secondary school.

How much time is allocated for the school day?

How much time do you estimate is devoted to *instructional time*?

How much time do you estimate is devoted to *engaged time*?

How much time do you estimate is devoted to *academic learning time*?

Class Activity 11.2
Violence in Schools

A recent spate of deadly school shootings, including the April 1999 massacre of 14 students and a teacher at a suburban Colorado high school, have given much attention to the necessary intervention needed in our schools. Researchers, politicians, and school personnel have focused on issues of bullying, student-teacher ratio, gun control, and zero tolerance. Read the following paragraphs on these issues and answer the questions that follow.

- The phenomena of bullying are often described using such terms as harassment, teasing, and peer abuse. Bullying can include a wide range of hurtful behaviors, encompassing physically injurious actions, as well as verbal forms of harassment, and indirect means of hurting others. In schools, verbal harassment is the most commonly observed form of bullying; physical bullying the least. Although boys and girls may engage in all these behaviors, indirect bullying is more commonly found among girls; physical bullying among boys.

- A high student-teacher ratio makes it nearly impossible for teachers to effectively monitor student behavior. Teachers are unable to notice acts of aggression which precede violence in large classrooms, lunchrooms, and playgrounds. Discipline problems and crime increase because of the high student-teacher ratios. It also makes it difficult for teachers to maintain control, and reduces the opportunities for teachers to form supportive, personal relationships with the students. Many educators and experts believe that reducing class size is one of the most important ways to help ensure school safety.

- Child behavior experts and school officials say it's unclear whether so-called "zero tolerance" is making schools safer or putting violent kids back on track. Zero tolerance is the practice in which disciplinary action is taken immediately following the serious violation of school policy. Although zero tolerance tends to provide a feeling of safety, there is little solid evidence it is curbing violent behavior in schools. Zero tolerance policies may be causing a "near epidemic" of suspensions and expulsions that ultimately may encourage at-risk students to drop out of school altogether.

- Gun violence among young people continues, despite the fact that it is illegal for anyone under 21 to buy a handgun and anyone under 18 to buy a rifle or shotgun. This increased violence among young people has created an atmosphere of fear that has driven more young people to carry weapons. According to a recent report issued by the Department of Education, over 6,000 students were expelled in 1996-1997 for bringing guns to their public schools. A 1995 survey conducted by the Center for Disease Control found that two in 25 high school students reported having carried a gun in the last 30 days.

Class Activity 11.2 (continued)
Questions for Reflection:

How could bullying be reduced in the schools?

How do you think reducing bullying in the schools would decrease violence?

In what ways can schools reduce student-teacher ratio?

How do you feel reducing the student-teacher ratio will affect school violence?

What kind of policies do you think would necessitate zero tolerance?

Do you think zero tolerance is effective? Why or why not?

Do you think stricter gun laws would reduce the occurrence of school shootings?

What preventative measures could schools generate to curtail the incidence of school violence?

AVAILABLE RESOURCES ON-LINE
The Innovative Classroom
innovativeclassroom.com /Class_Management/
This website provides four sections, labeled Bell Work, Class Certificates, Center Focus, and Organization Tips. Bell Work ideas are short and simple activities that students may complete independently while teachers are completing their morning tasks. Every week this website presents a new class certificate for teachers to download and use in their classroom. The certificates are in full color and may easily be mounted and laminated to create extra special incentives for students. The Center Focus section is a great resource for all teachers using centers in the classroom. There are hundreds of original activities covering all grade levels and subject areas. The majority of the centers are designed to be completed independently by students to help them become responsible learners. Organization Tips provides hundreds of great tips for organizing the classroom. The ideas deal with the organization of materials and supplies, tips dealing with behavior issues, and suggestions for implementing class routines.

The Teachers Guide
www.theteachersguide.com/Classmanagement
The Teachers Guide provides lesson plans to teach behavior modification, and techniques for improving classroom discipline. The techniques include "11 Techniques for Better Classroom Discipline," "Discipline Techniques That Backfire," "Four Stages of Discipline," and "Four Steps for Classroom Discipline." This website also provides feature resources, including The Well-Managed Classroom: Promoting Student Success through Social Skill Instruction, Positive Discipline: A Teacher's A-Z Guide, Teacher Smart!: 125 Tested Techniques for Classroom Management and Control.

Mary's Teaching Hints
members.nbci.com/_XOOM/teach2000/teachingtips/index.html
Mary's Teaching Hints provides information on ways to better manage the classroom like: being consistent with your expectations and follow through, having a daily routine posted somewhere in the room on word cards or a sheet of paper, and reminding students of their manners if needed. It also provides links to many other websites for teachers, students, new teachers, and specific subjects.

Calico Educational Software
www.calicoed.com/
The Calico Educational Software Inc. develops quality software tools for educational and personal purposes. The programs are available to help teachers manage their classrooms. Calico offers free software for teachers to try before buying. Fasttracker is a complete classroom management system with advanced functionality. The gradebook ledger, automated task wizards, attendance tracking, and 'One Click' professional reports make FastTracker an efficient teaching tool. Calico is soon to release TestWeaver which will help in exam creation.

RECOMMENDED VIDEOS FOR CHAPTER ELEVEN
Classroom Management at Its Best
Price: $159
VHS Video (35 minutes)
Published by Insight Media, New York, NY (1999)
Order #UAA1980
This video clarifies the difference between order and control in classroom management. It teaches fundamental approaches to discipline; describes effective teaching procedures, rules, and consequences; and provides examples that illustrate the efficacy of various management strategies.

Discipline and Achievement
Price: $159
2 VHS Videos (30 minutes each)
Published by Insight Media, New York, NY (1999)
Order #UAA1597

This two-volume set shows how classroom discipline can improve student achievement. The first volume teaches preventive techniques that minimize conflict, maximize cooperation, and reduce the potential for frustrating power struggles. The second shows how to develop and implement effective boundaries that focus on positive outcomes rather than negative consequences.

Managing the Disruptive Classroom: Strategies for Educators
Price: $295
VHS Video (60 minutes)
Published by Insight Media, New York, NY (1994)
Order #UAA720
This video explains how meeting students' basic needs – inclusion, achievement, enjoyment, freedom to make choices, and survival – can curtail disruptive behavior. It shows teachers as they apply reality therapy to typical classroom situations.

Planning for Prevention
Price: $149
VHS Video (26 minutes)
Published by Films for the Humanities & Sciences, Princeton, NJ
Order #ECU4511
To stop problems before they start, teaches must clearly define what is expected of students from the outset and establish routines that make best use of classroom time. It this program, teachers explain and demonstrate unique, effective styles of communicating expectations and initiating class procedures.

HANDOUTS TO ACCOMPANY YOUR LESSONS:

H 11.1	Kounin's Six Key Classroom Management Strategies
H 11.2	Ways to Respond to Misbehavior
H 11.3	Example of a Behavior Contract

H 11.1

Kounin's Six Key Classroom Management Skills

1. **"With-it-ness"** - teachers are attentive and observant to everything that is going on in the classroom.

2. **Coping Simultaneously With Numerous Situations** -teachers need to manage overlapping activities in the classroom.

3. **Rating Momentum and Ensuring Smooth Transitions** -spend as much uninterrupted time on an activity as needed before switching to another activity.

4. **Involving Every Student** -Calling on students at random will maintain students' attention because they are uncertain when their turn will come.

5. **Generating Enthusiasm and Keeping Lessons Interesting** -Teachers should use a variety of teaching approaches and styles to maintain student interest.

6. **Criticizing Students Constructively** -Criticism is specific, clear, and focuses on inappropriate behaviors rather than on the individual.

H 11.2

Ways to Respond to Misbehavior

1. Using "I" Messages

- An "I" message is a clear, direct, assertive statement about exactly what a student did that constitutes misbehavior, how the misbehavior affects the teacher's ability to teach, and how the teacher feels about the misbehavior.

2. Assertive Discipline

- A method of responding to misbehavior that is clear, firm, and direct. Teachers make their expectations clear and firmly state the consequences for misbehavior. They then follow through with these consequences if appropriate.

3. Deciding Who Owns the Problem

- When analyzing a problem with a student, a teacher must decide who owns the problem and why it is affecting the teacher. If the problem is the students, the teacher can help the student find a solution. If the teacher owns the problem, the teacher must direct the student to solve the problem.

4. Active Listening

- Teachers can allot the time to listen to a student in an active and concerned manner. This technique involves paraphrasing and encouraging the student to work through the problem.

5. The No-Lose Method

- This method of problem solving is productive because neither the student nor teacher feels like they lose. Both parties evaluate possible solutions and select the best solution.

H 11.3

Example of a Behavior Contract

<u>**Behavior Contract**</u>

This is an agreement between Joe Brown and Mrs. Smith. This contract begins on January 5, 2001 and ends on June 5, 2001.

The terms of this contract area as follows:

Joe will remain in his seat during class until he requests permission from Mrs. Smith.

Mrs. Smith will allow Joe to spend 2 minutes of leisure time during recess on the computer for each time he appropriately requests permission to leave his seat during class. The time spent on the computer will not exceed the length of recess.

If Joe completes his part of the agreement, Mrs. Smith will provide Joe with the computer time in the agreement above. If Joe does not request permission before leaving his seat he will lose 2 minutes of computer use during recess.

_____   _____
Student's Signature   Teacher's Signature

_____
Date

Chapter Twelve
Classroom Teaching

The instructor's manual for this chapter contains:
- A *Chapter-at-a-Glance* chart that reviews all chapter related material
- A detailed chapter outline to highlight main points of the chapter
- A list of transparencies from Transparencies - Educational Psychology IV that correspond to this chapter
- Several activities to deepen student understanding
- An annotated list of additional resources including internet sites
- Handouts to accompany your lessons

CHAPTER-AT-A-GLANCE

Chapter Outline	Objectives	Instructional Aids
1.0 Why Understanding Classroom Teaching is Important to Teachers, p. 424	1. Discuss the importance to teachers of understanding classroom teaching.	- Test Bank Questions 1-4
2.0 Principles of Teacher – Centered Teaching, p. 426	1. Define teacher-centered teaching. 2. Describe the role of planning in teacher-centered instruction. 3. Discuss direct instruction methods. 4. Discuss meeting the needs of different students in teacher-centered teaching. 5. Describe the limitations of direct instruction.	- Transparencies T110, T111, T112, T113, T114, T115, T116, T117, T118 - Handouts 12.1, 12.2 - Activity 12.1 - Test Bank Questions 5-29, 57-60, 66-68, 71 - Video Segment 15
3.0 Principles of Student-Centered or Constructivist Teaching, p. 444	1. Define student-centered or constructivist teaching. 2. Describe constructivism in the classroom. 3. Describe how to create constructivist learning environments. 4. Evaluate learner-centered psychological principles. 5. Discuss the role of planning in student-centered or constructivist instruction. 6. Describe methods for teaching constructively. 7. Describe the limitations of student-centered or constructivist teaching.	- Transparencies T119, T120, T121, T123, T124, T129 - Handouts12.3, 12.4, 12.5 - Activity 12.2 - Test Bank Questions 30-56, 61-65, 69, 70, 72 - Video Segment 16-17

DETAILED CHAPTER TWELVE OUTLINE

I.   Why Understanding Classroom Teaching is Important to Teachers

- A solid understanding of the many ways to conduct a class will improve your efficiency and flexibility, allowing you to accomplish more with students in less time.

- Knowing a variety of teaching techniques will help you hone your instincts and develop more insightful solutions to problems.

- Teacher-centered learning approaches view students as passive recipients of knowledge imparted to them by teachers.

- Student-centered learning approaches view students as active learners, constructing what they are learning in their own minds.

II.   Principles of Teacher-Centered Teaching

A.   The Role of Planning in Teacher-Centered Instruction

- **Individual Differences in Planning**
  - Good teaching depends on good planning done long before a teacher ever steps in front of a class to lead a discussion or give a demonstration.
  - First you must decide what general topics to cover.
  - Then you must develop teaching plans that chart instruction over the months and weeks of the school year.
  - From this level of information, you then plan what to teach throughout the week.

- **Limitations of Planning**
  - Expert teachers recognize the limitations of plans as well as their strengths.
  - Ineffective teachers tend either not to notice their plans are failing, or they press on with the plan anyway because they feel they must.
  - Research has shown that students learn more when their teachers are flexible in their planning and in their allocation of time instead of adhering rigidly to their plans.
  - The process of planning instruction evolves as you grow in competence and experience.

- **Learning Objectives**
  - Specific Objectives:

    Robert Mager believed that objectives should describe specifically what students should do to demonstrate their achievements, and how teachers can recognize student success in demonstrating their achievements.

    These specific types of objectives can take a long time to develop, but once defined they can assist motivated students in mastering the material.
  - General Objectives:

    Norman Gronlund sees objectives as general, focusing on cognitive goals.

    Students should understand that the specific tasks they are accomplishing are just a subset of many similar tasks they could tackle with the ability to think and reason in a new domain.
  - Using Objectives:

    The success of learning objectives depends on their appropriate use.

    Highly organized texts and teaching aids may reduce the need for teacher-defined objectives.
  - Limitations of Objectives:

    Poorly written objectives can confuse students before they have a chance to master a concept.

    Students often infer objectives too late to be optimally useful, thus teachers should always state their objectives early and often.

- **Taxonomies**
  - Cognitive Objectives:

    Knowledge consists of remembering or recognizing something, either with or without true understanding of it.

    Comprehension consists of understanding something, without necessarily relating it to other things.

    Application consists of being able to use a general concept in the solution of a problem.

Analysis consists of breaking a concept down into its constituent parts.

Synthesis consists of creating a new idea by combining other ideas.

Evaluation consists of judging the worth or value of something, particularly as it applies in a particular situation.

- Affective Objectives:

Receiving consists only of being minimally aware of something going on in the environment.

Responding consists of displaying some new behavior as a result of experience.

Valuing consists of showing some involvement or commitment.

Organization consists of changing one's value system to accommodate a new value.

Characterization by value consists of behaving consistently in keeping with the new value.

- Psychomotor Objectives:

Psychomotor taxonomies progress from basic reflexive actions to highly skilled movements.

For a teacher, it is important to focus on incremental improvements in skills over time.

B.   Direct Instruction Methods
- Lecturing and Explaining
  - Strengths of Lecturing:

Lecturing is a good method to use to communicate an overview of a topic to students, to describe detailed examples, and in general to tell a story about a sequence of events.

Use lectures to introduce students to topics and ideas that they can then further explore with your assistance through other teaching techniques.

  - Weaknesses of Lecturing:

Some students find it difficult to sit and listen and they may become disruptive.

Lecturing can leave behind students who are less prepared and who are unable or unwilling to interrupt the teacher with questions.

Lectures also demand that you be well prepared and organized.

  - Specific Lecturing Techniques:

The "big three" rules of effective speaking:

Begin by stating your objectives in giving the lecture and providing necessary context.

Present the content one step at a time, using body language that conveys enthusiasm, and using slides, overheads, or other tools to increase the interest level.

Review what was presented and show how it relates to other material that students have studied or will study.

David Ausubel's expository teaching approach suggests that well-presented verbal information and ideas, received and digested by the listener, result in meaningful learning.

Robert Gagné believes instruction should be based on the information-processing model of learning.

  - Adapting Lecturing for Different Learning Styles:

Students have individual learning and thinking styles that influence how well they learn from the lecture format.

Expert teachers are aware of the diversity of learning styles in their classrooms and do everything possible to broaden instruction in order to reach a range of students.

- **Recitation and Questioning**
  - Asking the Right Questions:

To be effective, think about distributing questioning across different objectives in order to create a well-rounded learning experience.

Younger and lower-ability students do best with simple questions that enable them often to answer correctly.

  - Methods of Questioning:

Wait time is the period of silence before and after a student answers a question that gives all students an opportunity to think.

Appropriate wait times give students a chance to process questions and think about answers.

  - Responding to Student Questions:

Responding appropriately to student questions encourages further learning and questioning.

Sternberg has proposed a seven-level model of teacher-child interaction in the questioning process where mediators who respond at higher levels better foster their children's

intellectual development.
- **Seatwork and Homework**
  - Making Seatwork and Homework Effective:
    To be effective, be sure the students understand the directions and the task you are asking them to complete.
    Express openly many implicit rules for doing homework and seatwork to help children unfamiliar with the rules and to refresh other students' memories.
  - How Much Homework?
    A recent study found no obvious relationship between the amount of homework assigned and the amount students learn, as measured on standardized tests.
    Effective homework reinforces classroom learning, enables students to succeed, is used as a normal part of instruction, and is graded promptly and returned to students.
  - Assigning Effective Seatwork:
    With young students, do not assign extended periods of seatwork.
    Avoid creating situations in which students simply copy to finish work quickly.

C. Meeting the Needs of Different Students
- **Aptitude-Treatment Interactions**
  - An aptitude-treatment-interaction indicates that individual students learn different things from the same instruction, as a result of background, abilities, and prior experiences.
  - Sternberg has advocated teaching to promote the development of diverse types of abilities, and teaching from different perspectives to reach students with diverse types of learning styles.
- **Adapting Instruction for Diverse Students**
  - Expert teachers remember that certain teaching approaches and activities benefit certain types of students.
  - Students with the benefit of prior knowledge are able to profit from many forms of instruction.
  - When students lack necessary background knowledge, the learning process must be designed to assist them in recognizing and learning the most important points so their attention is focused on what matters most.

D. Limitations of Direct Instruction
- Direct instruction has been criticized as limiting the types of thinking students engage in.
- Direct instruction has been criticized for placing students in passive roles.
- Some critics argue that direct instruction views teaching and learning as a process of mechanical transmissions of knowledge from teacher to student.

E. Implications for Teaching
- Carefully plan your instruction.
- Familiarize yourself with a wide range of direct instruction techniques.
- Remain attentive to issues of diversity in learning styles.

III. Principles of Student-Centered or Constructivist Teaching
A. Constructivism in the Classroom
- The most significant impact of student-centered approaches is that these approaches involve very different types of classroom instruction and activities.
- Student-centered approaches require thorough planning, tools and equipment, and in-depth knowledge of the students.
- Student-centered teaching has been the foundation of so-called open schools, a term often used to describe schools in which students are actively involved in deciding what and how they will study.

B. Creating Constructivist Learning Environments
- Student-centered teaching involves giving students real-world problems to solve, with all of the confusion inherent in such problems.
- Student-centered learning often involves social interactions with other students in varied formats, including group instruction, in which students learn, process, and discuss material in groups.

- Student-centered approaches involve using multiple representations of content in order to help the students generalize and transfer what they learn.
- Student-centered teaching requires teachers to use the principles and findings of cognitive and educational psychology to structure instruction so it best enhances intellectual development of the student.

C. Learner-Centered Psychological Principles
- The American Psychological Association developed a collection of Learner-centered psychological principles.
- These principles were intended to serve as guidelines for school redesign and reform.

D. The Role of Planning in Student-Centered or Constructivist Teaching
- It is necessary to define the main topic and overarching goals of the learning experience.
- Rather than drafting a precise lesson plan, teachers may choose to involve the students in the process of planning instruction.
- Expert teachers are adept at choosing topics that lend themselves to broad and relevant learning by students.

E. Methods for Teaching Constructively
- **Individualized Instruction**
  - Making Individualized Instruction Work:
    The teacher gives the students differing amounts of time to complete learning objectives.
    The expert teacher varies the actual learning activities that students engage in from one student to the next.
    Teachers can vary the actual instructional materials used with each student.
  - Limitations of Individualized Instruction:
    If frequent assessments are not built into the program, students may lack motivation to push themselves and may not learn as much as they ought to.
    Complex thinking skills are unlikely to develop as students work on their own.
    Individualized instruction is most effective for highly motivated students who are willing to push themselves.
- **Discovery Approaches**
  - Discovery learning is a process in which students use information supplied to them to construct their own understanding.
  - Unstructured discovery occurs when students make discoveries on their own.
  - Guided discovery occurs when the teacher assists the students in making the discoveries.
- Group Discussion
  - In group discussions, students do not just respond to teacher-initiated questions, they respond to each other's questions in an open discussion format.
  - Group discussions allow students to interact with one another directly, and thus to develop interpersonal skills.
  - Expert teachers know how to keep discussions on track by asking questions that keep students focused on central aspects of the issue or relevant controversial aspects of the issue.
  - Group discussions also allow students to see that their peers share certain questions and confusions about issues.
- Effective Cooperative Learning Approaches:
  - Cooperative learning groups develop students' interpersonal skills, and these skills are directly taught by the teacher.
  - When cooperative learning is successful, it increases the achievement of every student in the group.
  - Effective cooperative learning situations require students to interact in order to accomplish the goal.
  - Student Teams Achievement Divisions (STAD) is a formalized system for cooperative learning that creates learning situations most likely to result in desired outcomes.
  - Jigsaw is a method that encourages the interdependence of group members.

- Criticisms of Cooperative Learning:

    A review of 122 studies of cooperative learning supported the value of this approach.

    Some disadvantages of cooperative learning include the possibility that group interactions will negatively affect learning.

- Reciprocal Teaching

    - Reciprocal teaching is a method to increase students' understanding of what they read.

    - First, they summarize what they have read.

    - Second, they ask a question about an important point in the text.

    - Third, they clarify the difficult portions of the material.

    - Fourth, they predict what is likely to come next in the material.

    - After the teacher describes the strategies to the students, they learn to follow the steps on their own, with teacher guidance.

- The Role of Computers:

    - Effective Versus Ineffective Uses of Computers:

        Computer-assisted instruction is a type of individualized instruction administered by a computer and is an example of a meaningful learning activity enhanced through technology. Another important use of computers is word processing, complete with spell-checker and thesaurus.

    - Integrating Computers into Daily Classroom Life:

        Teachers must remain aware of different patterns of computer use among students of different groups.

        Computers can also be used effectively as part of student-centered learning situations.

    - Limitations of Computer-Assisted Learning:

        When material is presented in a form that produces especially vivid verbatim memories, children do better on rote memory tests, but they do worse on reasoning and inference tests of their ability to transfer material to new domains.

        Computer-based learning relies heavily on such strong visuals, which may improve children's verbatim memories at the expense of their reasoning ability.

- Limitations of Student-Centered Approaches

    - Critics of student-centered instruction point out that some teachers become so enamored with the activities and techniques of student-centered instruction that they lose sight of the main goal of education: meaningful learning.

    - Another criticism of student-centered instruction is that it is easy to lose control of students and their learning experiences.

    - Student-centered instruction takes more time than teacher-centered instruction, and is therefore more difficult to ensure coverage of the required material and curriculum.

- Implications for Teaching

    - Take steps to ensure active student involvement in learning.

    - Familiarize yourself with the different student-centered teaching methods.

    - Consider the increasingly important role of computers and technology in the classroom and use this technology as appropriate.

TRANSPARENCIES

- T110   Mager's Three-Part Objectives

- T111   Poorly Written Objectives

- T112   Gronlund's Combined Method for Creating Objectives

- T113   A Revised Taxonomy in the Cognitive Domain

- T114   Planning with a Topic Map

CLASS ACTIVITIES

Activity 12.1 Guidelines for Direct Instruction: Building Bridges

This activity provides students with guidelines for instruction. The guidelines provide brief tips on direct instruction. Also, the activity describes a classroom teaching story. The story demonstrates the techniques used for building bridges such as analogies, stories, demonstrations, and examples. The students are then asked to reflect on their favorite educational experiences that incorporated bridge building.

Activity 12.2 Classroom Observation Guidelines

This activity has the students complete a classroom observation. The observation can be in an elementary or secondary setting. The students are given a list of questions to answer during the observations. The students may then write a summary of the observation. The summary should include general impressions of the class and teaching philosophy. There is a rubric included to help students organize the assignment.

Class Activity 12.1
Guidelines for Direct Instruction: Building Bridges

Key features of direct instruction:

- Advanced organizers - previews - establish learning set

- Describe learning objectives - alert students to new, key concepts

- New material - use small steps, be organized, and be sequenced for easy following

- Elicit student response regularly (stimulate active learning) - ensure mastery

- Review main points - stress general integrative concepts

- Follow-up - exercises, encode in their own words, or application

* Use analogies, metaphors, and models
* Use vertical transfer for sequencing
Example: A famous teacher who was suppose to teach a class general mathematics had decided to teach algebra instead. When he informs the class, they respond, "If we could learn algebra, we wouldn't be in this class." The teacher tries to persuade the students that they can understand algebra. He tells the class how important it is to understand the concept of positive and negative numbers. He then tells a story. He says, "When you go to the beach and dig a hole in the sand. You put the sand next to the hole. The hole: minus two; the pile of sand: plus two. You see that? The hole is minus two, the pile of sand is plus two." Now he asks a student, "What happens when you put them back together, the plus two and minus two, what do you get?" The student resists and reluctantly answers, "Zero." The teacher says, "Zero, that's right. You know not even the Greeks understood zero. The Mayans, your ancestors, invented zero." The teacher demonstrates that he knows the subject matter. But more importantly, the teacher shows masterful ways of presenting the key ideas. He uses analogies, examples, stories, and demonstrations. He exemplifies the most important aspect of teaching today. He finds ways to connect new concepts and new ideas to the previous knowledge of students. The key to teaching is building bridges.

Think of your favorite example of bridge building (metaphors and similes, examples, stories, and analogies) from your school experience:

Class Activity 12.2
Classroom Observation Guidelines

__Directions__

Complete one observation of an elementary or secondary school classroom. If you observe in a junior or senior high school, observe for at least on entire class period. If you observe an elementary classroom, be sure to observe for at least one hour. As you are observing, try to answer the following questions:

1. What is the physical arrangement of the classroom? (Number of desks and students; Tables and chairs? Traditional? Learning centers? Position of teacher's desk? Etc.)

2. How did the teacher begin the lesson?

3. Were objectives of the lesson stated or written on the board?

4. What activities were completed by the students? (Describe each)

5. What exactly did the teacher do?

6. How did the teacher end the lesson?

7. Was homework assigned? What kind?

8. What type of discipline and classroom management techniques were employed by the teacher?

9. What did the teacher do to motivate students?

10. Did the teacher instruct the class about "how to study?" (Suggest specific strategies; Talk about self-testing; How to remember things better, etc.)

11. How much time and what kind of preparation was involved on the teacher's part to get ready for the lesson?

12. What kind of instructional and classroom management decisions did the teacher make?

After completing the observation, write a two-page typed summary of your observation including your general impressions of the class and your feelings about the teacher's particular "philosophy of teaching." Your paper should be organized and well-written. Clearly list the date you did the observation and the school and district at the top of the first page. Hand in this sheet with your notes taken while observing as well.

Please have the teacher you observe sign the bottom of this sheet.
Teacher's Signature:_____Date:_____

School:_____Grade:_____Time:_____

Class Activity 12.2 (continued)
Classroom Observation Rubric

1. Was observation completed according to directions?
   (Appropriate grade; classroom; time span;
   teacher signature obtained, etc.)

   _____

2. Are notes from the observation included with summary?

   _____

3. Is summary within page limits, free of typographical
   and grammatical errors?

   _____

4. Are "general impressions" of the class included
   succinctly but supported by specific examples from
   the observation?

   _____

5. Does the paper contain personal reflections on the
   observation that also reflect theoretical viewpoints
   discussed in class?

   _____

6. Using the details from the observation to
   support statements, does the paper address
   the teacher's philosophy of teaching clearly?

   _____

7. Is the paper well-written and organized?
   (It should be clear that the paper has been
   rewritten and gone through several "drafts")

   _____

Comments:

AVAILABLE RESOURCES ON-LINE
Constructivist Teaching Model
www.ehhs.cmich.edu/~dnewby/dt.html
This website provides steps involved in teaching constructively. It provides information on how to involve students in instructional activities and lists examples and nonexamples of ways to do so. Other information for teachers includes checking for understanding, providing hands-on activities, reflecting upon the lesson, and using an extension or independent activity.

WWW Constructivist Project Design Guide
www.ilt.columbia.edu/k12/livetext-nf/webcurr.html
This is a guide to initiate experienced educators into designing constructivist, cooperative learning projects around the World Wide Web. The introduction assembles relevant pedagogic and learning theory to inform planning for constructivist projects. The web page design is an introduction to the hows and whys of the World Wide Web for instructional use. Student surfing is a guide to helping students find and organize internet resources. Concept formation is a guide to helping students conceptualize and contextualize their findings.

Lecturing with Style
www.utc.edu/Teaching-Resource-Center/lecture.html
The University of Tennessee at Chattanooga provides information on when the lecture method should be used, disadvantages and advantages of the lecture method, how to build a lecture that works, different ways to organize lectures, and different presentation tips. It also provides links to media resources, software, and grants.

Computer Learning Foundation
www.computerlearning.org/
The Computer Learning Foundation is an international nonprofit educational foundation, dedicated to improving the quality of education and preparation of youth for the workplace through the use of technology. To accomplish its mission, the Foundation provides numerous projects and materials to help parents and educators use technology effectively with children.

RECOMMENDED VIDEOS FOR CHAPTER TWELVE
How to Improve Your Questioning Techniques
Price: $139
VHS Video (15 minutes)
Published by Insight Media, New York, NY (1998)
Order #UAA1776
Explaining why good questions benefit students' learning and thinking, this video shows how to make every question an interesting challenge for students. It reviews different types of questions; demonstrates questioning methods that keep students engaged, and discusses why teachers should encourage students to form their own questions.

Introduction to Student-Centered Instruction
Price: $119
VHS Video (60 minutes)
Published by Insight Media, New York, NY (1998)
Order #UAA1616
This video explains inquiry-based learning, a student-centered instruction method that produces a student-generated model of a given concept, process, or knowledge base through cross-disciplinary study, critical thinking, and structured research with students' learning styles.

Focus on Learning
Price: $169
VHS Video (55 minutes)
Published by Insight Media, New York, NY (1998)
Order #UAA2097
The active tutorial approach provides an opportunity for the exploration of many educational themes.
Stressing the importance of maintaining a focus on learning, this video illustrates many simple and easy-to-use reviewing techniques and exercises, and presents the basic educational model that underpins the work.

Building Character Through Cooperative Learning
Price: $139
VHS Video (38 minutes)
Published by Insight Media, New York, NY (1999)
Order #UAA1650
This video features Spencer Kagan's discussion of the value of cooperative learning in character education.
It explains that cooperative learning is an effective strategy for developing such core virtues as personal
responsibility and respect, and illustrates how to incorporate cooperative learning strategies into classroom
instruction.

HANDOUTS TO ACCOMPANY YOUR LESSONS:

H 12.1   Bloom's Taxonomies

H 12.2   Making Seatwork and Homework Effective

H 12.3   Creating Constructivist Learning Environments

H 12.4   Making Individualized Instruction Work

H 12.5   An Evaluation of Cooperative Learning

H 12.1

Bloom's Taxonomies

Cognitive Objectives	Affective Objectives
1. Knowledge • Consists of remembering something, either with or without true understanding of it.	**1. Receiving** • Consists only of being minimally aware of something going on in the environment.
2. Comprehension • Consists of understanding something, without necessarily being able to relate it to other things.	**2. Responding** • Consists of displaying some new behavior as a result of experience.
3. Application • Consists of being able to use a general concept in the solution of a problem.	**3. Valuing** • Consists of showing some involvement or commitment.
4. Analysis • Consists of breaking a concept down into its constituent parts.	**4. Organization** • Consists of changing one's value system to accommodate a new value.
5. Synthesis • Consists of creating a new idea by combining other ideas.	**5. Characterization by Value** • Consists of behaving consistently in keeping with the new value.
6. Evaluation • Consists of judging the worth or value of something, particularly as it applies in a particular situation.	

H 12.2

Making Seatwork and Homework Effective

Seatwork	Homework
Effectiveness	**Effectiveness**
• Be sure students understand directions and the task they are being asked to complete	• Be sure students understand directions and the task they are being asked to complete
• Openly express the rules for completing seatwork to refresh students' memories	• Openly express the rules for completing homework to refresh students' memories
• Seatwork assignments should be short and be combined with explanation and demonstration	• Be sure that homework is challenging, but within students' skill level and relevant to the class
• Make sure students show their work and reasoning when doing seatwork	• Assign more frequent, smaller assignments as opposed to long, infrequent assignments
• Teachers should make themselves readily available to students who may have questions	

DETAILED CHAPTER THIRTEEN OUTLINE

I. Why Understanding Standardized Testing is Important to Teachers

- Over 40 states require standardized tests as part of their annual assessment of students.

- Standardized tests also are used to compare the performance of teachers, schools, districts, states, and even nations, with one another.

- In 1997, President Clinton proposed a national standardized test for all students in fourth and eighth grades.

- Expert teachers understand the strengths and weaknesses of standardized tests in order to use them fairly and effectively.

- Part of being an expert teacher is attaining and understanding the confusing array of standardized test scores and being able to interpret these scores for others.

- Expert teachers understand some of the pitfalls of standardized testing, so they can avoid them to the extent possible.

II. What Are Standardized Tests?

- A standardized test is a test given to many individuals to develop appropriate content and scoring comparisons, and it is administered and scored according to uniform procedures.
    - Norm-referenced tests compare each test-taker's scores with the performance of all the test-takers.
    - Criterion-referenced tests measure a student's performance relative to what the student should know, rather than to the performance of other students.

- Researchers and expert teachers recommend several techniques to encourage and help students give their best performance on standardized tests.
    - Make the importance and purpose of the test clear.
    - Take the mystery out of standardized tests.
    - Provide good testing conditions.
    - Prepare yourself.

III. Types of Standardized Tests

    A. Test of Intelligence

- **Individual Tests**
    - The Stanford-Binet Intelligence Scales can be used for children as young as 2 years up to adults to measure intelligence according to Alfred Binet's conception.
    - The Wechsler Scales yield an overall score, as well as separate verbal and performance scores.
    - Kaufman Assessment Battery for Children is based on a biological theory of intelligence.
    - The Differential Abilities Scales provide a large number of subtests as options, from which the examiner decides which tests to administer.
    - The Learning Potential Assessment Device (LPAD) measures not children's developed potential, but rather their zone of proximal development.

- **Group Tests**
    - Omnibus tests, such as the Otis-Lennon Ability Test and the Henmon-Nelson Test of Mental Abilities, intermix multiple kinds of test items.
    - Another type of group test is divided into parts, or subtests, in which each part is typically timed separately.

    B. Intelligence Test Scores

        - Binet suggested that we can assess children's intelligence on the basis of their mental age, or their level of intelligence compared to an "average" person of the same physical age.

        - William Stern suggested the intelligence quotient (IQ), a measure of intelligence comparing

mental age (MA) to chronological age (CA).
- There are several problems with concept of mental age:
  Whereas chronological age increases indefinitely throughout a person's lifetime, mental age does not.
  Although mental age implies a continuous distribution of intellectual development, we know that intellectual development is not wholly continuous.
- Today people generally use what are called deviation IQ scores, calculated on the basis of how high a person's score is relative to that of other people of his or her age.

C. Tests of Aptitudes and Interests
- Aptitudes are abilities developed over a period of years that predict success in particular areas of endeavor, such as music, writing, or reading.
- Among the most widely used aptitude tests are the Differential Aptitude Tests, used to help students with curriculum or vocational planning.
- Tests of specific aptitudes, such as the Bennett Mechanical Comprehension Test and the Seashore Tests of Musical Aptitudes, are used for narrower purposes, such as selection or vocational placement.
- A vocational interest test such as the Strong Vocational Interest Blank, helps students decide where their vocational interests lie.

D. Tests of Achievement
- An achievement test measures accomplishments in either single or multiple areas of endeavor.
- Five of the most commonly administered achievement tests are the Iowa Tests of Basic Skills, the SRA Achievement Series, the California Achievement Test, the Metropolitan Achievement Test, and the Stanford Achievement Test.

E. Implications for Teaching
- Take into account the purpose of each type of score.
- Pinpoint strengths and weaknesses.
- Combine test scores with other evaluations to better assess performance.
- Evaluate the performance of the class as a whole.

IV. Assessing Test Quality
A. Populations and Samples
- The population is the complete set of individuals to which a set of results will be generalized.
- A sample is a subset of a population.
- In a random sample, every member of the population has an equal chance of being drawn for the sample.
- In a stratified sample, the test constructors make sure they proportionately take into account all of the characteristics that might be relevant to the scores that people receive.
- A good stratified sample in which the balance of relevant attributes in the sample is the same as that in the population is called a representative sample.

B. Reliability
- Reliability is the consistency of test results.
- Reliability is usually expressed as a proportion, on a scale that ranges from 0 to 1, with decimal numbers near 0 indicating low reliability, and numbers near 1 indicating high reliability.
- Test-retest reliability can be measured when test constructors give the same test to the same group of students more than one time.
- Alternate-forms reliability determines whether measurements from two or more slightly different versions of the same test are consistent with one another.
- Internal-consistency reliability is determined by comparing students' performance on one part of the test with their performance on another part.
- Split-half reliability is determined simply by dividing the test questions in half and comparing the two halves of the test.

- Inter-rater reliability determines the extent to which two or more evaluators of a given response rate respond in the same way.
- The reliability of standardized tests varies according to the method used, but it is generally high.
- A second major factor affecting reliability of the test results often is the variation of the individuals being tested in terms of the construct being assessed.

C. Validity
- **Predictive Validity**
  - Predictive validity refers to the extent to which a test predicts a performance that will be demonstrated after the test has been taken.
  - Predictive validities are expressed using a correlation coefficient, which range from -1 (perfect inverse relation) to 0 (no relation) to 1 (perfect positive relation).
  - Most predictive validities are greater than 0 but less than 1.
  - Predictive validities are lowered when there is restriction of range, the difference between the highest and lowest scores.
- **Content Validity**
  - Content validity is the extent to which the content of a test actually measures the knowledge or skills the test is supposed to measure.
  - Content validity must also be considered in terms of the particular curriculum used in a classroom, school, or district.
- **Construct-Related Validity**
  - Construct-related validity is sometimes called simply construct validity.
  - Construct-related validity is the extent to which a test completely and accurately captures the theoretical construct or attribute it is designed to measure.

V. **Interpreting Standardized Test Scores**
  A. Statistical Concepts Underlying Test Scores
  - **Frequency Distributions and Graphs**
    - Frequency distribution is a numerical display of the number or proportion of student scores at each score level or interval.
    - The relative frequency represents the number of students that received a given score.
    - The cumulative frequency represents the number of students that received scores up to that level.
  - **Measures of Central Tendency**
    - The mean is the arithmetic average of a set of numbers:
      - The mean takes into account the information at each data point.
      - The mean is generally the preferred measure of central tendency.
    - The median is the middle of an ordered set of values:
      - The median is less affected by extreme values.
      - The median takes into account less information than does the mean.
    - The mode is the most frequent value of an ordered set of values:
      - A distribution may be bimodal, having two modes, or multimodal, having two or more modes.
      - The mode takes into account less information than does either the mean or the median, and typically is least affected by extreme values.
  - Measures of Dispersion
    - The range is the distance between the lowest and the highest values in a distribution.
    - The standard deviation is the average dispersion of values around the mean.
    - The standard deviation is a measure of variability, telling us how much scores differ from the mean, on average.
    - Sometimes dispersion among scores is measured by an index called the variance, the value of the standard deviation squared.
  - Normal Distribution
  - In a normal distribution, most data values cluster around the average value of the distribution.
  - The normal distribution of scores is symmetrical: half the scores fall below the average, and the other half above.

- Measured values rapidly decline on each side of the center of the distribution and then tail off more slowly as scores get more extreme.
- Most people have scores relatively close to the center of the distribution and relatively few people have scores at the extremes.

B. Types of Scores
- **Raw Scores**
  - The easiest score to understand is the raw score, typically the number of items correctly answered.
  - Because raw scores are hard to interpret on standardized tests, these scores are often converted into other types of scores, such as percentile scores.
- **Percentile Scores**
  - The percentile is the proportion of other students' scores that equal or fall below a given student's score, multiplied by 100.
  - Percentile scores are a measure of comparison against other students, rather than of direct performance.
- **True Scores**
  - An observed score is the score someone actually receives on a test.
  - A true score is the hypothetical score someone would get if he or she took a test an infinite number of times with no practice effects in taking the test.
  - Practice effects are changes in score that occur as a result of increasing familiarity with the particular items, the test as a whole, and the experience of taking the test.
  - A confidence interval is the probability that a person's true score falls within a certain range of the observed score.
  - The measure used to express a confidence interval is called the standard error of measurement.
- **Standard Scores**
  - Standard scores, also called z-scores, derive from converting a raw score into units of standard deviation.
  - Standard scores are arbitrarily defined to have a mean of 0 and a standard deviation of 1.
  - Standard scores are useful because they make it possible to compare results that initially are on different scales.
  - The z-score tells teachers how many standard deviations above or below the mean a raw score is.
  - A variant of the College Board-type score is the T-score which has a mean of 50 and a standard deviation of 10.
  - Another type of standard score, the stanine, has a range of 1 to 9, a mean of 5, and a standard deviation of 2.
- **Grade Equivalent Scores**
  - The grade equivalent score is a measure of grade-level achievement compared with the normative sample for a given test.
  - Grade equivalents are often misleading and should be used cautiously, even avoided when possible.

C. Implications for Teaching
- Be prepared to explain the scores.
- Explain errors of the measurement.
- Focus on the entire student.
- Use tests to set teaching and learning goals.
- Use achievement tests to build self-esteem.

VI. Issues and Concerns in Standardized Testing
A. Test Bias
- Test bias refers to a test's being unfair for members of some groups but not for others.
- A test is biased if there is a difference between groups in scores.
- A test as biased if the content is judge by a panel of experts to favor certain groups over others.

- A test is biased if it either overpredicts or underpredicts some criterion or set of criteria for members of one group versus members of another:

    In overprediction, the test predicts a higher level of performance than a student actually achieves.

    In underprediction, the test predicts a lower level of performance than the student actually achieves.

B. The Cultural Context of Testing
- **Culture-Relevant Testing**
  - Culture relevance is the extent to which a task or test is an appropriate measure, given a person's cultural background.
  - Making a test culture-relevant means not only translating it into a language a person can understand, but also ensuring that the content is meaningful to the person, given his or her cultural contexts.
- **Culture-Fair Testing**
  - A culture-fair test is a test that has the same meaning for members of all cultures.
  - Culture-fairness is virtually impossible to achieve because people in different cultures have different language and educational backgrounds, different social backgrounds, different experience with and attitudes toward tests, and even different notions of how to perform in a testing situation.
- **Culture-Free Testing**
  - A culture-free test is unaffected by culture or cultural context.
  - It is hard to imagine how one might construct a test that is wholly unaffected by culture, because the very act of taking a test is a cultural act, and people bring to the testing situation their cultural background.

C. Misuses of Tests
- **High Stakes Testing**
  - This use of test scores as the sole basis for making important decisions about a student's placement or admission to educational programs is sometimes called high-stakes testing.
  - Many school districts and states even use readiness tests to measure the extent to which a student is prepared to learn something.
  - The minimum-competency test measures whether a student has attained the minimum level of overall achievement necessary for a particular purpose.
  - Forty U.S. states use minimum-competency tests, although not all of those states base graduation decisions on test scores.
- **Overuse in Measuring Accountability**
  - If the objectives measured by the standardized test in use do not fully match those of the school or school district, students may score low on objectives because they are not emphasized by the students' teachers.
  - Schools and school districts in many areas have found themselves in a competition to have students with the highest percentile scores.
  - Teachers and administrators in schools under financial and social pressure to keep normative scores high have resorted to unethical methods for raising school averages.
  - The multiple-choice, norm-referenced standardized tests commonly used to evaluate school performance may not be able to measure some educational outcomes that are valued by society.

D. New Directions in Standardized Testing
- One of the most important trends in standardized testing is the development of what are known as authentic assessments, tests designed to allow students to show their achievements or abilities in a real-life context.
- Different forms of authentic assessments have been developed, including performance tests, which require students to solve problems hands-on, and assemble their best work into a collection.
- Performance assessments are often scored by means of rubrics, or formal specifications of criteria for evaluation.

TRANSPARENCIES:

- T130   Norm-Referenced versus Criterion-Referenced Tests

- T131   Frequency of Scores Forming a Normal Curve

- T132   Describing Measurement Data: A Histogram

- T133   Example of Grading on a Curve

- T134   Two Tests with the Same Mean and Different Standard Deviations

- T135   Percentile Ranking on a Normal Distribution

- T136   Taking on "The Test": Problem-Based Learning

- T137   Stanines and Percentiles

- T138   Four Types of Standard Scores

- T139   Relationship Between Various Types of Scores

CLASS ACTIVITIES

Activity 13.1 Computing Measures of Central Tendency and Variability

This activity requires students to compute the mean, median, range, and standard deviation for a set of 20 test scores. Students are to record their computations for each measure. This activity would best be used as a homework assignment, or used as an individual or paired during class activity.

Activity 13.2 Standardized Testing and Achievement

This activity provides a summary on the effect standardized testing has on achievement and accountability of school systems. Students are to read the summary and then respond to questions requesting their opinion on this issue. This activity can be used as a homework assignment, and then students can share their responses during class discussion.

Activity 13.3 Outline for Test Evaluation

This activity provides students the opportunity to evaluate a standardized test according to the given guidelines. Students could work in pairs outside of class to research the material or as an individual project. The researched material could be presented to the class in short presentations.

Class Activity 13.1
Computing Measures of Central Tendency and Variability

For the following set of scores, determine the mean, median, range, and standard deviation, and place your answers in the space provided. Show your computations.

Pupil	Score	$|n-X|$ (Absolute Value)	$|n-X|^2$ (Absolute Value)	median
Holly	90	____	____	____
Nellie	55	____	____	____
John	88	____	____	____
Shaquelle	72	____	____	____
Marcie	61	____	____	____
Danielle	95	____	____	____
Charles	70	____	____	____
Naomi	59	____	____	____
Jennifer	81	____	____	____
Lekeisha	67	____	____	____
Ricarto	54	____	____	____
Timothy	92	____	____	____
Melissa	77	____	____	____
Sheldon	52	____	____	____
Lucas	51	____	____	____
Dontez	99	____	____	____
Tracy	65	____	____	____
Trevelle	85	____	____	____
Bonita	73	____	____	____
Norberto	94	____	____	____

Median =

Range=

Mean=

Standard deviation=

Class Activity 13.1
Computing Measures of Central Tendency and Variability
Answer Key

For the following set of scores, determine the mean, median, range, and standard deviation, and place your answers in the space provided. Show your computations.

Pupil	Score	$|n-X|$ (Absolute Value)	$|n-X|^2$ (Absolute Value)	median
Holly	90	16	256	51
Nellie	55	19	361	52
John	88	14	196	54
Shaquelle	72	2	4	55
Marcie	61	13	169	59
Danielle	95	21	441	61
Charles	70	4	16	65
Naomi	59	15	225	67
Jennifer	81	7	49	70
Lekeisha	67	7	49	**72**
Ricarto	54	20	400	**73**
Timothy	92	18	324	77
Melissa	77	3	9	81
Sheldon	52	22	484	85
Lucas	51	23	529	88
Dontez	99	25	625	90
Tracy	65	9	81	92
Trevelle	85	11	121	94
Bonita	73	1	1	95
Norberto	94	20	400	99
	1480		4740	

X=1480/20   s=4740/20   72+73=145

X=74   s=237   145/2=72.5

                     s=$\sqrt{237}$

                     s=15.4

Median = 72.5

Range= 99-51=48

Mean= 74

Standard deviation= 15.4

Class Activity 13.2
Standardized Testing and Achievement

Read the following summary and respond to the corresponding questions.

Although standardized tests were originally used to determine achievement levels, they are more frequently used to assess the competence of the educational system, including teachers, principals, superintendents and students. Some researchers argue that standardized tests fail to accurately measure student achievement and that they do not measure how effective school systems are. Despite these arguments policymakers still feel that the benefits outweigh the limitations in providing information on a school system's performance.

A report by Dr. John Jacob Cannell, known as "the Lake Wobegon report," suggested that statewide test scores rank above the national average. Dr. Cannell became suspicious of these results when reviewing West Virginia's statewide results on the Comprehensive Tests of Basic Skills (CTBS). West Virginia was above the national average at all grade levels, but also had the highest percentage of adults without a college education, the second lowest per capita income, and the third lowest college entrance scores in the nation. He found similar results for the majority of the states. This information led to conclusions that these tests allow 90 percent of school districts to be above average, and more than 70 percent of the students to be told that they are performing above average. The exaggeration of scores may not provide an accurate view of how well students are mastering certain skills. Instead, it reflects undesirable instructional practices that raise scores more than achievement.

Some critics suggest that Dr. Cannell provides inaccurate information and misleading figures in his report. Many of the figures he lists are interpreted incorrectly, distorting his conclusions. The report also did not recognize the important difference between the average scores of districts and the scores of the average students in those jurisdictions. Although some of these errors are of significance, his basic conclusion is still sufficient enough to call into question.

Dr. Cannell suggests two reasons for the Lake Wobegon phenomenon: test publishers and educators. He feels that inaccurate norms and teaching to the test may cause high scores. While teaching to the test requires the help of teachers, administrators pressure teachers to raise test scores. Also, malfeasance and technical weaknesses in testing programs may distort test scores.

Questions

1. Do you agree with Cannell's conclusion about standardized testing?

2. Do you think standardized tests make schools accountable?

3. Do you think teachers are pressured to raise test scores by teaching to the test?

Class Activity 13.3
Outline for Test Evaluation

Choose a standardized test and evaluate it according to the following criteria.

➢ General Information

- Title of test (including edition and forms if applicable)

- Author(s)

- Publisher, date of publication

- Time required to administer

- Cost (booklets, answer sheets, other test materials, available scoring services)

➢ Brief Description of Purpose and Nature of Test

- General type of test (e.g., individual or group, performance, multiple aptitude battery, interest inventory)

- Population for which designed (age range, type of person)

- Nature of content (e.g., verbal, numerical, spatial, motor)

- Subtests and separate scores

- Type of items

➢ Practical Evaluation

- Qualitative features of test materials (e.g., design of test booklet, editorial quality of content, ease of using, attractiveness, durability, appropriateness for examinees)

- Ease of administration

- Clarity of directions

- Scoring procedures

- Examiner qualifications and training

- Face validity and examinee rapport

➢ Technical Evaluation

- Norms
- Type (e.g., percentiles, standard scores)
- Standardization sample: nature, size, presentativeness, procedures followed in obtaining sample, availability of subgroup norms (e.g., age, sex, education, occupation, region)

- Reliability
- Types and procedure (e.g., retest, parallel-form, split-half, Kuder-Richardson), including size and nature of samples employed)
- Scorer reliability if applicable
- Equivalence of forms
- Long-term stability when available

- Validity
- Appropriate types of validation procedures (content, criterion-related predictive or concurrent, construct)
- Specific procedures followed in assessing validity and results obtained
- Size and nature of samples employed

➢ Summary Evaluation

- Major strengths and weaknesses of the test, cutting across all parts of the outline

AVAILABLE RESOURCES ON-LINE

Fairtest

www.fairtest.org/

The National Center for Fair & Open Testing is an advocacy organization working to end the abuses, misuses and flaws of standardized testing and ensure that evaluation of students and workers is fair, open, and educationally sound. This web site provides information concerning standardized test, technical assistance and advocacy on a broad range of testing concerns, and focuses on three areas: K-12, university admissions, and employment tests, including teacher testing. FairTest publishes a quarterly newsletter, *The Examiner*, plus a full catalog of materials on both K-12 and university testing to aid teachers, administrators, students, parents and researchers.

All the Tests

www.allthetests.com/introtests.shtml

This web site provides information on many different tests, including the SAT, GMAT, GRE, LSAT, and MCAT. It tells how the tests are structured, how the tests are scored, and what kinds of questions you can expect to see on the day of the test. It presents some of Kaplan's best strategies for dealing with each question type and discusses when and how to guess when you don't know the answer. Finally, it provides practice sets of test-like questions arranged in increasing levels of difficulty, just like on the real tests, so people can learn to pace yourself for optimum performance on test day.

Thurbers Educational Assessments

www.thurbers.net

This web site provides information concerning testing resources, educational web sites, online reference books, and information about colleges. There is information about standardized achievement tests for grades K through 12. It has thousands of links to educational web sites, internet resources for homeschooling gifted children, online reference books for elementary, middle and high schools, and information about colleges, admission tests, and financial resources.

Achievement Tests: Kindergarten to Grade 12

ednet.edc.gov.ab.ca/k_12/testing/achievement/ach_default.asp

Alberta Learning provides information for students, parents, teachers and administrators concerning Achievement tests in grades 3, 6 and 9. This web site also provides the 1998 and 1999 achievement tests and answer keys so teachers and students can use them in the classroom throughout the year. Subject bulletins provide students and teachers with information about the achievement tests scheduled for the 2000-2001 school year.

RECOMMENDED VIDEOS FOR CHAPTER THIRTEEN

Intelligence Testing

Price: $199

VHS Video (114 minutes)

Published by Insight Media, New York, NY (1996)

Order #TAA1454

This three-volume set features noted experts discussing aspects of intelligence testing. Arthur Jensen defends his contention that intelligence is a genetic fact of nature that correlates with certain physical attributes, Jonathan Baron offers a more social definition of intelligence, and Richard Burian responds to each contention.

Performance Assessment: Moving Beyond the Standardized Test

Price: $129

VHS Video (28 minutes)

Published by Films for the Humanities & Sciences

Order #EIH10265

In an age of multicultural classrooms and new understandings about multiple intelligences, what role should standardized tests play? And what direction should performance assessment take in tomorrow's schools? In this timeless program, experts address the urgent need to create viable alternatives to standardized tests that can measure creativity, problem-solving, and cooperation.

Alternatives to Standardized Testing
Price: $149
VHS Video (30 minutes)
Published by Insight Media, New York, NY (1996)
Order #TAA1270
Hosted by Monty Neil, this video argues that standardized testing is harmful to the educational health of most public school students and discusses alternative assessment systems.

HANDOUTS TO ACCOMPANY YOUR LESSONS:

H 13.1   Guidelines for Preparing for a Classroom Test

H 13.2   Guidelines for Taking a Test

H 13.3   Implications for Teaching: Using Standardized Tests and Explaining Test Scores

H 13.4   Factors to Consider When Assessing Test Quality

H 13.5   Issues Concerning Standardized Tests

H 13.1

Guidelines for Preparing for a Classroom Test

1. **Know when test will be given** - what date, time, etc. Will you have the entire class period to complete the exam or will it be given at the beginning or end of class? Will this be a timed test?

2. **Know what test will cover** - what chapters, what notes, etc. Will there be questions asking you to apply information to new situations not specifically discussed in class or in your textbook?

3. **Know your teacher** - Would your teacher give detailed questions about specific dates, numbers, distances or names? Will your teacher allow you to ask questions concerning words you do not understand or how to interpret a question? Will your teacher allow you to use external aids such as dictionaries, tables and calculators while taking the test? Ask your teacher about these and other concerns before the test date.

4. **Know what kind of test you will be taking**. Will there be fill-in-the-blank, completion, essay, multiple-choice, or true/false questions?

5. **Know how to study**. Which study methods will work best for the material you need to learn and the type of test you will be given? Plan your study ahead of time so you will have ample opportunity to learn all the material. Do not engage in last minute cramming. Ask your teacher for suggestions concerning how to study. While studying, predict material or questions that are likely to be on the test.

6. **Know yourself**. What are our test-taking strengths and weaknesses? What types of questions are most difficult for you? What type of material is most difficult for you to study? Plan methods you can use to overcome your weaknesses and capitalize on your strengths. Ask your teacher for suggestions. Also, rest, proper nutrition, and exercise are important for good test performance.

Strategies for Learning and Remembering, Rafoth, Leal, and DeFabo. Copyright 1993. Washington, DC: National Education Association. Reprinted by permission of the NEA Professional Library.

H 13.2

Guidelines for Taking a Test

1. Take time to read test directions carefully before answering the questions. Watch for changes in directions.

2. Skim or look over the entire test before you begin answering individual questions.

3. Do not read more into a question than is actually there.

4. Place a question mark in front of any question you are uncertain about rather than spend too much time deliberating over it and becoming frustrated. Return to this question after you have answered the other questions. Eliminating the obvious incorrect answers when responding to multiple-choice questions.

5. For those items that are difficult to answer underline key words.

6. Read all choices before making a selection on a multiple-choice exam.

7. Look for absolute words such as "all," "none," "never," "always,"; keep in mind there are not many absolutes in our world.

8. All parts of a True/False question must be true before the statement can be true.

9. When matching, first answer items that are known and then go back to remaining items and make the best choice.

10. If you have time, go back and reconsider your answers. Always proofread your test before turning it in.

11. Never change an answer unless you understand clearly why you are doing so.

12. Ignore the pace of other students.

H 13.3

Implications for Teaching: Using Standardized Tests

- Take into account the purpose of each type of score.

- Pinpoint strengths and weaknesses.

- Combine test scores with other evaluations to better assess performance.

- Evaluate the performance of the class as a whole.

Implications for Teaching: Explaining Test Scores

- Be prepared to explain the scores.

- Explain errors of the measurement.

- Focus on the entire student.

- Use tests to set teaching and learning goals.

- Use achievement tests to build self-esteem.

H 13.4
Factors to Consider When
Assessing Test Quality

Population - the complete set of individuals to which a set of results will be generalized.

Sample - a subset of a population.

Reliability - the consistency of test results.

- <u>Test-retest reliability</u> - giving the same test to the same group of students more than one time.
- <u>Alternate-forms reliability</u> - giving the different versions to a group of students and compare the results on each version.
- <u>Internal-consistency reliability</u> - dividing the test questions in half and comparing the two halves of the test (*split-half reliability*).
- <u>Inter-rater reliability</u> - the extent to which two or more evaluators of a given response rate the response in the same way.

Validity - the degree to which a test provides measurements that are appropriate for its intended purpose.

<u>Predictive validity</u> - the extent to which a test predicts a performance that will be demonstrated after the test has been taken.

<u>Content validity</u> - the extent to which the content of a test actually measures the knowledge or skills the test is supposed to measure.

<u>Construct-related validity</u> - the extent to which a test completely and accurately captures the theoretical construct or attribute it is designed to measure.

H 13.5

Issues Concerning Standardized Tests

Test bias - a test that is unfair for members of some groups but not for others.

Culture-relevant testing - the extent to which a task or test is an appropriate measure, given a person's cultural background.

Culture-fair testing - a test that has the same meaning for members of all cultures.

Culture-free testing - a test that is unaffected by culture or cultural context.

High-stakes testing - the use of test scores as the sole basis for making important decisions about a student's placement or admission to educational programs.

Readiness tests - measures the extent to which a student is prepared to learn something, or the extent to which a child is ready for a grade placement.

Minimum-competency test - measures whether a student has attained the minimum level of overall achievement necessary for a particular purpose.

Chapter Fourteen
Classroom Assessments

The instructor's manual for this chapter contains:
- A *Chapter-at-a-Glance* chart that reviews all chapter related material
- A detailed chapter outline to highlight main points of the chapter
- A list of transparencies from Transparencies - Educational Psychology IV that correspond to this chapter
- Several activities to deepen student understanding
- An annotated list of additional resources including internet sites
- Handouts to accompany your lessons

CHAPTER-AT-A-GLANCE

Chapter Outline	Objectives	Instructional Aids
1.0 Why Understanding Classroom Assessment is Important to Teachers, p. 507	1. Discuss the importance to teachers of classroom assessments. 2. Compare and contrast formal assessments with informal assessments. 3. Explain the concept of evaluating student achievement. 4. Compare and contrast formative assessment with summative assessment. 5. Compare and contrast norm-referenced assessment with criterion-referenced assessment. 6. Describe how the goals of assessment affect how students study and what they learn.	- Transparencies T140, T141 - Handout 14.1 - Test Bank Questions 1-12, 51-54, 66
2.0 Traditional Assessments p. 512	1. Explain the goals and types of traditional assessment. 2. Discuss how to decide which material a test should cover. 3. Discuss the when and how of testing. 4. Describe how to develop five different types of objective test questions. 5. Describe how to develop, and then evaluate, essay tests.	- Transparencies T142, T143, T147 - Handout 14.2 - Activities 14.1, 14.2, 14.3 - Test Bank Questions 13-20, 55-59, 63, 64, 67
3.0 Authentic Assessments p. 526	1. Explain the rationale of using authentic assessments. 2. Describe Gronlund's four types of performance tests. 3. Define characteristics of good authentic assessments. 4. Describe two kinds of portfolios and how portfolios are created. 5. Describe exhibitions as a form of authentic assessment. 6. Discuss how to evaluate performance on authentic assessments.	- Transparencies T144, T145, T146, T148, T149 - Handout 14.3 - Activity 14.3 - Test Bank Questions 21-30, 60-62, 65 - Video Segment 18

| 4.0 Grading and Reporting, p. 533 | 1. Describe the how your grading system impacts student learning.
 2. Discuss the general grading guidelines of expert teachers.
 3. Compare and contrast relative improvement versus absolute performance.
 4. Compare and contrast criterion-referenced grading systems with norm-referenced grading systems.
 5. Describe total-point grading systems.
 6. Describe percentage grading systems. | - Transparencies T150, T151, T152, T153
 - Test Bank Questions 32-50, 68
 - Video Segment 19 |

DETAILED CHAPTER FOURTEEN OUTLINE

I. **Why Understanding Classroom Assessment is Important to Teachers**
  A. Formal and Informal Assessments
  - Formal assessments are objective and rigorous methods for obtaining information about student learning, such as tests, quizzes, book reports, and assigned in-class presentations.
  - Informal assessments consist of observations teachers make of students in the classroom, doing work, and talking to the teacher or to other students.
  - The key difference between formal and informal assessment is that formal assessment usually results in information collected in a uniform manner on all students, whereas informal assessment consists of information collected opportunistically on some students, but not always on others.

  B. Evaluating Student Achievement
  - Measurements are data on student performance and learning that are collected by teachers.
  - Evaluation is the process of making judgments about individual students' learning and performance based on the information at hand.
  - Reliability describes the consistency of a measurement, or the extent to which the method of measurement can be relied upon to provide consistent information every time the method is used.
  - Validity describes the extent to which an assessment measures what it is supposed to measure.

  C. Formative and Summative Assessment
  - The purpose of formative assessment is to discover the strengths and weaknesses in prior learning.
  - Formative assessment reveals a student's developmental stage in the area being tested.
  - Formative assessment is diagnostic in that it is often used to assist teachers and others in making decisions about where students should be placed.
  - Summative assessment is the typical final test of student learning in a particular area.

  D. Norm-Referenced versus Criterion-Referenced Assessment
  - In a criterion-referenced grading system, a grade represents a specific set of accomplishments, which can be identified for one student independently of the performances of other students.
  - A norm-referenced grading system represents how well a student has done compared with other students, or assigning a student a grade relative to the other students who took the same assessment.

  E. The Goals of Assessment
  - **Assessment, Motivation, and Learning**
    - Assessment provides information that serves as a guide to the effectiveness of teaching strategies and as a mechanism for improving teaching.
    - Assessment influences motivation and learning in other ways.
  - **Assessment as Student Feedback**
    - Constructive feedback if designed to show students specifically what aspects of their performance need improvement, and also to provide specific suggestions for how to improve.
    - Expert teachers often start out with positive feedback to place a student in a receptive and

nondefensive mood and then proceed to giving constructive feedback that shows what one must do to improve.

- **Assessment as Teacher Feedback**
  - Assessment of student performance also provides important feedback to teachers about the quality and success of their instruction.
  - Feedback on teacher performance, reflected in student assessment, is used widely by principals, other administrators, and school boards.
  - Most parents wish to be involved in their children's school experiences, and knowing how well their children are doing is essential to keeping their at-home interactions with the children on target.

F. Implications for Teaching
- Make assignments meaningful to students.
- Ensure that assessments are objective and as fair as possible to all students from all backgrounds.
- Ensure that assessments are neither so easy that all students do well with little effort, nor so difficult that no students do well despite having worked hard.
- Use methods of assessment frequently enough that students get practice in being assessed, and that the assessment process is demystified for students.

II. Traditional Assessments

A. What Material Should the Test Cover?
- **Consulting Published Sources**
  - Before designing a test on your own, examine the tests provided with your instructor's manuals and other teaching materials.
  - The advantage of using these published test questions is that they have often been checked for errors or potential problems in phrasing.
  - The disadvantage of using published test questions is that they may not accurately reflect what you taught.
- **Using Instructional Objectives**
  - The most important part of designing a good test is to make sure the test reflects what the students were taught.
  - Your test should cover the same basic content as the instructional objectives, and the number of questions should correspond to how much time you spent on the topic in class.
  - A precise way to accomplish the goal of matching assessment to instruction is to use a behavior-content matrix.
  - A behavior-content matrix lists the topics you covered down the left column, and the types of thinking or behaviors that students should be able to engage in across the top row.

B. The When and How of Testing
- **More Frequent, Shorter Tests**
  - Students will study more if they are tested more often.
  - The use of many shorter tests helps test-anxious students overcome the paralyzing fear of being given only one opportunity to show what they know.
  - By scheduling frequent tests, you encourage students to actively process and use the material.
- **Considering Testing Conditions**
  - Poor conditions can depress test performance.
  - Give students explicit instructions regarding how long they will have to complete the test.
  - Keep a close watch on students so you are available to answer questions if students need help with interpreting instructions, and so that your presence will discourage cheating.
- **Ensuring Clear Directions**
  - Go over a sample test question to demonstrate the task that is required.
  - Return the tests as soon as possible, while the students are still interested in how they did and why.
  - Have students share their correct answers with the class to incorporate testing as an instructional activity in itself.

C. Developing Objective Test Questions
- **Multiple-Choice Items**
  - Multiple-choice items permit the teacher to test a great deal of information in one sitting.
  - Multiple-choice items are useful for measuring factual knowledge.
  - Each multiple-choice question contains a stem (consisting of the question or incomplete statement) and a group of options.
  - The incorrect options are called distractors because they serve to distract students who are unsure of the correct answer.
  - Multiple-choice items can also be used to measure higher order learning and reasoning.
- **True/False Items**
  - A true/false item is one in which the test-taker is presented with a statement and must judge whether it is true or false.
  - True/false items are also good for young students who are not yet adept at writing out their answers.
  - Be sure each statement contains only one idea to be judged as true or false.
- **Matching Items**
  - Matching items include a group of stems and a group of options from which to choose the answers.
  - The best matching items are those in which the same answer can be used several times.
  - Matching items are useful for measuring students' ability to discern the exact definitions of a group of terms.
  - To avoid confusion, matching lists should not be longer than roughly ten items.
- **Fill-in-the-Blank and Short-Answer Items**
  - Fill-in-the-blank and short-answer items require the test-taker to complete a statement by filling in the missing information, or to compose a short answer to a question.
  - Although this procedure seems very straightforward, items requiring the completion of missing information can be very confusing.
  - There are often several potentially correct answers that the teacher may not have considered.
- **Evaluating Objective Items**
  - You should show the draft of the test to a colleague, then pilot the test on a friend or a student not in your class.
  - After administering the test, you should remain alert to potential problems with individual items.
  - Keep a record of the student input you get in response to each item.

D. Developing Essay Tests
- Essay tests require students to be actively involved in defining a question as they answer it, and in composing and defending their answer.
- Essays are best used for measuring high-level, complex learning.
- When they score essays, expert teachers ensure that they follow appropriate guidelines regarding fair grading policies and procedures.
- The essay question is the best format for probing student understanding and reasoning at a complex level.
- Provide clear input about what the answer should cover, so the essays do not drift from the main point.
- When including more than one question, suggest how students should divide their time among the questions.
- Avoid making essay tests too long, to keep fatigue and writer's block from undermining students' ability to show what they know.

E. Evaluating Essay Tests
- For situations in which there is one long essay rather than multiple short essays, first read through all of the essays and then divide them into piles according to best and worst.
- Begin by writing a model answer to each question that contains all the fact and main issues you want your students to cover.

- Model answers should show the point totals a student will earn for each portion of the correct answer.
- This technique is well suited to grading essays designed to elicit factual recall and direct exposition.

- Begin by developing a scoring key that is generic and can consequently be used for many different types of essays.
- To ensure you are grading the essays fairly, score all students' answers to one question before moving on to score the next question.
- Try to grade all responses to a particular question at a single sitting.
- Have students place their names on the backs of their papers, so you are not biased by knowing the identity of the students during grading.

F. Implications for Teaching
- Count on well-designed, traditional assessments to provide valuable information about student learning and progress.
- Plan well-organized lessons and tailor assessment questions to the level and content of classwork and homework.
- Use frequent, short assessments.
- Use objective test questions to assess a wide range of student learning in a short time.
- In using essay tests, be careful to ensure uniform and fair grading of essays.

III. Authentic Assessments
A. Types of Authentic Assessments
- Norman Gronlund describes four types of performance tests that simulate real-world performances to differing degrees.
- The least like real-world performances is the paper-and-pencil test.
- Next is the identification test, in which students are asked to describe things to show their knowledge.
- Next is the simulated performance, in which students perform under conditions created to simulate the real world.
- There is the work sample assessment, in which real-world performances are scored as assessments.

B. Characteristics of Good Authentic Assessments
- Often an authentic assessment is open-ended as far as time allotment is concerned.
- Authentic assessments often require collaboration with other people in the planning, developing, or enacting of the performance.

C. Portfolios
- **Types of Portfolios**
  - An artistic portfolio includes a written statement of professional goals, and the range of her talents and her development as an artist.
  - An author's written portfolio consists of a selection of short stories, poems, essays, or critical pieces of work that show the writer's range and strengths.
  - A student can prepare a portfolio in any area of study.
- **Creating Portfolios**
  - Students should be encouraged to include pieces of work that represent self-reflection improvement, and the ability to learn from criticism.
  - Portfolios should include material that reflects the different activities that students engaged in while doing coursework.
  - One of the advantages of portfolios is that they engender pride in the students who have developed them.

D. Exhibitions

- An exhibition is a public performance before an audience that may involve people who will judge the performance.
- Exhibitions that represent good authentic assessments will reflect a great deal of time and preparation, and this preparation will have helped the student understand a wide range of material.

E. Evaluating Performance on Authentic Assessments
- The evaluation of either a portfolio or an exhibition should be criterion-based, or based on an analysis of whether or not the portfolio or exhibition has met established standards.
- The proper use of authentic assessments includes giving students clear feedback and directions regarding how to improve in the future.
- Authentic assessments can be biased, unreliable, and invalid, just as traditional assessments can be.
- One way to reduce subjectivity in the scoring of authentic assessments is to develop ahead of time clear and unambiguous scoring guides that are uniformly applied to every student's performance.

F. Implications for Teaching: Authentic Assessment
- Use authentic assessments to test students on skills and knowledge required to solve real-world problems and complete real-world tasks.
- Recognize the diversity of authentic assessment options and take advantage of different testing formats.
- Score authentic assessments, including portfolios and exhibitions, as objectively and rigorously as possible.

IV. Grading and Reporting
A. Impact of Grades
- The importance you assign during grading to different types of work will directly influence how much importance students assign to these activities.
- If you act as though a grade is a final judgment of a student's ability, rather than simply a reflection of a student's performance at a particular point in time, you will encourage students to view bad grades as an irreparable disaster rather than as evidence of the need for more focused, hard work and improvement.

B. General Grading Guidelines
- Grades should be based on multiple sources of information.
- A teacher should grade only when he or she has determined that a grade is really necessary.
- Help each student feel that he or she is capable of working toward learning goals, by stressing effort and improvement and by being encouraging.
- Explain the system clearly to the students, perhaps by distributing a written guide to the grading system.
- Teachers must remember that they may be called upon to document individual students' performance.

C. Relative Improvement Versus Absolute Performance
- Teachers often incorporate an estimate of a student's effort into their calculation of the student's final grade.
- A more formal system of separately rewarding absolute levels of performance and relative improvement is usually fairer than an often subjective judgment.

D. Criterion-Referenced and Norm-Referenced Grading Systems
- **Criterion-Referenced Systems**
  - In a criterion-based grading system, the teacher describes to the students what levels of competence are associated with individual grades on each test, project, assignment, and in the course in general.
  - Every student theoretically can earn an A if each student works very hard.
  - One way to handle grading by a criterion-referenced system is to give students specific grades on

many individual objectives, rather than one overall grade, to show the extent to which a student has mastered each objective.

- **Contract Systems**
  - In a contract system, the teacher creates a contract with the class in which specific standards are established that correspond to specific final grades.
  - The key to a successful contract system is specific guidelines about the quality and quantity of individual pieces of work.
  - The requirements for earning a given grade are demystified, and students tend to have less anxiety about grades and evaluations.
  - A good contract system should not be so lenient as to make it easy for students to receive the higher grades.
  - One difficulty with a contract system is its potential to result in disappointment on the part of students who complete all of the work with enthusiasm, but who lack the ability to do high-quality work and thus may receive a lower than expected final grade.
- **Norm-Referenced Systems**
  - With this system, called grading on the curve, students are graded in comparison to other students, so that how others do affects a given student's grade.
  - The statistical principle behind the concept of norm-referenced grading is called the normal curve.
  - One problem with grading on the curve is that often only one point on an entire test may separate students receiving a B- and a C+.
  - Another problem with grading on the curve is that sometimes a teacher has a small class, or a class whose students are generally excellent or generally poor.

E. Total-Point Grading Systems
- With the total-point system, the teacher decides how many points each test, paper, report, assignment, and so on, is worth.
- It is important when using this system to ensure that two tests or assignments worth the same number of points cover the same amount of material and are approximately equal in difficulty.
- One way to compute final grades is by adding up the total number of points earned by each student, and then ranking the students, and assigning letter grades based on the percentage of each student's letter grade.
- Another way to handle the task is to convert each score on each test and assignment to a percentage, and then appropriately weight and then average the percentages, rank the students, and assign letter grades.

F. Percentage Grading Systems
- A percentage grading system consists of assigning grades on the basis of the percentage of the material a student has learned.
- The teacher scores each test or assignment on a zero-to-one-hundred percent scale, representing the percentage of the knowledge a student has demonstrated.
- One problem could by if some teachers fail to assign appropriate weight to different tests and assignments when they compute a student's overall percentage score.
- Another potential problem with a percentage system is that it is not possible to know how much "total knowledge" a student has mastered in a specific area.

G. Implications for Teaching
- Take grades as seriously as do your students.
- Employ defensible objective criteria when assigning grades.
- Assign grades separately to both effort/improvement and absolute performance.
- Review the various grading systems and speak to your principal and colleagues before choosing one.

TRANSPARENCIES
- T140 Table of Specification for a Chemistry Unit
- T141 What Do Teachers Assess?
- T142 Analyze Essay Questions
- T143 Comparing Objective and Essay Tests
- T144 Characteristics of Authentic Tests
- T145 Assessment Criteria for a Science Concept Map
- T146 Sample of Criteria for Evaluating Students' Writing Ability through Portfolio Assessment
- T147 Scoring Guidelines for Spelling
- T148 Sample Scoring Rubric: Targeted Performance, Performance Criteria, and a Description of Performances at Different Score Points
- T149 A Sample Checklist Form for Assessing Student Performance in a Laboratory Experiment
- T150 Example of a Performance Assessment Activity
- T151 Self and Peer Evaluation of Group Learning
- T152 Example of a Daily Report Card
- T153 Assign and Justify Grades

CLASS ACTIVITIES
Activity 14.1 Selecting Specific Objective-Type Items for Classroom Tests
This activity is designed to prepare teachers to choose tests that appropriately measure a specific learning outcome. Students are to read the examples and choose from the best measure. Students are to then provide two specific examples of what different tests actually measure. Students can do this activity as a homework assignment, or can brainstorm examples together in pairs.

Activity 14.2 Constructing Multiple-Choice Items
This activity provides the opportunity for students to construct examples of multiple-choice items based on different instructional objectives. Students can use examples from previous courses or an area in which they would like to teach. Students are to also write down the type of learning outcome from the multiple-choice question. This activity can be done in groups or as a homework assignment. Students can share their multiple-choice questions with their peers.

Activity 14.3 Guidelines: Teacher-Made Classroom Assessment
This activity asks students to construct a test in their area of concentration according to suggested guidelines. A grading rubric is provided for this assignment. Students should be asked to do this assignment as homework, and may share their tests with their classmates in a group discussion.

Class Activity 14.1
Selecting Specific Objective-Type Items For Classroom Tests

- Choose the type of objective test item that is most appropriate for measuring each of the specific learning outcomes listed below.

> Short-answer or completion
> True-false or alternative response
> Matching
> Multiple-choice

1. Relates dates and events.   _____

2. Distinguishes between fact and opinion.   _____

3. Recalls algorithmic formulas.   _____

4. Identifies the antonym of a word.   _____

5. Reduces factions to lowest terms.   _____

6. Selects the most likely causal effect of an action.   _____

- State two specific learning outcomes that can be most effectively measured by each of the types of questions listed.

Short answer or completion:

True-false or alternative response

Matching:

Multiple-choice:

Class Activity 14.2
Constructing Multiple-Choice Items

In some subject area you have studied or plan to teach, construct one multiple-choice item for each of the general instructional objectives listed below. Write in the space provided and state the specific learning outcome for each item.

Knows basic terms

    Outcome:

    Item:

Knows specific facts

    Outcome:

    Item:

Understands principles (or facts)

    Outcome:

    Item:

Applies principles or facts

    Outcome:

    Item:

Class Activity 14.3
Guidelines*
Teacher-Made Classroom Assessment

*These guidelines are not intended to include every characteristic of a good teacher-made test. Specifics have been covered in class and in your text. Your notes and text should be consulted in developing your test. This is a general checklist only.

- Construct a test in your area of concentration.
- The test should cover a unit, not an entire semester's work.
- Stay with grade levels 3-12.
- Include a list of the general objectives for your unit, with specific outcomes under each, on a separate sheet (no more than a page), and **note special characteristics of your target population**, especially age and grade.
- Utilize short answer, true/false (2-choice), and multiple choice questions (write 10 of each) and include one essay question and one performance assessment activity. Avoid matching unless you are certain it lends itself especially well to your material.
- Be sure to include a separate set of directions for each type of item.
- Appearance does count. Double space between each format. If you use graphs or diagrams, be sure they are clear and readable. Print must be dark and clear enough to allow for good reproduction. If your personal printer is inadequate, utilize printers on campus. Overall format should be appropriate for the age of your target population.
- Include your scoring plan on a separate sheet. Be certain to include:
    - number of points for each item
    - a scoring system for your essay
    - a scoring system for your performance assessment
    - a procedure for grading the entire test
    - a scheme for number of points equal to an A, B, etc.
- You may include the score on the performance assessment as part of the test grade, or not, at your option.
- Choose **either** hearing impairment, visual impairment, or learning disability (specify type of LD) and discuss in one paragraph how you would modify your test for a student with this disability. Please do not say you would just have a resource teacher administer the test. That is not a modification.

Grading Rubric

The project will be graded with regard to thoroughness; quality of items; directions and scoring procedures with regard to guidelines discussed in text and class; appearance; correlation with stated goals of your unit; and level of appropriateness for your population (see definitions of terms and point system below.) Be **sure** to measure every item against the criteria for a good item of that types.

- <u>Thoroughness</u> - Are all types of required test items and number of items present? Is there a separate set of directions for each section? Have instructional objectives and scoring plans been included on separate sheets? Is there a paragraph regarding modification for disability?

    All types of items present?
    Correct number of each type of item?
    Modification paragraph absent?
    Overall scoring plan absent?
    Instructional objectives in at least 3 areas (knowledge, understanding, application)?

- <u>Quality of Items</u> - Are items free of contaminating characteristics that reduce validity and reliability? Is the modification for disability appropriate?

    Weak item?
    Poor item?
    Inappropriately written outcome?
    Limited quality of disability modification?
    Limited quality of creativity of performance assessment?

- <u>Quality of directions</u> - Are directions clear and relevant to the type of item for which they are intended?

    Each short answer type
    Essay
    Performance Assessment
    Maximum points that may be lost for directions

Grading Rubric (Continued)

- <u>Scoring procedures</u> - Does attached scoring sheet include an adequate point system for fixed choice items? Are the systems of evaluation for the essay question and authentic assessment clear? Appropriate?

    Overall plan
    Essay
    Performance Assessment

- <u>Appearance</u> - Is test typed? Double space between sections? Diagrams and graphs clear? Print dark enough and large enough? Place for name of student and date? Title present? Etc.

    No vertical placement of response options
    Poor General appearance
    Grammar and punctuation errors
    Spelling and typos
    No name of student, etc.
    No lines for fill-in

- <u>Correlation with goals of unit</u> - Do important aspects of what was taught appear in the test? Is emphasis appropriate for different objectives and outcomes? Is type of item appropriate for that objective? Is duplication of content in items avoided?

    Appropriate use of material
    Material in objectives present

- <u>Appropriate for population</u> - Level of language used and phrasing appropriate for age and grade? Format in keeping with developmental level of students with regard to perceptual overload?

Be sure to include a key.

Classroom Test Assignment developed by Dr. Victoria Damiani, Dept. of Educational and School Psychology, Indiana University of PA and used with permission.

AVAILABLE RESOURCES ON-LINE
Classroom Assessment: Principles and Practice for Effective Instruction
cw.abacon.com/bookbind/pubbooks/mcmillan2_ab/
This web site is based on the book by James H. McMillan, *Classroom Assessment: Principles and Practice for Effective Instruction,* and features several tools to help study each chapter of the text. The learning objectives focus on the key points in each chapter. Online practice tests for each chapter include multiple-choice questions and essay based questions on chapter content. Net search will provide key words for each chapter to assist with the internet search engines. Net news contains subscription information for several news groups related to assessment. The Destinations section provides links to numerous web sites with information on assessment.

Center for Excellence in Learning and Teaching
www.psu.edu/idp_celt/CATs.html
This web site provides classroom assessment techniques used by the Center for Excellence in Learning and Teaching (CELT) of Pennsylvania State University. The techniques by Angelo and Cross are outlined for them to be easily used, interpreted, and modified for different classrooms. This site also includes examples of how some of these techniques have been adapted and implemented by Penn State teachers.

Classroom Assessment Techniques
www.hcc.hawaii.edu/intranet/committees/FacDevCom/guidebk/teachtip/assess-1.htm
This site provides information from the book *Classroom Assessment Techniques, A Handbook for College Teachers, 2nd Ed.* by Thomas A. Angelo and K. Patricia Cross. Classroom Assessment is an approach designed to help teachers find out what students are learning in the classroom and how well they are learning it. This site provides the characteristics of the approach, seven assumptions to classroom assessment, and five suggestions for a successful start.

Student Assessment
www.utc.edu/Teaching-Resource-Center/assessment.html#top
This site provides seven assumptions of classroom assessment, student assessment techniques, and ways to design test questions. Included in the student assessment techniques are techniques for assessing course-related knowledge and skills, techniques for assessing learner attitudes, values, and self-awareness, and techniques for assessing learner reactions for instruction. This site also provides descriptions of uses, advantages, disadvantages, and tips for writing test questions in the numerous formats.

RECOMMENDED VIDEOS FOR CHAPTER FOURTEEN
Construction Teacher-Made Tests
Price: $129
VHS Video (25 minutes)
Published by Insight Media, New York, NY (2000)
Order #UAA2085
Intended for teachers of grades K through 12, this video presents strategies for constructing teacher-made tests. It defines the purpose of testing, explains how to create a test with multiple evaluation uses, and stresses the value of tests designed in the service of specific education objectives.

Good Practices in the Classroom
Price: $149
VHS Video (30 minutes)
Published by Films for the Humanities & Sciences
Order #EIH6672
This program surveys alternative assessment practices. Evaluation expert Carol Rolheiser and Paul LeMahieu of the Delaware Education and Development Center discuss the importance of portfolio assessment to the evaluation process, how this and other innovative methods work, and what factors to keep in mind when assessing the whole student.

Developing Performance Assessments
Price: $399
VHS Video (60 minutes)
Published by Insight Media, New York, NY (1996)
Order #UAA1768
Touring a series of innovative schools, this video show how educators are developing and using creative performance tasks such as portfolios, presentations, and interviews in assessments. It explores tasks that develop students' ability to think, solve problems, and apply learning. It also shows how to integrate performance-based assessments across every subject area and grade level.

Reporting Results
Price: $149
VHS Video (29 minutes)
Published by Films for the Humanities & Sciences, Princeton, NJ
Order #EIH6674
Today's parents have a difficult time understanding alternative assessment strategies. This program looks at techniques schools might adopt in order to communicate better with parents, the media, and the community regarding student performance and expectations. Professor of Education Administration Mark Holmes talks about the need for education al accountability, parental input, and more creative assessment and evaluation methods. Research professor Gareth Morgan addresses the pitfalls of relying too heavily on hard data as the sole indication of student success.

Portfolio Assessment
Price: $319
VHS Video (58 minutes)
Published by Insight Media, New York, NY (1993)
Order #UAA913
These videos explore the role of portfolios in student assessment. They explain how to assemble, manage, and evaluate portfolios, and how to help parents interpret them.

Fair Grading Made Easy: Assessing Student Achievement
Price: $119
VHS Video (23 minutes)
Published by Insight Media, New York, NY (1999)
Order #UAA1997
Grades rarely reflect the whole story of student learning and achievement. This video addresses such problems with traditional grading approaches as the standardized definition of failure; explains why, though sometimes problematic, the practice of assigning grades is important; and considers the visual-interpretation grading method as a possible solution to the grading dilemma.

HANDOUTS TO ACCOMPANY YOUR LESSON:

H 14.1   Formative versus Summative Assessment

H 14.2   Evaluating Essay Tests

H 14.3   Implications for Teaching: Authentic Assessment

H 14.1

Formative versus Summative Assessment

Formative Assessment

- Its purpose is to discover the strengths and weaknesses in prior learning.

- It reveals a student's developmental stage in the area being tested.

- It is often used to assist teachers and others in making decisions about where students should be placed.

- An example would include a math test to find which math level a student belongs to.

Summative Assessment

- It is the typical final test of student learning in a particular area.

- It is used to summarize prior learning.

- An example would include a swimming test at the end of the semester.

H 14.2
Evaluating Essay Tests

Approach 1

- Read through all of the essays and then divide them into piles.
- Using five piles, the first pile should contain the best essays and the fifth pile the worst.
- After sorting the essays, skim the piles once again to ensure that they have been sorted fairly.
- Finally, award grades that correspond to the piles.

Approach 2

- Begin by writing a model answer to each question containing fast and main issues that students should cover.
- The model answers should show the point totals a student could earn for each portion of the correct answer.
- Good writing can earn more credit.

Approach 3

- Begin by developing a scoring key that is generic and can consequently be used for many different types of essays.
- This scoring key consists of anchors explaining what each score reflects.
- A '1' reflects a poor essay that makes few or no appropriate points and is nearly incomprehensible.
- A '5' reflects an excellent essay that is well argued, well written, and filled with numerous facts that support its arguments.
- Scoring can begin without reading through all of the essays.

H 14.3

Implications for Teaching: Authentic Assessment

- Use authentic assessments to test students on skills and knowledge required to solve real-world problems and complete real-world tasks.

- Recognize the diversity of authentic assessment options and take advantage of different testing formats.

- Score authentic assessments, including portfolios and exhibitions, as objectively and rigorously as possible.

NOTES

NOTES

NOTES

NOTES

NOTES

NOTES

NOTES

NOTES

NOTES